About Marta Becket . . .

"Tears came to my eyes. Marta represented to r
The spirit of the theater. The spirit of creativity.

———, AUTHOR

"*To Dance on Sands* reveals the inner life of a creative child for whom art always mattered more than anything else. The story of course, is what ultimately makes the book worthwhile."

—ROBIN FLINCHUM, *PAHRUMP VALLEY TIMES*

"*To Dance on Sands* is a breathtakingly beautiful book. The ones you keep, the ones you remember are the ones that represent beauty."

—ERIC KAMPMANN,
PRESIDENT MIDPOINT TRADE BOOKS

"Long before anybody invented the term performance art, Marta Becket was doing it, in an abandoned opera house in Death Valley Junction. She restored it and it restored her. With serene tenacity, she set down roots, working hard for decades, caring as well for endangered animals, including wild burros, until the world began coming to her."

—*BOSTON GLOBE*

"Becket's saga epitomizes the eternal struggle of the artist for personal expression."

— *CHICAGO TRIBUNE*

"The forthright artist went on with what essentially was her own private show. She choreographed and performed her own dances, at first to an audience of tumbleweeds. But over the course of years, she painstakingly developed another audience — the Renaissance-looking crowd she painted in elaborate murals to fill her Amargosa Opera House with gawking spectators. Eventually Becket was discovered by living audiences, mostly appreciators of art, who have gone to great lengths to see her work. Becket overcame much and worked hard to get where she is today, a relatively unknown artist in the middle of nowhere. But she loves her unique place in the world."

—*SAN FRANCISCO CHRONICLE*

"If this were fiction — if Marta Becket were not a real person — then the whole oddball-in-the-desert scenario might seem like something dreamed up by David Lynch. Or Sam Shepard. But Becket is very much the real thing, and she has made quite a name for herself out there in the desert."

—*NORTHERN CALIFORNIA BOHEMIAN*

"On stage there is a warble to her voice. She is thin, but her expressions are as varied and fluid as shifting sand dunes. To say that Becket was beautiful when she was young, as evidenced by photographs in her program is to do a disservice to the beauty she still holds."

—*Los Angeles Times*

"There's something really wonderful about the fact that she picked the most desolate spot in America to do this. It says you can have your life on your own terms, but you'll have to sacrifice. It says the process is the point. And people come away from there inspired."

—Todd Robinson, Director, *Amargosa*

"There is indisputably a whiff of eccentricity about Ms. Becket's enterprise. And if one might expect the woman herself — dark haired, trim, with the visible sinews of a dancer — to carry an eccentric air, she doesn't, though there is a faint haughtiness of the artiste about her. Ms. Becket is self-aware, perfectly willing to admit that her shows and her painting have been her obsessions. In explanation of what amounts to her self-imposed exile, she said, 'I couldn't have created another world anyplace else'."

—*New York Times*

"Death Valley holds a special mystique for Europeans. You can find them among the locals in the 120-seat house, along with the occasional journalist or ghost-hunter — the place has a reputation for being haunted."

—*Dance Magazine*

"Occasional mesquite trees and patches of recalcitrant desert grass signal the only shade in a landscape of bleached earth and twisted rock that stretches for hours in every direction. And there, rising mirage-like from the sands at a lonely crossroads that serves as the gateway to Death Valley, the hottest, lowest, hardest place on the continent stands an opera house. For the past 30 years Marta has provided her homespun programmes of dance, mime and musical revue for a ragtag collection of patrons, many of whom have inspired the characters that people her shows; Mormons, truckers, cowboys, farmhands, hippies, dreamers, tourists, and gamblers burned on the roulette tables across the Nevada border nearby, even the femmes de nuit from local bordellos."

— *The UK Guardian*

To Dance On Sands

AMARGOSA
OPERA HOUSE

To Dance On Sands

The Life and Art
of Death Valley's Marta Becket

Stephens Press • Las Vegas, Nevada

Editor: Ginger Mikkelsen Meurer
Copy Editor: Don Clucas
Designer: Sue Campbell

Becket, Marta.
    To dance on sands: the life and art of Death Valley's Marta Becket /
Marta Becket ; edited by Ginger Mikkelsen.
328 p. : photos ; 23 cm.
    In this autobiography, Marta Becket tells of her life from her childhood
in New York in the 1920s and 1930s to her career as a painter and dancer to
her unusual artistic rebirth as the owner, choreographer, and star performer
at the Amargosa Opera House in Death Valley Junction, California.
                        ISBN: 1-932173-81-1
                    ISBN-13: 978-1-932173-81-9
1. Becket, Marta, 1924- 2. Ballet dancers—United States--Biography. 3.
Artists—United States--Biography. 4. Amargosa Opera House (Death
Valley Junction, Calif.) I. Title. II. Mikkelsen, Ginger, ed.
[B] 792.802'8092 dc22   2007   2005932561

STEPHENS PRESS, LLC
A Stephens Media Company

Post Office Box 1600
Las Vegas, NV 89125-1600
www.stephenspress.com

Printed in Hong Kong

Dedication

I am grateful to my mother, Helen Beckett, for the happy creative childhood I had. The Christmas she gave me in Rose Valley was the most beautiful Christmas of my life. I thank my father, Henry Beckett, for exposing me as a four-year-old to the operetta ballet performances and stage presentations which helped me know that theater was the life I wanted and had to have. I am even grateful to Sioma Glaser who challenged me to create a dance company based on Oriental scenarios. Although he never came up with the money to back the venture, it woke me up to what I could do and the marvelous possibilities that created my Turkish fairytale, *The Mirror, The Carpet, and The Lemon.* From that challenge came Nat Jerome, a theatrical agent who, when watching me audition all the parts in *The Mirror, The Carpet, and The Lemon,* encouraged me to work on a one woman show of my own, playing all the parts instead of relying on a company of dancers. Thus was launched my program of dance pantomimes. I thank George Michaelson and Harold Alford for booking me on my first two tours for the University of Minnesota. Yes, and I thank Tom Williams for bringing me to Death Valley Junction where I began my second life. Most importantly I thank Tom Willett, affectionately known as Wilget, for sharing my creative and personal life for the last 23 years, from installing all the theater seats in the Amargosa Opera House to playing many parts in the twelve stage productions we staged together. Last but not least, I thank McDonald Harris for encouraging me to write my autobiography, for without that encouragement, this book might not have been written.

Contents

PROTEUS: *Say that upon the altar of her beauty*
You sacrifice your tears, your sighs, your heart:
Write till your ink be dry, and with your tears
Moist it again, and frame some feeling line
That may discover such integrity:

For Orpheus' lute was strung with poets' sinews,
Whose golden touch could soften steel and stones,
Make tigers tame and huge leviathans
Forsake unsounded deeps to dance on sands.

After your dire-lamenting elegies,
Visit by night your lady's chamber-window

With some sweet concert; to their instruments
Tune a deploring dump: the night's dead silence
Will well become such sweet-complaining grievance.

This, or else nothing, will inherit her.

—*Two Gentlemen of Verona*
Act Three, Scene Two
Duke's Palace

Overture

All my friends and acquaintances from New York thought I had lost my mind when I told them about this old theater that had been abandoned for twenty years. When I told them I was planning to leave New York for good and make a new life for myself out in the desert, they were convinced that I was now a hopeless case and gave me up for good.

Fifteen years passed before I heard from any of them. Perhaps they saw my picture and an article about me in a *National Geographic* they saw in some dentist's office. The article told a story about this dancer from New York who performs every night in an abandoned theater in the desert whether anyone shows up or not. In fact, they even said I painted a Renaissance audience on all three walls of my theater so that I would be guaranteed an audience each performance night. This of course is untrue. I painted a Renaissance audience to surround my performance with an atmosphere complementary to what I performed.

Of course, much of what has been written about me makes me seem crazy. It makes for good press. And of course, it makes gossip more fun.

In 1967, on my birthday, I settled in the town of Death Valley Junction. When I arrived, this place wasn't deserted. There was the old Amargosa Hotel which was operated by several families who were given a place to live in return. This of course did not mean they knew anything about operating a hotel. There was also a filling station across the road. "Death Valley Junction Service," it read over the porte-cochere.

Around the corner from our old post office and vacant general store was the Lila C Café. The same folks who ran the filling station ran the café as well. When business was brisk, the station hand, Smitty, could be seen climbing out from under a truck he was working on to fix a hamburger for a customer in the café without even bothering to wash his hands.

When business was slow, they would close up for the rest of the day and invariably a tour bus would round the corner with passengers hoping to find a place to eat. The closed sign would signal them to go on.

For a while there was a milk cow housed in a pen she shared with two jackasses by the filling station. An old bathtub inside the pen provided drinking water. She was milked every day. I never did find out if her milk was served in the Lila C Café. But the thought did enter my mind.

To me, the most important building was Corkhill Hall, an empty theater left from the 1920s when the town served as a company town for the Pacific Coast Borax Company. This building is the reason I was here. It's the reason I'm here now. This building, now the Amargosa Opera House, has been home to me. Nowhere else could I attain the artistic fulfillment I have found here.

When I first came, I was to many, the crazy lady who moved out into the middle of the desert to run an opera house. To many I am not crazy anymore. Perhaps this is due to the fact that the Amargosa Opera House has survived and become successful. I enjoy the public approval. However, if my Opera House had not become successful, I would still be here struggling to support my art. This is not because I think my art to be great. It is because my art is necessary to me. The early years here were difficult. I was misunderstood, gossiped about, and even heard tales of my death more than once. I am very much here and very much alive. And now, almost forty years later, I am pleased to present my life.

Marta poses with a hoop on the roof of the Empire State Building at age 13.

ACT ONE: *Childhood*

New York Beginnings

I was born August 9, 1924, the same year Corkhill Hall, my future Amargosa Opera House, was built.

My first home was at 405 Bleeker, a walk-up three story red brick building in New York City. Inside, the two and one-half room apartment held an Italian sofa, a fireplace, a grand piano, and a Victrola, with a big wing chair facing them. The rear windows looked out onto a courtyard lined with fire escapes. The sunlight made its way down this shaft only at noon. Each day Mother would set me out on the fire escape for my sun bath.

Mother was melancholy most of the time. She would play sad songs on the piano and sing softly to herself. I began to associate Mother with sadness.

Each afternoon Mother would take me down the street to Washington Square in an old wicker baby carriage. The butcher would give me a discarded chicken foot to play with on the way home.

The voices of the street vendors, the bargaining housewives, and laughing children faded away on the trip back. Once we entered the dim light of our home, all the imposing pieces of furniture seemed to be waiting for something to happen. The Italian sofa was not at all comfortable. The wing chair was erect and hard, facing the piano as if waiting for the concert to begin. The Victrola was really the only functioning piece in the room, for it outplayed Mother's sad pieces on the piano with its turntable constantly revolving to pour forth Paderewski, Kreisler, Caruso, Chopin and Schubert. I danced to them constantly.

When Mother put me into the crib in the half room at dusk, she would give me a dozen colored handkerchiefs to play with. The neon light from the street corner shown in the window and I would make them dance, fluttering them over my head.

One morning, I was carried into the front room and transferred into the arms of a man. The man rocked me from side to side and told me he was my father. He smiled at me, but his face seemed stern. He wore silver rimmed glasses that glinted in the dim light. Behind the glass panes, his eyes were blue. Mother's were brown. My eyes were brown, also. "For this reason, I am closer to my mother," I thought.

My father's name was Henry Beckett. Mother's name was Helen. I called my father by the nickname of Mana, because he was a man. I could never get used to the idea of calling him "Father."

Sometimes we all three went out to dinner. Once after dinner Mana took us on a double-decker bus ride up to Lewisohn Stadium to see the Denishawn Dancers. We sat on great stone steps far from the stage and watched groups of dancers move like great tidal waves, to the accompaniment of Liszt's Preludes. At home, Mother put me in my crib with the handkerchiefs. I would try to duplicate what I had seen.

The next day, after my sunbath and nap, I awoke to find a pile of brilliant colored skirts and old evening dresses on the floor. The Victrola was playing the Preludes. I picked up a piece of lavender chiffon and floated around the room with it. Later, I discovered a huge tablet of newsprint on the floor and some crayons. I drew what I remembered from the magical performance of a few evenings before.

Mana appeared again one afternoon and we took an underground train to a place where neon lights and theater marquees announced what was inside the huge structure. Mana showed a card to a gentleman standing at the entrance. He was dressed a bit like a tin soldier. Among the balustrades stood more soldiers whose only function was to show us to our seats.

First there was a movie, then the curtain rose to reveal a fantasy land come to life. The orchestra played ballet music, and down on the stage a fairy tale unfolded starring Patricia Bowman and Leonide Massine. In my short life, I had never imagined such perfection.

A line of beautiful ladies wearing feathers and plumes paraded out and I decided then that this was the life I wished to live.

Later Mana took us backstage. It was like entering a magic box. I met the feathered ladies and was introduced to the real Mr. Roxy.

Mana received free passes for theatrical events. His job was to write about them for the newspaper. Thanks to Mana's work, I saw Harold Kreutzberg and Tilly Losch, the theater of Angna Enters, the Carnegie Hall concerts of Jascha Heifetz, Ignace Paderewski, the monologues of Ruth Draper and a one-woman show of Cornelia Otis Skinner.

Aside from culture, Mana took me to Coney Island. The sound of barkers, roller coasters and music fused with the smell of popcorn and salt air, conjured up images that found their way onto my drawing tablet. Then there was the evening at Palisades Amusement Park. Here the crowds participated in the spectacle. The theater and ballet were both too exquisite to allow the audience to participate, just a peek, and then the memory to cherish.

One day when Mana appeared, Mother gently and reluctantly ushered me toward him but didn't go along.

"Are we going to the theater again?" I asked. In silence my father put his arm around me and led me down the stairs.

This was the first time we were alone. We walked to the entrance to the subway and as we waited, I kept wondering why my mother wasn't with us. Mana said little.

The train came, and after a few stops we got out and emerged into the street at the southeast side of Central Park. Mana led me to a horse drawn carriage, while a strange lady rose from one of the park benches and came toward us.

"This nice lady will be riding with us in the carriage," Mana said.

I wanted to run home. Mana lifted me into the carriage. He sat me in the middle. The nice lady made small talk. Mana looked his stern self and I was numb.

These outings with the nice lady sandwiched themselves between outings with Mother. I was beginning to notice Mana would leave money under the lid of the Victrola. Mother seemed to ignore it until after he had gone. Then she would reluctantly remove it.

By the time I was five years old, Mana had saturated me in Richard Wagner, with the complete *Ring Cycle*. I did not care too much for these, they were long and everyone on stage seemed like immovable objects planted in the ground. I preferred to dance to Chopin and Kreisler.

Hansel and Gretel was given every Christmas at the old Met. I went to the show in a red silk dress sent to me by my Aunt Anne, a hand-me-down from her daughter Betty Ann, a child prodigy at the piano. I had a small red silk purse that exactly matched the dress. Queena Mario sang Hansel.

After the opera was over, we stepped out of this exquisite world onto the street. I wanted to stay and hold onto this experience which was decidedly more beautiful than the real world.

Victor Herbert's *Babes in Toyland* at the old Century Theatre, also led me to wonder why it all had to end. The next day the sun would shine brightly, the same way it had before, but the memory of my glimpses into fantasy lingered on.

I cut the cherry colored satin sleeves from one of the evening dresses and put them on my legs for tights. I made a chiffon tunic from another evening dress and danced to Rosamund until I could no longer stand.

Mother enrolled me in the Greenwich House Preschool. In interpretive dance class, we ran around with rainbow china silk scarves to Chopin. We had art lessons and listened to classical music sandwiched between naps, lunch and spoonfuls of liquid vitamins in the form of chocolate milk or orange juice.

One day during our nap, I heard someone downstairs playing Chopin's *Prelude in A Major* on piano. I rose from my cot, snuck to the balcony and looked over the railing. In the corner of the big empty room was the piano with a teacher playing. I crept downstairs. The woman playing didn't notice. I began to dance to the music. When she finished playing, I stopped my dance and held a pose on the final chord.

A woman came out of the shadows, lifted me up and carried me back to my cot. For a short time the real world didn't exist. I knew whatever motivated me to dance was not confined to home. Whether anyone watched me was unimportant. There was something inside me that was my reason for living.

Frequently I was taken out alone where Mana could meet the nice lady. My father called her Helen. Mother's name was Helen, too. I wondered if all women were named Helen and all men Henry. Perhaps when I was grown, my name would be Helen, too. Maybe Martha was just a child's name.

I began having terrible nightmares. The light bulb which hung over my head from a giant "octopus" of electric wires would dim on and off and a woman's voice singing an eerie song would emanate from it. The creases in my bed sheets would lengthen and become serpents. I would let out a scream and Mother would come in and try to comfort me. When she turned off the light and left, the dreams returned.

That afternoon Mana came to take me away from Mother to meet the "nice lady."

A long cardboard box lay on the floor in front of her. Mother and Mana were both smiling at me. Mother said, "Open the box, it is your birthday present from Cousin Jane."

Inside lay an enormous rag doll almost as large as I was. I lifted her out of the box. She stood as tall as I.

"Cousin Jane made this rag doll for you," Mother said.

I looked again at the doll whose broad face smiled back at me from a row of stitches, "I will name her Echo," I said.

She went with me everywhere and sometimes her presence seemed to subdue the nightmares. She was more friend than toy. I had a little wooden duck which I also considered a friend.

One Christmas I was given a set of building blocks. They were oblong, square, cylindrical, and curved with instructions on how to build. It didn't take me more than one afternoon to decide they were to become people. Only the curved blocks remained for building, and these became rows of seats as if in a theater. The other blocks became people who sat in the seats, and the tall cylindrical and oblong blocks became the cast in a play which I made up as I went along.

Echo watched the plays and went with me for my sunbaths, too. From my vantage point, I noticed the empty storeroom on the first floor of our building. I saw Mother behind the clouded window.

Later, Mother took me inside and I noticed the storeroom filled with pieces of furniture you would find in a museum. Mother let me stay while she worked. Tables with legs representing winged griffins standing on lion's feet stared back at me. Mother was recreating a whole world of the past on these rejected pieces of furniture she had bought from junk stores.

Mother's preoccupation with this new interest kept her busy. She seemed happier.

My interlude at Greenwich House ended and I was put in a private preschool. The children there were the offspring of famous people — writers, actors and professionals — my father was simply a newspaper reporter. Mother was a housewife.

This new school specialized in group activities. Either we were all building a bridge, mining coal, or group singing. Dance class tried to make us conform, doing the same movements at the same time. The freedom I had at Greenwich House was gone.

Mother now had a determination in everything she did. "We are going to Harrisburg," she said. "That's where I was born, and you and I will live at Grandmother's for a few days."

When I asked if Mana was going too, Mother's "no" gave me a sense of relief.

The move was completed by the end of my fifth summer.

Marta sits in front of the fire at her first childhood home, 405 Bleeker Street in New York City, at age 5, 1929.

Scene Two

Harrisburg

other took me to Maude Firestone's boarding house. Maude and mother had been friends since childhood. Mother had an exciting life before she married Mana, but Maude remained home to help her mother run the boarding house.

"You'll be staying here until I come for you," Mother said. "I must go back to New York and get another load of our things then we'll live with Grandmother until we can find an apartment."

She kissed me and then left me in the hallway. I looked up at Maude. She smiled, and then shepherded me into the front parlor where her elderly mother sat in an overstuffed chair.

The room was filled with furniture, a large brown velour davenport, chairs, and a small table with a lamp wearing a fringed lamp shade.

A huge dark wood box sat up against the wall opposite the davenport. It had a cathedral-like design with knobs in a row.

Maude turned several of the knobs and the room filled with the sounds of Dixieland jazz. I was transfixed. The cathedral radio, was the source of many an evening's entertainment: *Amos and Andy, Guy Lombardo, Lowell Thomas,* and *Major Bowe's Amateur Hour.*

When Mother finally came for me to take me to Grandmother's, there was a little sadness upon leaving the boarding house. But I was happy to be with Mother again.

Grandmother's house was a large brick house in a row of other large brick houses. A small hall led into the dining room filled with light. The hallway seemed to bypass a dark parlor on the left which had heavy drawn drapes and sheets spread over huge pieces of sleeping furniture. In the corner of the dining room stood a grandfather clock with a smiling sun and moon which slowly played hide-and-seek with each other as time ticked on. My grandmother was a tiny subdued lady with pitch black hair, even though she was very old.

When we arrived, Cousin Jane and her mother were there as were a number of other relatives. We didn't stay long at Grandmother's.

Mother seemed happy for the first time, and I remember the two of us walking down the brick sidewalk. I looked up at her contented, and she was humming to herself. She actually looked beautiful. I told her that I liked her look.

When we left Grandmother's, our taxi stopped in front of the house kitty-cornered from a huge stone library. Next to a small flight of marble stairs was a storefront window full of Mother's beautiful period furniture.

In the front hallway Mother unlocked another door with a glass window at the top and we stepped inside a huge front room, the light streaming in from the store window which looked out on Walnut Street. Inside was more of Mother's furniture. The grand piano was there, but the Victrola and the big wing chair were gone.

In the corner was a crate full of my block people, my costume box, and my newsprint sketch pad. Echo was seated on top.

"We're home," Mother said. I ran into her open arms.

There was a combined happiness and a sense of relief knowing that we could live our lives without Mana.

After a bite of lunch, Mother began unpacking, while I opened up my crate and spread my fantasy world in the back room with my block people who now could continue their lives. The rich and the well-to-do block people lived in Broudrich Farms. The poor lived in Polecat Ridge.

That fall I was enrolled in the Bose School uptown from where we lived. It was a sprawling one story building with a front yard for recess. I loved it and made friends quickly.

These children were very different from those in New York. There was Nana, with bangs all the way around the head. I begged Mother to let me have my hair cut like hers, but she would have none of it. Then there was Geraldine, who wore a different freshly starched dress each day, but all the same style. She had a shingle bob.

I had to keep my hair shoulder length and wear lace-up shoes instead of Mary Janes. Worse than anything, I grew taller than everyone else. I was a string bean. Even though I was unlike the others, this was one of the happiest of times of my childhood.

Others walked to school by themselves, but Mother always accompanied me. I asked her why she didn't let me go by myself. She reluctantly told me she was afraid I would be kidnapped and taken back to New York. We had moved away from Mana, but that did not mean he ceased to exist.

Reading and writing came naturally for me. The simple art lessons, painting a flower pinned up on the blackboard, were confining.

After mother's furniture business got a little busier, she hired a black girl named Alice to walk me to school. Alice decided to take me the round-about route through her neighborhood.

She lived in a house in an area the neighbors referred to as "dark town." She took me inside and introduced me to the entire family, which consisted of her grandma, grandpa, mother, and younger sister and brothers who were playing on the cracked linoleum floor strewn with toys and chewed chicken bones. A large dog in the corner of their parlor had a litter of puppies.

I enjoyed these visits to Alice's house, with the smell of brand new oilcloth on the table and a faint aroma of dog. They seemed more relaxed than anyone I knew. When I got home, I made sketches on my newsprint pad.

This was the way mother found out that Alice had not taken me to school, but home to meet her folks. There were also a few notes of absenteeism from school. So Alice was relieved from her responsibilities.

One day while playing, I happened to find some letters in Mother's desk. Deciphering what I could, I learned the letters were from Mana. The final paragraphs revealed that he was coming to Harrisburg to take me back to New York. My eyes welled up with tears. I couldn't believe it. I ran to Mother.

"Yes" she said, "He's even been here when we didn't know it. This is why I take you to school."

Mother dried my tears and said, "I have to tell you something dear. I've put it off as long as I could, but now I can not wait any longer, and time is running short. Mana is coming next week to visit, but I'll be right near by. I won't let him take you."

Mother and I hugged each other and sobbed. I finally cried myself to exhaustion.

Mana turned up with presents under his arms. There was no joy in this reunion, just the somber look of resignation on Mother's face, and silent submission on my part.

With Mana, there was anxiousness in his face whenever he looked at me. We walked to the Susquehanna River Park. Mana sat on a bench and I was shepherded by Mother to sit next to him. Then Mother went away and sat on a bench around the corner from the tree. She made sure that she could see me.

I felt safer knowing she was present. I wondered how I could divide myself in two so that each one could have a half of me. "Would they be happier?" I thought. I wondered if my existence brought them any happiness. If not for me, they wouldn't have to see the other again.

Mana brought out the presents, the book *Jacques at the Window*, a game called "Stick-Stack" and a box of pastel colored peppermints. After the visit, Mana said he'd be back in two weeks.

Grandmother was ailing and she was going to be sent to a nursing home or hospital. However, prior to this she came to visit for a few days. Although the apartment and storeroom were small we all managed to sleep in the combined quarters.

Unfortunately, I was beginning to have the nightmares again. The same phantoms I had endured in New York were returning. This was very hard on Grandmother. She was soon sent away. Not long after Grandmother was gone, there was great sobbing in the front room. Mother had always idolized her mother, as if on a pedestal.

Not much was ever said about Grandfather whose image in the family portrait was of a dignified mustachioed gentleman seated in a painted garden with a wife and six children. There had been seven children, but the first, a daughter named Ruth, died from "blue heart."

I found old photographs of my grandfather holding me in his arms after I was a few months old. All I ever learned was that he was a steelworker who worked in Steelton, Pennsylvania, took the trolley to work, and drank beer.

Grandmother worked hard to raise the six children; cooked, ironed, sewed all their clothes, cleaned, and baked pies. Grandmother was a saint in Mother's eyes. However, Mother said Grandfather did the laundry in a washing machine he built in the basement.

There were happy times in Harrisburg. Summer evenings we went to the dance boat, which docked on the river on weekends. A dance band played, while women in flowered georgette dresses and the men in white linen suits danced. Colored lanterns bobbed to and fro in the warm breezes. It prompted me to wonder where my mother fit in all of this. I was constantly reminded

Mother had no one. In my childlike way I tried to be that someone for her, but even in our good times when we laughed and played together, I felt inadequate.

Periodically a woman named Mrs. Orth would come and visit Mother. She had papers with her, and the conversation was about money. Mother began not opening her furniture shop until afternoon. In the mornings now she left the apartment and went to a place she called her office. After she took me to school each morning she got to her office at ten o'clock and remained there until three o'clock. Then she would pick me up at school.

Mother had a few orders, and even had a large order from an Anglican minister's wife. But these orders were few and far between. Her interest in her shop was dwindling and her office took precedence.

Mrs. Orth took Mother and me to lunch at the Harrisburger hotel, and I enjoyed my bacon and tomato sandwich on toast and a glass of chocolate milk in the elegant dining room. The conversation between Mother and Mrs. Orth was very uninteresting to me. Again it was about money; money that might be there if they made the right move.

Mother took me to her office, which was a busy place consisting of an audience seated on chairs in front of a narrow platform on which two boys darted about changing numbers on a big blackboard that covered almost the whole wall. Above this big blackboard was a long narrow lighted window with a Trans-Lux with faded numbers and symbols on it. A glass bubble spewed out tape and clicked nervously. Businessmen stood at this bubble reading from it obsessively. Mother sat in the front row with her eyes glued to the Trans-Lux as if nothing else existed.

Her moods followed the market, and the mother I thought I knew and loved was now turning into an obsessed and frightened woman. Her furniture store was neglected, and it was impossible for me to penetrate her new world.

Nevertheless, I was still happier than in New York. My schoolmates and I got along very well. There was Clarabelle Lovelace who came home with me and we played, and Honora, an Italian girl who lived around the corner through the back alley.

Then there was Jack Born next door. We played, pretending we were climbing like monkeys. The Fager boys lived next door, too. Their father, Dr. Fager had his office on the first floor.

On my eighth birthday, Honora and Clarabelle came over to celebrate. While sitting and pouring over my presents on top of stairs leading into the back yard, I fell and broke my arm.

Mother rushed me to Dr. Fager where my arm was supposedly set right. However, it was set incorrectly which resulted in it being broken and set over and over. The visits to Dr. Fager for these nightmares continued well into early winter.

Mother took me to see an acquaintance, an osteopath named Dr. Ruth Deeter who planned to heat bath my arm. Dr. Deeter wore a gray cape and her presence was slightly intimidating. She seemed to have a lot of influence over Mother.

The doctor had a country place, and she invited Mother and me to go there on weekends. I loved going there. It was just Mother and me and I love the country. Dr. Deeter's house was full of antiques. Even her china was antique. The old house provided me with a temporary peace. I loved it there so much, I hated to leave.

One weekend we went on a trip to see my Uncle Paul Bittner. He lived in a huge old farm house with his twelve children. His wife had died and now Uncle Paul went every Sunday to a spiritualist tent out in the country to receive messages from a medium.

Once we all went to go to the tent meeting with him. It was starting to drizzle. Everyone was huddled under the huge tent while a woman stood in the center with a large horn through which messages from the other world came.

There was also Edna who wore a long black dress and a small white cap tied under her chin. She, too, had a daughter named Martha, about the same age as I, who was being groomed for missionary work.

There was another distant cousin who lived in Hazelton. Mother allowed me to go alone on the trolley to visit occasionally. It was another large family who lived in a wooden farm house next to a huge corn field. At dinner time the table was amply laid with corn on the cob, mashed potatoes, boiled beef, and a plate piled high with white bread. Milk was constantly poured into glasses as soon as they emptied.

When Mother came with me to Hazelton, the middle daughter, Rosey, was asked to go put on her costume and do her dance. Eagerly she returned in a pale green tutu and pink toe slippers. At a cue from her mother she went up on her toes for a moment, and then slowly sunk down into a split. I was transfixed.

"What do I have to do to become as beautiful as that?" I wondered.

Rosey struggled to her feet and ran shyly to her mother who explained, "That is what she'll learn in her next lesson, how to rise out from the split gracefully, isn't it dear?"

For weeks I asked my mother to let me take toe dancing lessons so that I could do what Rosey did. No one taught toe dancing in Harrisburg and even if there had been a teacher, Mother couldn't afford it.

Mother moved us into the rear apartment and gave up the store. The apartment in the rear was roomy, and I had my own bedroom. The yard was all mine now, and Mother allowed me to dominate the apartment with my world of block people.

The gentleman who had occupied the apartment taught singing and had a very beautiful wife, an American Indian. She died there in a huge four poster bed. He left the bed to us when he returned to New York. It was difficult for me to sleep in a bed where I knew someone had just passed away. However, I did get used to it and didn't even have nightmares about it.

Mana still came to visit each month. Later in the evening mother would invite a girlhood friend of hers named Esther Allen and her son Roger to come help dispel the tension generated by the visit from Mana. Roger and I played with poster paint and newsprint followed by hot cocoa and marshmallows.

At Christmas Cousin Jane gave me a beautiful lavender flowered organdy dress. After a visit from Mana, Roger and his mother were expected in the evening to celebrate the holiday. I put on the lavender organdy dress and stood by the Christmas tree like a stiff doll for the entire evening. No one could budge me. I stared straight ahead as if my eyes were glass doll's eyes. I didn't care what Roger and his mother thought. I was a doll and it seemed Mother wasn't concerned in the least. I was a doll wearing a beautiful lavender organdy costume.

There was a movie theater in Harrisburg that for one performance only was presenting Singer's Midgets for a matinee. Mother made sure I was to see this attraction and made arrangements to pick me up at school early that day. I felt privileged as I walked out of the school earlier than anyone else.

When we arrived at the theater and got settled in our seats right down front, we were first presented with an *Our Gang* movie, then came the overture. Suddenly the stage lights hit the red velvet curtain like a bombshell of color. The small orchestra sounded the cue for the curtains to part. On stage was an elaborate north pole scene, complete with icebergs and frozen mountains, and, in the distance, thirty tiny penguins stood looking like miniature nuns. Suddenly they moved to the music in unison and trailed around the set between the icebergs and frozen cliffs with perfection. It was sheer magic. The curtain had yawned open to a magical world that allowed us out front to peek at for a short while. Then all too soon the curtain closed leaving us in a sort of stupor, out in the real world again. I wondered whether the penguins continued to dance between the icebergs even though the curtain closed.

Dr. Deeter came often to check on Mother's health. Mother's office activities caused her to worry. She would be happy one day, sad the next. The roller coaster moods went up and down like a chart, and I began to be affected by them. Even my block people reflected these moods.

Mother was talking to herself at the dinner table and sometimes would turn to an invisible entity next to her. I asked who she was talking to.

"Someone I never was able to tell how I feel. Just unsaid things dear." she murmured dramatically.

I realized at this point I was out of control of everything, but myself. I delved more and more into the cave of my imagination.

Henry Beckett takes a boat ride around Manhattan with
Helen Brown, his second wife, "the nice lady," 1930s.

SCENE THREE

Rose Valley

Toward the end of our third year in Harrisburg, Dr. Deeter came quite often and discussed plans with Mother. The doctor had a brother named Jasper ("Jap"), a close friend of Mother's from childhood. He founded the Hedgerow Theatre and established a repertory group in Rose Valley. They presented everything from original plays to classics on a rotating schedule. Ann Harding was discovered at Hedgerow and Paul Robeson appeared in *The Emperor Jones*.

Since Mother had hit on hard times, her old friend Jap, offered to pay our rent and give us our meals if she would come and help sew costumes. Perhaps in time he would even give her a few small parts. So we moved to Rose Valley.

I was happy to hear that we would be living in the country. The small tastes I had from our visits were so lovely I longed to be in the country all of the time. I also had high hopes that this move would be the end of Mother's office and perhaps the visits from Mana.

I felt happy to be surrounded by rolling green hills, shade trees, the grass and flowers, and the quiet of nature. We moved into a small two story stucco house surrounded by a garden. Our landlady's house was just a few yards away through the trees.

I had my own room upstairs, and pretty much the whole house and garden to myself.

When we arrived, it was late summer, going into fall. The woods we walked through to the theater was dark even in the daytime because of the thickness of the trees.

The theater on the main Rose Valley road was a stone structure with two carved wooden horses on each side of the entrance. Inside it was dark and smelled the way a theater should, damp and musty. I could feel the presence of magic penned up in the costume trunks just waiting to fulfill their destiny.

Jasper was a tall, thin, distinguished gentleman. The actors and actresses and general theatrical fringe surrounding this man consisted of some over-educated graduates from Bryn Mawr University to aspiring young thespians from the Midwest. Everyone seemed to be an authority on something. I would sit on the sidelines of the green room and watch rehearsals, or go up in the costume room where Mother was working on costumes for *Twelfth Night*.

When no one was around I was allowed to go back stage and play with a few costume rejects. I began to feel very much at home around the theater.

There was a feeling of past wealth in Rose Valley. The great depression was in full swing, but the people in Rose Valley did not let it affect their attitude of superiority.

The little woods by the theater was certainly not affected by the depression. To walk through these woods at night when the dew was falling was magical. The tree trunks glowed with phosphorus. The fireflies sparkled in the black night. Frogs croaked in a pond. An occasional glimpse of a star appeared overhead when a breeze lifted a branch or a broken twig underfoot frightening a hoot owl into the night would all awaken a theater within me.

I felt more at home in the woods than backstage. Hedgerow Theatre belonged to others; the little woods were mine!

Mother had been given a small part in a play called *Turnstyle*. She was away a lot. Late one night when I was lying in my bed upstairs half dozing, a hoot owl shrieked through my open window, sending me downstairs as fast as I could go. Terrified, I turned on all of the electricity downstairs making the small house a beacon in the dark night. I huddled on the sofa with a book of Hans Christian Anderson's fairy tales.

It was long past midnight when Mother arrived. She was in full theatrical makeup. As Mother tried to comfort me from behind her painted face, her apparition was the grand finale of the evening's terror.

Mother decided we should move closer to the theater. We were forced to move into a one and one-half room quarters with shared bath and kitchen.

The move was made to the other side of the little woods which meant those lovely walks to get to the theater were over.

I slept on an old couch with broken springs that dug into my ribs. The one and one-half room quarters used to be a porch. Once walls were built around the porch to make it a rentable room. It was discovered the couch was too large to move out the doorway, so there it stayed.

The Italian sofa was in the bigger of the two rooms, and mother slept on that. The piano was gone and so was the big wing chair. There was one window in my room, and it was broken. The landlord promised to fix it before winter.

Our new landlord's name was Billy Walton. He had a wife named Rose and a teenage daughter named Rachel who spent the day in a big stuffed chair in the living room eating peanut crackers and reading dime novels. There was a brother who came to visit on holidays from where he lived in a mental institution.

The landlord's sister Julia was constantly peeling vegetables which left mountains of skins in the sink causing an odor of rot heavily permeating the house. Julia would put on a white sheet and sit in a lawn chair on the grass with the palms of her hands flat on the ground. Looking up at the sky she would claim to be getting some kind of energy from the earth.

One day Julia didn't make an appearance, so Rose went upstairs to see her. Upon opening the door, Rose discovered Julia lying in a sort of stupor on the bed with an empty Hershey bar carton full of wrappers from at least two dozen chocolate bars. Julia was sick, but she finally fulfilled her greatest ambition which was to live in an insane asylum. She was sent away to an institution soon after.

Jasper was preparing a play called *Thunder on the Left*, by Sherwood Anderson. There were two children's parts in it, and he came to our home with a script in his hand to try me. I got one of the parts. The other was given to Patricia Edmonton, a little girl who lived down in the hollow. I got to know her pretty well from rehearsals. Being on stage speaking lines seemed to be perfectly natural to me.

There was one scene in which we ate an entire dinner on stage, complete with boiled meat, mashed potatoes, and string beans followed by a piece of coconut layer cake. To this day coconut layer cake reminds me of *Thunder on the Left*.

Mother made me a pink organdy dress to wear on my ninth birthday because *Thunder on the Left* was on the bill for that night. However, the performance was canceled when the Pennsylvania child labor law office threatened to close the theater down if they continued using children. I cried bitterly at this news. My dress just hung over the doorway. I don't remember wearing it. To me it was a costume.

During the summer I learned to swim at the Rose Valley swimming pool. Mother supplied me with tablets of newsprint. After swimming I would sketch the swimmers. It was a good chance for me to study muscle formation since legs and arms were not covered.

Once while concentrating on my drawing, I looked up and saw Mana's face looking at me between some ferns. He smiled. It was unexpected. I ran to my mother where I would feel safe. When I told her I saw Mana in the bushes, her face dropped into an extremely darkened expression. She took my hand and together we hurried along the woods back to the theater where we could get inside. This happened several times, but then fall came and I stopped going to the swimming pool.

Then one day Mana turned up for a visit. He sat on a stone wall with me while Mother could look out the window in the upstairs costume room of the theater.

On his visit he gave me a large cardboard box, a present from the "nice lady." In it were two beautiful new dresses and a witch's costume for Halloween, complete with peaked hat and broomstick. I pretended to be pleased. After the visit, Mana promised to return as soon as he could. To me, this was more of a threat.

Mother came down. Numbly, I pointed to the dresses and said, "I don't want them. I'll give them to Betty Shay."

Betty's parents hosted a Halloween party which practically the whole valley was invited to. I don't really know why I gave the Halloween costume to Betty because her mother could have afforded the very best. However, Betty accepted it eagerly and even her mother was impressed at the fine material from which it was made.

Betty wore the costume throughout the entire evening. I wore a ballet skirt Mother made from old curtains. I loved it, and had a good time watching Betty enjoy her costume. It was wonderful to finally be not so different than the other children.

Mother began talking about getting a divorce. I didn't know much about it, except I was hoping it would mean there would be an end to Mana's visits. Mentioning my mother's divorce to Betty, Patricia, and Marion Gillman suddenly made me the center of attention.

"My mother wants to get a divorce too," Marion said, "And she doesn't know how to go about getting it. Perhaps your mother could give my mother some advice. Mom and dad are always yelling at each other. Besides, it's the latest thing."

When I asked Mother if she would give Marion's mother divorce advice, I thought it would make mother feel important. Instead she just looked off in the distance and murmured that everyone's situation is different and Marion's mother should go and see a lawyer.

When Christmas neared, we were all allowed to take one day off from school to go into Philadelphia on department store journeys. We were expected to write about it and then read it in front of the class.

The first stop in Philadelphia was a short visit to Mother's office, followed by Wanamaker's Fantasyland. Oh what a thrill to walk through the maze of snow, angel hair, mechanical snowmen in a land of enchantment. This stage set was not being observed from a theater seat. We were actually walking through it.

After a nice lunch we went to Snellenburg's department store to see their fantasy land which was a feast for the eyes and then on to Gimbel's. At the end of the walking journey through fairyland, there was a performance of mechanical dolls played by people; real people. One doll in a red sparkling tutu rose on her toes. So exquisite was she that I insisted we go through fairyland again. There were eight performances every afternoon and we went to all of them.

All the way home, I could think of nothing but that doll in the red tutu. "How can I become like that? Can I be that? Where can I go to learn how to be as beautiful as that?" Going to sleep that night my dreams were not of sugar plums; they were about the doll in the red tutu.

We had a really nice Christmas, even though the snow came through the broken window. It was still cozy; just Mother and me. The tree she set up was beautiful. She spent all Christmas Eve setting it up. I could hear her from my little room where I was supposed to be sleeping. The sound of tissue paper unwrapping ornaments, an occasional ringing bell, and strings of Christmas lights being unwound. Then under the door I saw the electric light go out and there remained, creeping through the crack, the warm theatrical glow of the colored lights of Christmas. I lay there in my warm covers feeling a very deep love for her, too. I turned and fell into a short sleep.

Christmas lights were just the beginning. I was always attracted to theatrical lights. Billy Walton and the WPA road crew were always repairing country roads in Rose Valley. At night they set up rows of oil lamps which flickered through the crisp air to signal travelers of detours. I used to love to go where the oil lamps were set up at night and slowly walk down the road between them pretending to be an Inca princess in a processional ceremony. I would take an old curtain with me and drape it over my head and walk down the avenue singing to myself. I was alone, but in my imagination there was a procession of fictitious characters walking behind me. I would come to a turn in the road, and there before me stretched more rows of oil lamps as far as I could see.

Mother decided to look for another place to live. She took me room hunting one day, and we traipsed up a rather steep hill to the right of Rose Valley Road. Through a large forest down the right side of the hill, I could hear a waterfall and see an old mill. It was all very beautiful and I was looking forward to reaching the top to see what was there. A large mansion stood at the top.

We went up to the door and knocked. A large woman wearing a red chiffon-velvet negligee with white marabou around the collar and cuffs opened the door. I detected the strong odor of perfume. "Yes?" she said in a broad voice.

"We came to look at the room for rent," Mother said.

"Oh yes," the woman replied. "Come with me and I'll show it to you. It's thirty-five dollars a month."

We followed upstairs and through hallway after hallway, past several bedrooms and baths, sitting rooms with sheets draped over the furniture and finally ended up in the servant's quarters.

"This is it," she said. "The bath is down the hall, and you can have use of the kitchen, and also the dining room."

"We'll take it," Mother said. "You're sure it's heated in the winter?"

"Yes," the woman replied, "We provide heat here. By the way, I'm Mrs. Scott, in case you need anything."

Mrs. Scott had a maid named Mary who had a room on our floor but spent most of the time in the kitchen. There were two daughters, Barbara and Janet, who were grown up now. Janet was engaged. Mr. Scott was no longer living. At one time, the big mansion had servants, two butlers, a chauffeur, and, I imagine, a limousine and several automobiles. Thanks to the depression, many of the rooms were closed.

I was given full rein to wander about the house at will. Echo often went with me. It seemed I had the mansion to myself most of the time. Mother was commuting to Philadelphia daily to her office.

One day I stumbled on Mrs. Scott's bedroom. A large double bed with an ornate headboard was covered with an old rose satin quilted spread which dominated the room. Opposite the bed was a huge dresser covered with cut-glass perfume bottles, lotions, powder puffs and pastel shades, a vase with flowers, and a collection of old family photographs.

I took care not to linger, although I was fascinated. I was afraid I would be discovered.

The living room downstairs was the most elegant of all. Windows overlooking a mowed meadow with big trees. A large fireplace was the central point. The grand piano was by the window. There were Queen Anne chairs, a coffee table, and a large sofa, behind which stood a long table with a vase of flowers. Drapes softened the light from the ceiling to the floor windows.

I liked Mrs. Scott, although Mother criticized her for wearing gaudy clothes and strong perfume. I always felt Mrs. Scott liked me, too. She stood up in my defense when Mother would scold me.

We ate breakfast together in the dining room. A young man who also rented a room ate his breakfast about the same time we did. Every morning I put a large stuffed Felix the Cat in the young man's chair so that when he came downstairs he could see it sitting in his place. Upon seeing it, he would pretend to be angry and punch the cat out of the room and down the small hall. We all laughed.

Sometimes I would hover around the kitchen where Mary would be preparing breakfast and humming to herself. Her favorite song went "The object of my affection's to change your complexion from white to rosy red" and so on. I used to wonder if she knew what the song meant, because her skin was dark, and her skin couldn't change from white to rosy red. Mary and I had many good times together.

Mother again fixed a cozy Christmas. We had a tree, complete with all of the familiar ornaments. The closeness I had with Mother that previous Christmas at the Walton's, however, was replaced by more of a feeling of independence on my part. My imagination became my companion while Mother's office occupied her time.

Winter came and went, and the most beautiful summer I've ever had in my life was spent at Mrs. Scott's. I romped over the grassy meadows with her German shepherd and sheep dog. I climbed the stone steps to the top of the silo and pretended it was a miniature castle. I wandered afternoons in the forest behind the mansion which was immense compared to the little woods near Hedgerow Theatre.

Sometimes Mother and I would pack a lunch and have a picnic in the forest. She would rest on a fallen tree and read while I explored the forest nearby. Most of the time I was alone and the forest seemed endless.

The forest was alive after dark. The fireflies filled the night with their tiny explosions of light while frogs croaked like castanets echoing through the forest. The close chirping crickets and their sudden hush at the sound of my footsteps reminded me I was an intruder. I wished I could stay in this world; become a fairy or an elf.

I became immersed in fairy tales: Anderson, Grimm, Russian, Japanese, and finally the French fairy tales. The French fairy tales were my favorite. They went on and on, and I remember spending many an afternoon in the forest reading.

At the end of summer, Mother asked me if I would like to go live in Philadelphia where I could perhaps take art lessons, piano, and go to the theater and possibly the ballet again. She said we'd look for an apartment and not tell Mana where we were. I was hesitant. I thought of the forest, but winter was coming and the lessons sounded wonderful. Perhaps with no visits from Mana, Mother would be happy again, which meant I could be happy, too.

I yearned to know more about my father who came in and out of my life like a shadow, so I summoned my courage and asked Mother. It was painful for her to answer these questions, but my need to know was strong. I learned the "nice lady" had been Mother's best friend when they both worked in Cincinnati on the newspaper. Both their names were Helen. The "nice lady" was one day older. My father worked on the *Cincinnati Post*, too. He met my mother first. They courted and became engaged. But before they married, Mana went off to fight in World War I.

Mother left the *Post* to work on a newspaper in Alabama so she could be near Mana while he was in combat training. The "nice lady" replaced Mother who had written a column for the woman's page. When Mana returned, he and Mother were married, and settled in Greenwich Village. He got a job as a reporter for the *New York Herald*.

The "nice lady" turned up, and the two Helens continued their friendship. Mother and Mana decided to go on a writing trip all over Europe, earning their way from country to country. Many years later I found old letters written from Mother to the "nice lady" during this time in Europe. There was never a mention of Mana in these letters. Instead, the writing was mostly descriptive of the spirit of Europe at that time. Mother would write about how dangerous it was for a woman alone to walk the streets of Naples where she was constantly pinched by Italian men. You would think from these letters that she was traveling alone. When Mother and Mana returned to New York they decided to have me. Mana became acquainted with the "nice lady" and began spending time away from home, either at the office or more than likely with the "nice lady."

Mother said that she had me all by herself and that Mana wasn't even there when I came into the world. Now I knew why my mother was so sad all the time. She had been trying her best to live from day to day while her marriage was falling apart.

Mother had been divorced from Mana on the 4th of July, and Mana and the "nice lady" were married the next day, somewhere in Mexico. I had the mistaken notion that this meant he had divorced me, too, and that Mother and I would now be free to live our own lives in peace.

Our new apartment was in west Philadelphia at 4434 Chestnut Street. It was a first floor apartment. There was a rear room overlooking a back yard with ailanthus trees, and as one stood to cook at the stove or to wash dishes in the sink there at the window, the yard was a restful sight. There were elegant sliding doors which separated the front room from the rear. The doors came in handy later when I played theater.

The bathroom had its own window. I was impressed with the shadows of the trees dancing on the frosted glass. The tub had elegant lion's feet, and the whole apartment seemed quite a luxury after having lived in one room at the mansion.

We had all of our belongings moved in a van. The grand piano returned and stood proudly in the corner by the big window. All our things looked so elegant in this high ceiling room and our rent was just twenty-five dollars a month.

Mother started going to her office on Broad Street almost right away. She took me there on Saturdays. The big board numbers here changed electrically; an improvement from Harrisburg. Mother would sit in the front row because she was nearsighted. Her eyes clung to every symbol that passed from left to right. I usually sat way over in a corner somewhere. When mother was in her office nothing else existed, not even me.

Mother met a woman there named Mrs. David who appeared to notice me when I came in. She asked Mother if I was artistic, and Mother said she didn't know, but had moved with me to Philadelphia to find out.

Mrs. David gave Mother an address and the following week Mother collected all of my drawings and sketches. The description of the colorful neighborhood belongs as a stage set to the music school which provided art and music to the local Jewish children of immigrants. The neighborhood looked like Old Europe.

On Saturday, mother took me on a trolley that went down Catherine

Street which was like a trip into the past. Horse drawn push carts with bolts of fabric to produce and vegetables lined the street. We walked toward a large brick building that covered almost a whole block. It seemed as if the building would burst with sound. Over the entrance, big letters spelled out "Settlement Music School."

The instant we stepped inside I remember feeling intoxicated. The sounds of practice filled the lobby, and from downstairs to the left, the aroma of paint, wet clay, varnish and linseed oil beckoned. I was home at last.

As the receptionist, a Miss Finnegan, spoke, the daylight reflected in her glasses, so her eyes were not visible. "You should have come during the summer," she continued. "That is when we start our enrollment for the following season. I'm sorry, but we can't take any more."

"You'll have room for this one," Mother answered. "I insist you look at her portfolio before you shut your registration book; and test her ear for music as well. If you find there is still no room then we will leave."

Miss Finnegan rose slowly from her seat in a daze, and descended into the basement. Mother and I stood waiting. She had my portfolio of sketches under one arm and with her free hand she held mine tight. Miss Finnegan returned and told us to go down into the basement where the art class was being held and talk to the art instructor.

Mother pulled me to the stairway and we went down into a room filled with easels, long tables laid out with poster paint and sculpture stands with figures of clay standing poised in various degrees of completion.

Children were concentrated on solitary projects. A few adults scattered about the room worked on large canvases or imposing figures of clay. A man in a smock walked toward us. He wiped paint from his hands, and then extended his hand in greeting.

"I'm Antonio Cortizas" he said. Mother introduced herself and then pushed me forward to Mr. Cortizas who shook my hand.

"My daughter Martha has brought her folio, and we would like to show it to you," Mother said.

Mr. Cortizas led us to a table in the corner. Mother laid open the portfolio. There were countless drawings of bathers at the swimming pool with characters and houses in "dark town" in Harrisburg, where Alice lived. There were sketches of Renaissance statues Mother had in her shop and there were some early sketches done of the ballet performances back in New York.

"Were all of these done by your daughter?" Mr. Cortizas asked.

"Yes," mother replied, "All of them."

"So many styles, all different from each other, as if there were many artists, all in one person. And so young," he said. Mr. Cortizas left for a moment, bringing back some of the adults who were working on the other side of the room.

"What do you think, Alex?" he asked. A tall man with a full head of dark hair, wearing a blue smock examined my folio with great interest.

"Classes are every Saturday at ten." Mr. Cortizas said. "If you can come during the week, do so. Come and work as much as you can and when your school closes for the summer you can come and work every day." He went up the stairs to the lobby. The remaining artists continued to pour over my folio, while Mother stood with an expression of triumph on her face.

Mr. Cortizas returned, told us to see Miss Finnegan, and that he would expect me next Saturday at ten. Mother asked Miss. Finnegan what the art lessons would cost.

"Nothing at all," Miss Finnegan replied. "Mr. Cortizas has given your daughter a scholarship."

After all the necessary information was written in the registrar, she closed the book and said, "Mr. Weinberg will see your daughter now, upstairs in the Brahms Studio." Mother took my hand and we went up the staircase to the second floor to the Brahms Studio.

"Well, hello, I'm Herman Weinberg," the instructor said as he concluded a lesson. "I understand you have come for piano lessons. Have you ever had any music lessons?" I told him I hadn't.

He played a simple tune on the piano, about two bars, and asked me to sing what I had heard. I did that, and afterward he played something in a different key, and asked me to sing that, which I did. He then asked if I had a piano at home, and when I answered "yes," he was pleased.

"I believe I can make time for you about two in the afternoon next Saturday," he said. "I will want you to be prepared to buy some sheet music for beginners which I will assign you next week."

The music lessons too, were on scholarship. The creative impulse inside me had finally found a home! Out on the street in the fresh autumn air, I suddenly felt that life had a purpose for me. I was going to study art, and piano. Perhaps one day I would be able to sit at the beautiful grand piano in our living room and make beautiful music come out of it.

Then my thoughts went back to the beautiful dancing doll in the red tutu at Gimbel's, and Rosey in Hazelton in her pale green tutu rising on her toes. Yes, it was wonderful that I was now going to be able to study art and music, but where was I going to have the ballet lessons I yearned for? How I wanted to dance!

My school, the Henry C. Lea School, had two floors and occupied a city block. There was a big yard for recess. Push carts stationed outside the chain link fence sold colored ice in paper cones for one cent. The liquid, waiting in bottles to be poured onto the ice, came in brilliant hues. But whatever color was chosen, the flavor was the same; sweet.

All the classrooms were lined up side by side with a wide hallway between for assembly. Sliding doors between the classrooms were opened promptly at nine o'clock creating instant togetherness on the entire floor while we remained seated for starting the day.

Allegiance to the flag and singing the "Star Spangled Banner" opened the ceremony, followed by group singing of familiar songs such as, "Going Down to Rio" and "Oh, Give Me a Home." After the sliding doors were closed the day started with reading, writing, and arithmetic. A bit of geography and history interrupted the regular subjects twice a week. One art class a week, consisting of painting in watercolor the likeness of a flower. There were no rhythm or dance classes. At least if there had been scarf dancing I would have been able to stay in touch with the part of me that longed to move to music. But the day was mostly spent sitting at our small child size desks, or single filing out into the cool air for our calisthenics which did nothing either for body or for soul.

I liked school, and made close friends, and I liked all of the subjects offered, except arithmetic. I suffered through this subject even more than I did in Rose Valley. Each class was like a cross examination. Our minds were picked and challenged for answers I really didn't think mattered. To make matters worse, I couldn't see the blackboard because I was made to sit in the back of the room due to my tallness.

One day I heard my name called. I had been daydreaming. I was called again and was ordered to go up to the blackboard and figure out the problem. Standing beside the blackboard, I saw the numbers for the first time, but I didn't know what to do with them.

"Stupid," the teacher said. "All week we have been learning long division and where have you been? Dreaming? Go sit down."

My whole face was wet with tears. I went back to my seat in the last row. Not long after that, an eye doctor visited my school and discovered I was nearsighted. I don't know if Mother bought my glasses or if the school did, but I got a pair. Finally I could see the blackboard from the back row seat in the classroom. I could see the teacher's face and even her eyes. The world around me was no longer fuzzy but it also was not as beautiful as it had been before.

The walk home from school each day was enjoyable. I walked alone now, without fear of Mana. The children's voices, roller skate wheels, or the sound of a rubber ball bouncing on the pavement, chased by a little boy running past me, were all music to my ears. Mother bought me a pair of roller skates, and soon I was skating to and from school.

Once home, I dutifully practiced my piano and I painted, and then played with my block people. Mother would come home around five thirty p.m. and cook supper. Then we would share one of those close evenings together that added up through the years, creating a tight bond between us that no one in my life has ever been able to penetrate.

There were times I brought playmates home from school. We would play theater, using the sliding doors for a curtain. We played ghosts in a basement under the house. I remember Molly, Dorothy, and Betty as if it were yesterday.

I was the only child in school that did not have a father at home. Most of the children had a father who, because of the depression had no job and, so, sat by the window all day, or on the porch, or at the local bar. Mothers were usually sewing, baking, or making candy to earn money for groceries. Many of our neighbors thought I was illegitimate. Mother wasn't disturbed by this; she preferred to believe she had me all by herself. One day an old friend of Mother's from Hedgerow turned up and gave us a pair of tickets to the Sunday Academy of Music performance of *Col. De Basil's Ballet Russe de Monte Carlo*.

My Saturday art class was the perfect threshold for Sunday. I was working on large paintings in poster and tempera paint. The subject I worked on was my choice. The expert guidance came from Antonio Cortizas. He gently, and in a fatherly way, pushed me forward into creating my own worlds on these huge sections of photographer's paper with that creative confidence so many teachers try to take away for the sake of more academic training.

I would arrive at ten o'clock every Saturday morning and feverishly work on my painted project until one. Then a short lunch of a lettuce and tomato sandwich and a carton of milk was followed by piano lessons.

My piano lessons were something else entirely. I practiced every day but played so well by ear that my sight reading fell by the wayside. Even with my glasses it was difficult for me to see the notes on the page. The keyboard was fuzzy. When I took the glasses off, the keyboard was clear, and the notes on the printed page fuzzy. So my ear took over and I would play my Mozart *Minuet* and later on, *Fur Elise* by Beethoven, with confidence.

My creative energy started taking over and I began composing pieces of my own, always in the minor key. I would practice them to perfection so that if any one asked, I could sit down and give a concert. It wasn't long before I had a small repertoire of my own. However piano teachers did not react to this weakness of mine the way Antonio Cortizas did to my world in art. They frowned on this creative escapade, of composing my own music when I should be concentrating on basics assigned to me. This made my piano lessons less satisfying than art.

At home, at the big piano, I would sit and compose for hours. I taught myself to write down what I had composed on music paper.

The Academy of Music interior did not have the ornate decorations of the old Metropolitan Opera House. But, as the orchestra assembled in the pit, the sounds of the oboe and woodwinds topped by a violinist practicing a difficult passage added to the electric atmosphere inside the grand old building.

Our seats were an upper balcony. I could look down and see all the people dressed elegantly for the matinee. I wore a robin's egg blue dress with smocking around the neck, and my braids ending with ribbons to match.

The first ballet of the evening was *Swan Lake*. I had never seen anything so beautiful. The overture from the very start was tragic serenity. The curtain rose on a shaded glen as the handsome Prince Siegfried entered with his friends. The ballet starts with the exquisite portrayal of a group of ballerinas portraying swans and the swan queen herself, whose tragic mortal entity is locked up in the body of a swan, doomed to live under the spell cast upon her by the evil sorcerer Rothbart.

Up to this point, I had never seen tragedy in the ballet. I had only been witness to fairy tale spectacles. Now I had seen the tragic figure of an exquisite young girl, forever in the body of a swan, who brushed love for an instant in a simple pas de deux of beauty and sadness.

I learned later that the ballerina who danced the swan queen was Alicia Markova. She was magnificent.

The second ballet on the evening's program was *Gaite Parisienne* to the music of Jacques Offenbach. The array of characters and strong pantomimic style displayed by the dancers was an inspiration. It was choreographed by Leonide Massine, whose theatrical trademark made him one of my idols in years to come. This colorful and gay display of charming Parisian characters caught up in a nineteenth century Parisian fantasy was electric.

The final ballet of the evening was *Scherherazade*. From the time the overture started and the curtain rose on this setting of the sultan's luxurious palace, I was transported to a world completely foreign to me, and yet I understood it all. The gaudy trappings and rich hangings of the sultan's boudoir with languishing harem ladies dazzled me. It seemed I was breathing the sound and the spectacle through my eyes and my ears, and that my lungs were themselves becoming asphyxiated with the sensuousness of it.

I knew now that dance and pantomime were universal languages in the theater, where tragedy becomes bearable, even beautiful. I knew now that this was the language I wanted to speak. I wanted to be part of that world which had the ability to reflect life back to us beautifully.

Going through my daily routine was superimposed by the vivid pictures of what I had experienced at the ballet. Real life was transparent. I walked about in a daze. All the time my mind was going over everything I had seen.

During those years on Chestnut Street, I observed everything that went on around me. Little dramas that went nowhere presented themselves to me at every turn. On my side of Chestnut Street lived Dr. Steinmetz, his wife and their teenage son Charles. Mrs. Steinmetz was a Sunday school teacher in the local Baptist church. She recruited me for her class, and I went every Sunday. She wore a large brooch, which, during the lesson, went up and down as she breathed. She resembled one of the women in Ruben's paintings, even the auburn hair and fair skin.

Mrs. Steinmetz objected to roller skating on Sunday, which made it difficult for me because Saturday was spent at art and music lessons. So I roller skated in the back alley.

The Baptist Sunday school and church were a strange ritual to experience. I sat and watched the baptisms in a great marble pool. I sang hymns and listened to sermons I didn't understand. I watched the daylight through the stained glass windows. The music emanating from the choir and organ did nothing to create that sense of awe and humility one feels in God's house. However, I tried to feel something.

When Christmas came, there was a big church party. However, I decided not to go when I heard that Mrs. Steinmetz would not allow Elaine, my best friend in Sunday school class, to come. Elaine was one of thirteen children left to a man whose wife had recently died, and who had taken to drink rather heavily. I could no longer bear to sit every Sunday morning in a congregation of persimmon smiles and fake righteousness while children were being turned away at the door because of the sins of their fathers.

Mother decided to move to the apartment next door, 4436 Chestnut, because it was ten dollars a month cheaper. She called on a storage company to do the job. Mr. Bernstein, the owner, came and made an estimate. He became attracted to Mother, and she did nothing to discourage his visits.

He began taking us out to dinner and coming to our apartment on late Sunday afternoons. I would prepare a play with my block people and Mother and Mr. Bernstein would sit and watch. I enjoyed these Sundays, having an audience of my mother and perhaps a father figure to watch. It was all happy, until I heard there was a Mrs. Bernstein in the picture.

When I asked questions, Mother would only answer, "Well, his wife doesn't understand him. She wants children and he doesn't."

Mother was now the "nice lady," and Mrs. Bernstein was the wife who remained home. I was disappointed in my mother for doing to someone else the very thing that was done to her. I liked Mr. Bernstein, and we all had fun together, but underneath it all was the painful knowledge that there was someone in the background being hurt.

Often on Sunday afternoon, mother and I would go to the Philadelphia Art Museum. The hush inside its walls, the muffled sounds of voices discussing the paintings, and the special light provided made me feel that the only important thing in the world was art. From then on I decided to make everything I saw a scene in a play where something is about to happen. I decided to make everything I did a part of that play or a possible painting, or a stage set.

During the summer months, Mother and I would take long walks in and outside of our neighborhood. At the local candy store we'd buy seven caramels for one cent, and make them last all evening. We'd pass rows and rows of wooden porches. We'd pass a game of hop scotch or jump rope out on the sidewalk. We would put a handkerchief on our head to visit a beautiful Catholic church whose stained glass windows intrigued us.

My observations became reality in my drawings. The magic of the ballet however, had not yet made its way into these stage sets of my life. What I dreamed of since I had been to the Ballet Russe was still in another world. But the worlds of those around me seemed just as worthy of exploration on stage as the stories of *Swan Lake* or *Scheherazade*.

Life itself is a stage. Millions of plays are all going on at once. I didn't realize that I, too, was a part of this drama. I was too busy observing it and recording it.

Mother had made an impression with her dramatic personality at Settlement Music School. Because of her experience at Hedgerow Theatre in Rose Valley, she sold them the idea of teaching drama as an additional subject to music and art.

I soon learned they had dance all this time, and ballet too, taught by Madame Krupska. I scolded Mother for not bringing it to my attention.

"You knew I wanted ballet lessons more than anything else," I cried.

Mother retorted, "You would never have the strength it takes. Your diet would be more than I could afford. And don't forget, your father abandoned us. We are two against the world, dear. You have enough with your music and art."

I would watch the ballet classes from the doorway. The piano rang out through the halls with that romantic melancholy ballet music has. I longed to go inside and work along with the others to that beautiful music.

Christmas of that year, Mother's dramatics class was scheduled to give a play. It had gnomes and a princess in it. Mother did not give me the part of the princess. She thought that might show favoritism. I was the princess' friend. The anticipation of going out on stage to play a character other than myself was for me a happy anticipation.

In addition to the play, piano and violin solos, as well as the ballet class were scheduled to appear. After the play in the wings, I heard Miss Finnegan's voice announce, "Solo to be danced by Dania Krupska."

A vision in a romantic length tutu appeared and danced to Chopin's Waltz in C# Minor. I was so close I could almost touch her. The otherworldliness of her movements as she skimmed across stage on her toes, the poses, and the mood she evoked at each gesture brought tears to my eyes. I learned later that she was Madame Krupska's daughter. "Why can't I be allowed to have ballet lessons?" I wondered. "What harm would there be?"

Ballet could absorb all of me, physically and spiritually. In dance, I am the instrument instead of the player of the instrument. In painting, there again, I am only the eye behind the brush. In dance, I become the painting.

I was twelve years and I knew if I were ever going to take ballet lessons, I'd better not wait too much longer. I tried not thinking about ballet. But visions of Dianna Krupska, the Ballet Russe and the twirling doll in the red tutu kept interrupting me and each time there was that dull pain inside.

My playmates from school did not appreciate my obsession with the ballet. They thought toe dancing was for tiny tots who would one day grow up and have a photo of themselves on the mantle as a four year-old prodigy. I had witnessed ballet performed entirely by adults. I knew there was a world of art populated by adults. How could I get into this world?

Perhaps you have to be Russian, like the women in the Ballet Russe, I thought. From then on, I wanted to be Russian. Theirs was such a beautiful, colorful world. When the curtain fell, and they were no longer visible, I truly believed they continued to live in this world of beauty while we, out front, continued our humdrum lives.

I began composing pieces on the piano mainly in the minor key. When I wrote them down in manuscript, I signed them with a Russian name; Olga Marnoff.

In art class I worked on huge murals of the circus, side shows and jungle scenes complete with savages, elephants and tigers. In class I was treated as an adult and encouraged to dream with charcoal, paint, and clay. I would wake up on a typical summer day, dreaming of the project waiting for me down in the big studio. Nothing else mattered but getting down there to work on it.

Sometimes Mr. Cortizas would take me to the Europa Theatre to see a foreign movie. Because I was so thin, he felt I did not have enough to eat, so he gave me money one day to buy a sandwich before going home. I went into Woolworth's after he turned the corner and bought a lovely set of watercolors to take home with me instead. The only art materials I had then were those supplied by the art class.

There was to be an art exhibit down on Broad Street of all the adult artists in Mr. Cortizas' group. My jungle mural was to be included. One day while looking at my work, I decided that it was finished. Mr. Cortizas was not present, so I turned to Alex and exclaimed, "I believe it is finished. Any more would be too much." I put down my brushes and added, "If Mr. Cortizas returns and believes it is not yet finished and needs more work, be sure he lets me know. I cannot even look at it anymore."

Alex looked up and said, "All right I'll tell him."

Mother and I dressed up for the exhibit. After we were inside, we searched everywhere for my painting, but it was not there. Spotting Mr. Cortizas standing in a corner talking to a group of artists, I ran up and asked, "Why is my jungle mural not in the exhibit?"

"You weren't sure it was finished," he answered. "You had asked for my opinion," he continued. "It is not my painting, it is yours. I won't hang an artist's work unless he feels his work is finished."

Mother led me outside and wiped away my tears. I was deeply hurt. I was a disappointment to Mr. Cortizas who expected more of me.

Soon my desire to paint and sketch new works began to overshadow the lump in my throat. I began to realize my talent; this magnetic pull toward the studio and my creative pursuits was the best friend I had.

Fall was upon us. These golden afternoons of Indian summer roller skating to and from school, painting and practicing the piano, and anticipating the quiet suppers with Mother gave me a happy childhood.

The outings on two weekend Sundays a month with Mr. Bernstein were pleasant, and gave me the opportunity to go dine in Chinese restaurants, an exotic experience for me. I tried not to think of Mrs. Bernstein alone at home.

In school geography lessons, we were studying Holland, the land of tulips, dikes, windmills, canals, and wooden shoes. Mr. Lynch assigned me and a boy named Walter to paint a Dutch landscape on a piece of paper that would reach entirely around the room. Walter threw a fit because I was a girl.

"I will not work on the same project with a girl," he explained. "Girls cannot paint. They will never be able to paint. Either I go in with another boy, or paint the scene myself," he said.

I thought surely Mr. Lynch would side with Walter, being a man.

"You will collaborate with Martha on this Holland project, or she will paint it by herself," Mr. Lynch said.

"I'll work on the painting," Walter said meekly. Next day the paper was unrolled and the great scene was started. I was assigned one half of the room, Walter the other.

The poster colors were mixed from jars of brilliant powders. We were allowed to paint continuously until it was finished, and what a beautiful scene it was, the two halves of Holland surrounding the room until they met at the head of the class, and the rear. Walter would not allow his half to blend with mine. My being a girl must have made him feel that if our halves blended, his half would be contaminated. The space in between did not spoil the landscape. It was a triumph, and stayed pinned up around the top of the classroom for the rest of the year.

Underneath the apartment where Mother and I lived, were two ex-vaudevillians. Tony had played the violin all his life. Ralph had been a tap dancer. They would practice their old routines out in the backyard every evening. "Haven't you heard? Vaudeville's coming back. We must stay ready," they would say.

They had happy, wonderful times in the backyard. Though the countless afternoons, practicing in the backyard for the return of vaudeville would never amount to a return of their dreams, the hope colored by vivid memories of the great life they had shared years before was an experience unequaled by most people. I used to gaze out the window and watch them trying to preserve a dream.

Even when Ralph became terminally ill, it did not seem to change his behavior. They still practiced. Ralph, Tony, Mother and I went on an outing to the country and spread a picnic beside an old swimming hole. Ralph invited me to ride on the inside of a big inner tube while he navigated. From my vantage point in the inner tube, I watched this brave man, a tap dancer, who was going to die.

"Perhaps he refuses to believe it," I thought to myself as I gazed into his laughing face. I decided not to believe it either. But two weeks later, Ralph died. Tony had him cremated; his ashes put in an urn, and set on the mantle piece. The dream they shared had come to an end.

One day at school during one of our classroom sessions, the door opened and in walked a teacher from the principal's office. She went over to Mr. Lynch and handed him some papers and an envelope.

I was called to the front of the room. "Are these photographs of you?" the teacher asked as she removed snapshots from the envelope. The snapshots were of me, when I was three to five years old.

"Yes," I said meekly. "Why?"

The whole classroom turned in my direction. The silence was tense.

"You may be excused for the rest of the afternoon," said Mr. Lynch. "But first you must go to the principal's office."

In the principal's office he smiled at me and said. "I believe we have a surprise for you, Martha."

He made a gesture with his arm to the corner of his office where Mana sat in a chair beside another man from child welfare. The sobbing started from my heart and went through my entire body like tidal waves. They gave me a chair and I collapsed on it, and bent over so that my head could touch my knees. I felt cornered.

"Look at her," the principal said, "Martha is crying for joy at the sight of her father again, aren't you dear?" He came over and raised my chin with his hand.

I wondered how he could interpret this outburst as joy. I didn't want to believe Mana had found me. I was hoping against hope that this was all a nightmare, and that I would open my eyes from this terrible dream into reality.

I would never be able to walk to school alone again or go to the Settlement House Music School alone, roller skate alone, or play hopscotch in the back alley with my friends. I had been having such a happy life. How could he ever legally claim my love?

Suddenly the school bell rang. I remembered Mother was going to meet me after school. It was a bank holiday, and she didn't need to go to her office. I dashed out of the principal's office and ran out into the school yard, through the crowds of children to Mother who stood waiting for me on the other side of the chain link fence. She was smiling, but her smile faded when she saw the look of terror on my face.

Behind me she could see the principal walking with Mana and the man from the child welfare office. When I reached Mother, I fell into her arms and the sobbing started all over again.

Mana came out through the gate and made an attempt to approach us. "I would like to see you and talk about something," he said to Mother.

"I think I'd better take Martha home now," Mother answered. "She seems to have had quite enough for one day."

The next day Mother kept me at home. She told me to bolt all the doors and not to let anyone in. She had to go to her office.

"What will be my excuse for staying home?" I asked.

"A sore throat," Mother answered.

She drank her coffee, hugged me nervously and assured me that she would be home around four thirty p.m. Then she left, and I was very much alone. Even my block people could not help me now. I didn't want to draw or paint or compose at the piano. I just sat there on the sofa in my bathrobe, feeling numb. I felt hunted.

Suddenly, there was a knock at the door. I stood motionless, unable to breathe.

"It's Dr. Rennslaar," a voice called out. "Your principal from school. Open the door, you needn't be afraid. I'm alone."

I opened the door, and Dr. Rennslaar stepped in. He looked around the bare room, looked at our furnishings and all my drawings strewn around the place with a critical expression which told me he regarded the apartment as a mess.

"Where is your mother?" he asked. "Why are you not in school and why are you still in your bathrobe?"

Meekly I answered that Mother had to go to the store, and that I had a sore throat.

"Your mother is afraid your father is going to kidnap you, isn't she?" Dr. Rennslaar said.

"Well yes," I answered.

"Your father wouldn't do anything like that," Dr. Rennslaar replied "He only wants the very best for you; he wants to watch out for your welfare. I want to see you in school tomorrow morning. If you are absent again we'll have to send the truant officer after you. Please give this message to your mother when she returns."

When Mother returned, she was furious. "What right has the principal of a school got to meddle in the family problems of a student? I'm a mother, and I have the right to keep my child home from school if she is in jeopardy."

The next morning she again told me to bolt the door against intruders, then stormed off to school and had it out with the principal. After this incident, he backed off and Mother said he even apologized for his intrusion.

I was in school the next day. In assembly, Dr. Rennslaar talked to us and said, "As you grow up into adults and observe the world around you, we see that there are many who are not as fortunate as ourselves. Most of us come from warm, cozy homes where a mother and father are always there for emotional as well as physical support. Many of you have brothers and sisters, combined to make what we refer to as the family. The other day," he continued, "I had reason to visit the home of one of our more unfortunate neighbors. The apartment was stripped of the comforts of life. No comfortable chairs, no rugs, no carpets, no drapes at the window, and no radio. It was practically bare. To make things worse, there was no mother in sight and no father present at all, ever. If any of you might possibly be acquainted with such a neighbor, I hope you will observe this tragic situation and not take yours for granted. Give this neighbor a helping hand instead of looking down on him, or feeling superior. As you grow into adulthood, it is a good thing to start accepting the fact that we are all brothers and sisters in this same world, and that no one is any better than anyone else just because he happened to be born under more fortunate circumstances. This is my message for the day."

He bowed his head and went out. I felt all of the eyes in the assembly were upon me. No one even turned to look. However, my close playmates knew how I lived, and I could not help but think that their mind's eye would be picturing me during Dr. Rennslaar's vivid description.

Following this turn of events, Mana again began to visit on weekends. The man from child welfare was not with him. Mana came alone, with presents. The visits were uncomfortable, but at least Mother and Mana were congenial to each other.

"How would you like to take a trip to New York?" Mother asked out of the clear blue.

"I guess that would be nice. Are we going to go to the ballet?" I asked.

"No," she answered. "Mana is having us visit New York so that you can hear the symphony concert at Carnegie Hall. He feels that it is important for you to hear Arturo Toscanini, the greatest conductor of them all."

"Can't we go to the ballet, too? We're going to be right there where it is? We used to go."

"No," Mother answered. "We're going to go apartment hunting. If we find an apartment, we'll move back to New York and Mana is going to pay our rent and food, and you can continue your art and music there."

"Aren't we happy here?" I asked. "Why do we have to go back to New York?"

"We won't be hungry in New York, dear," Mother answered. "I can hardly manage any more, and this will be a great help."

When it was time for the first bus trip to New York, all I told Mr. Cortizas was that I wouldn't be down to the art class that Saturday because mother was taking us to New York. I remember Mr. Cortizas looked concerned over this news, but he said nothing.

As the end of our long bus ride neared, mother pointed her finger out the window and exclaimed, "Look, the New York skyline."

I raised my eyes to see the island of lighted skyscrapers, huddled together, reaching to the sky. My heart pounded. Those skyscrapers; I had been born in there somewhere. The ballet was there somewhere. The memories of six years ago were now swarming through my mind. Maybe it will be all right after all I thought.

Mother and I went to the YWCA where we stayed in a dormitory with other ladies. I took a warm bath in a communal bathroom where rows of bath tubs on lion's feet stood at the ready.

The next three days were a whirlwind merry-go-round of activities only to be found in New York. Mana met us the next day at the Metropolitan Museum of Art. We had lunch at the Central Park Zoo. That evening we went to Child's Restaurant.

After dinner we walked up to Times Square to Carnegie Hall to hear the symphony conducted by Arturo Toscanini. The elegant white and red interior brought back a swarm of memories. The awesome hush before the storm of applause greeting the white-haired Toscanini as he walked to his place on the podium generated a wave of nostalgia and awe.

Toscanini raised his arms, held them slightly up for a moment, the baton poised a bit higher. Then suddenly, down they went as he seemed to literally pull Beethoven's pastoral symphony out of the air.

The next morning Mana was there waiting for us in the lobby of the YWCA, and we went across the street to Rikers Quick Food restaurant for toasted English muffins and hot cocoa.

The day started on the Third Avenue elevated train which took us to the Staten Island Ferry. The vibrations from the center of the ferry were overwhelming, like a tremendous animal clearing its throat before a cry. The green-brown water around us began to churn, and looked like a glassy marble surface set in motion. The great whistle blew, the gates clanged, and the lattice like accordion fence closed us in as the ferry majestically moved out into the bay.

An accordionist on board serenaded young couples and amused small children. I watched brothers and sisters play as I sat on the bench of the ferry. I wished I had a sister but instinctively knew I would never have one.

I also observed affection between the many mothers and fathers. When I would turn to look at my mother and father, they would be sitting stiffly in their own worlds looking out at the bay.

At the end of the ferry ride, Mana quickly skirted us around through the park in between the bench-lined walks to the aquarium. Inside the aquarium it was dark, and round. Lighted windows with fish inside, hundreds of species, circled us. Voices echoed, and the screams of small children reverberated into a deafening pitch. I noticed how oblivious the fish were to us and all that went on outside their glass window.

We made a trip to the Natural History Museum during this weekend in New York. Past the great dinosaur and the progression of skulls from the ape to the homo sapian there were painted miniature stage sets of the Western prairie and American deserts which stood as background to coyotes, eagles, buffalo, and smaller creatures. I was struck with their placid beauty; the sandy space with interruptions of brush evenly spaced, converging in the distance to become merged in a horizon which touched the sky.

"Was there such a place?" I wondered. The serenity and peace, endless space of pale colors of sand and sky seemed like a perfect canvas for dreams.

That evening after supper at Horn & Hardart, we went to a movie and stage show at Radio City Music Hall. Stepping inside the great lobby with its luxuriant soft carpet underfoot was not unlike the feeling of the old Roxy Theatre. The chandeliers, the curving grand staircase, the ceiling to floor mirrors, and hushed voices of the crowd gave that feeling of anticipation.

Stiff men in military type garb stood at the entrance of each aisle leading into the great theater, and like recordings, answered questions and directed the crowds to the seating area. We went up the grand staircase and were ushered to seats in the center of the first balcony.

The great Wurlitzer organ was playing popular tunes of the day. Suddenly the orchestra pit mechanically rose from out of a deep well. The spotlight hit the orchestra from above, the great Wurlitzer organ stopped, and the conductor turned around and bowed. The orchestra played "Orpheus in the Underworld" and "Dance of the Hours."

The curtain rose in its spectacular contour fashion to display a mythical scene revealing Apollo in his sun chariot surrounded by a swarm of dancing maidens in pastel chiffon dresses. The maidens, who seemed to float on air about the stage, caught my eye. I closely watched the ballet unfold. I knew once again that theater was the world I wanted, and that dance was the medium I wanted to express myself with.

Following this exquisite glimpse into the world of illusion was a dog act, two people who played ping-pong and a couple who sang operetta selections, followed by the Rockettes who stretched clear across the stage and kicked until applause sprang up all around us.

Finally the great curtain fell, the orchestra disappeared, and the Wurlitzer organ played a short march introducing the *March of Time* news. The *March of Time* was followed by the feature film which was *It Happened One Night*.

It was indeed a whirlwind weekend of sightseeing and I knew it was about over. Mana and Mother made arrangements to do it all over again, which we did later on that spring.

That summer, Mother and I made our final trip to New York to look for an apartment. We stayed this time with an old friend of hers who also had been divorced and had two little girls, Ellen and Sue. They lived in an apartment in Greenwich Village on Waverly Place.

Ellen and I played together between excursions with Mana. Meantime, Mother found an apartment at 44 Greenwich Avenue, first floor.

Our new apartment had once been inhabited by the well known American artist, Thomas Hart Benton. It had a wonderful back porch with two French doors through which you could step from the living room. The back porch looked out onto a series of roof tops with skylights over which bent countless ailanthus trees. The large living room had a rough board floor and an exposed kitchenette that we hid with a folding screen with big flowers on it.

I had my own small bedroom off the porch which also had a glass door. The bathroom was under the stairway which led to the apartment upstairs. I remember having to bend over in order to get into the tub.

We decided I would continue my music and art lessons at Greenwich House. I wanted to go to the same school Ellen did. Since it was a private school, Mana paid the tuition, along with our rent which was forty dollars a month, and ten dollars a week for food.

This final visit to New York was the happiest visit of all. Along with all the concerts and theater Mana took us to, I remember so well the festive Fifth Avenue double-decker bus ride, which provided an elephant ride-like view of Manhattan's Washington Square all the way up to the cloisters near Fort

Tyron Park. I had my picture taken on top of the Empire State Building with a big hoop we had bought at Macy's.

Returning to Philadelphia this last time was painful. I didn't want to leave Settlement Music School, Mr. Cortizas, or the slow pace of the life. Mr. Cortizas had planned that I would join his life class and adult groups the following winter, and my move to New York was a great disappointment to him. He wouldn't talk much and didn't want to stay in touch at all. Our parting was very final.

Marta wears her La Source costume at age 15.

Scene Four

Returning to New York

I continued my piano lessons with a Miss Edwards at Greenwich House and my art lessons with a Mr. Cavelito. While Mother and I were standing in the large lobby in the Barrow Street building, signing me up for my music lessons, I could see the auditorium where I had improvised to Chopin's *Prelude in A Major* during naptime many years ago.

I noticed children and young adults all going through the doorway with practice bags and black felt acrobatic sandals clutched in their hands. Inside, an exotic woman in a long purple chiffon dress was leaning over the grand piano talking to the accompanist. She clapped her hands and everyone ran and took a folding chair for the first exercise. The woman began to move and demonstrate while the class followed.

I insisted we stand in the doorway and watch after Mother finished paper-work. I was so strong in my insistence that she had little choice.

"Mother," I asked, "Why can't I go to that class, please?" Mother went over to the registration desk and asked how much the rhythms class was.

"Twenty five cents," the woman seated at the desk answered.

"All right," Mother answered, "I guess we can afford that."

I sighed the largest and most meaningful sigh of my life. I felt a glowing inside, an anticipation of being completely alive at last. Now I will be able to express with my body what up until now was expressed with brush and piano. The door to this world that had been shut to me for so long was now open. True, I was not going to have ballet lessons, but I was going to dance through space and become a part of the music instead of a listener.

I was not used to the new kind of school which I was going to go to, labeled "progressive." Certainly today, if I were a parent, I would not consider a school such as this one. However, at age thirteen it seemed perfect. I thought it was a waste of time to study a subject you disliked and were not good at. Why not devote all your time and energy to cultivating something you enjoy. So as far as arithmetic was concerned, it was completely left out of my school schedule.

Instead, there was art, folk singing, modern dance, and many sessions discussing political issues of the day. A new subject loomed up on the horizon too; adolescent problems which were discussed in the cloakroom, only to find their way to the classroom.

The children were all a bit snobbish, and again, as in my preschool days, were offspring of famous people. One or two of them were problem children whose behavior was being studied. I remember sitting next to a boy named Owen who would suddenly turn and start beating on me. The teacher was taking notes on what he was doing and to my reaction to the beating!

Music class consisted mainly of Southern spirituals and work songs. The modern dance class was simply stomping around a large room to the accompaniment of a drum, acting oppressed. I wasn't happy at this school, but I knew if I could make it through until high school without arithmetic, I would be safe. I had heard of music and art high school where I could major in art, and Washington Irving High School where I could also major in art, and could drop arithmetic if so desired.

At this time Ellen started taking real ballet lessons from a Mrs. Van Dyke. Although I was taking the twice a week rhythms class at Greenwich House, I couldn't help feeling a slight pang of envy at seeing the new pink Capezio ballet slippers, tights and black leotard her mother bought her. My mother had not been able to buy me the black felt acrobatic sandals like the others in the class, but I didn't dwell on this for at last I was taking dancing lessons. Pink ankle socks were good enough.

At this time there was a French film which had just been released called *Ballerina*, starring Mia Slavenska and Yvette Chavier. I am still impressed by this film. When the leading ballerina of the Paris Opera retires at the height of her career to marry, the star pupil asks her, with tears in her eyes, "Why do you stop, what else is there?" With a patronizing pat from the ballerina on the child's shoulder she answers, "When you grow up you will understand."

I have grown up many times and I still do not understand!

I was beginning to imitate what I saw in the film, and my dance classes with Ingaborg Tarrup were now taking hold in my body so that movement was no longer foreign to me. I was no longer just a spectator, I was really dancing.

Ellen and I used to roller skate afternoons on the sidewalk which circled the Woman's House of Detention. I had taught myself to do pique turns on roller skates, and one particular day I was having a glorious time turning when a woman passing by stopped me.

"Your pique turns are very good," she said. "How long have you studied?"

When I told her I took rhythms classes, she shook her head.

"You need a real ballet teacher," she said. "You have the makings of a very good dancer."

I was ecstatic, no one had ever noticed I had any talent to dance, yet alone a perfect stranger. Perhaps it wasn't too late after all.

My piano lessons were alright, but uninspiring. However, I did compose one selection rather Mozartian in style and structure. Miss Edwards thought it was good enough to play in the spring recital. I played my own compositions so much better than my musical assignments, so I guess Miss Edwards decided my own work would show me off to better advantage.

All the parents came to hear their little geniuses display what they had accomplished during the year. Mother and Mana came, and they even sat next to one another. The thought even went through my head that if I played well enough, and made them both proud of me, I could perhaps create a togetherness.

After the recital was over and we were on the way out, Mana said he overheard a woman behind him say, "I don't believe that child wrote that piece. Someone helped her!" I wasn't too happy about this remark.

This recital gave me great impetus to write more compositions. I attempted to copy them down through carbon paper and go into the publishing business by having piles of manuscripts. It was hard; the carbon would slip. To solve this problem, Mana treated me to a Christmas present of a hundred mimeographed copies of my *Gavotte* and my *Nocturne in A Minor*.

I designed a cover for these published selections which consisted of colored paper with the ghost of a large G clef stenciled on the front, surrounded by a field of lightly spattered poster paint. On the back cover was printed, "Coming next week, Prelude in G Major, Waltz in A Minor, Minuet in C Major, Sonotina in F Minor, and Spanish Dance." I named my publishing company the Marnoff Publishing Company. I thought, as everyone else did at this time, to be Russian in name would win immediate respect and instant success.

I took my published works and piled them in a little red wagon and toted them up and down Greenwich Avenue selling them for five cents each. I commissioned for myself a terrible schedule. Now I had to get these pieces out and published by the following week because the back cover said so. However, Mana advised me to sell my *Gavotte* and *Nocturne in A Minor* first before publishing the rest of my repertoire. This was just good business, he advised.

Soon the Marnoff publishing wore itself out. After a few people on the block had bought a composition or two, I still had a pile of one hundred sheets of manuscript.

Mother continued to go to the board room in the Pennsylvania Hotel daily. On Saturday mornings I went along so she could keep an eye on me. I would sit out on the second floor balcony with my sketch book and draw the cleaning women with their mops and buckets swabbing down the marble staircase. After the market closed at noon, we went for a hot dog and orange drink. Then we'd go window shopping and perhaps a museum.

Mana was beginning to make insinuations about Mother not looking for a job. I could not imagine her holding down a day-to-day job.

I had a well-to-do aunt on Mana's side of the family whose daughter did charity work for a small thrift shop on Eighth Avenue between Fortieth and Forty-first Street. She helped Mother get a job which paid seventy-five cents an hour.

With visible lack of enthusiasm Mother started working at the family thrift shop. After school, I was told to answer the phone just in case her broker called with information regarding her stocks. In this there was to be secrecy as well. I was not supposed to let her broker know that she had a daughter, so when I answered the phone I did so with the drawl of a maid fresh from the South. Mr. Marquis, her broker, seemed satisfied with my message taking, and I remember hearing Mother chuckle when she told me how impressed he was with the nice homey sounding maid who answered the phone.

Mother was now beginning to get presents from Mr. Marquis, and soon, when he had proven himself to be a trusted friend as well as a good broker, she told him about me. Soon the three of us began going out to dinner together.

Mr. Bernstein still visited New York periodically, and he too would take us out. Mana would come and take us out every weekend now that he was providing for us regularly. The conflict of colliding social engagements, plus the secrecy of her stock market activities, kept mother jumping.

I felt she was wanted now by two different men, and my company was always welcome.

Somehow I had a feeling of family.

When I would roller skate up to the family thrift shop to meet Mother so that we could go home together, Miss Sydell, the shop's manager, would look up and smile. Until closing time, I would browse. The shop was piled high with hat boxes on shelves and racks of 1910 to 1930 suits, dresses, and evening clothes, as well as umbrellas, parasols, and rows of the narrow pointed ladies shoes with fancy buckles. Piles of lace slips and camisoles, and boxes of novelties like stick pins and feathers occupied the center aisle. The smell was musty. It reminded me of Hedgerow Theatre.

One particular evening dress caught my eye. It was almost my size. It had a silver lamé bodice with a dropped waist line. From the dropped waist line hung tiers and tiers of pink tulle pointed like the petals of a rose. I looked at the evening dress longingly. I yearned to wear it and dance in it. Each time I went to meet Mother, there it was. The price tag was sixty-five cents. For six months I roller skated up and met Mother at the thrift shop, always ending my browsing with the evening dress.

One day I was browsing about the store and I stopped short where the evening dress hung and it was not there! My heart sank. Somehow I had begun to feel that the evening dress was mine and now it was gone!

At school we had an end of the term play which we presented as the big dramatic accomplishment of the class. It was a play about tenement life and street gang fights, with a murder at the end. It supposedly pointed a finger at the injustice of our social system, allowing the spoils of poverty to go as far as this theatrical display revealed.

I really didn't care about the message this play was trying to convey. What I did care about was that I was assigned to create the stage set, paint it, and play the important part of the murdered boy's mother. This venture absorbed all of my time and enabled me to get out of all class subjects, such as arithmetic.

The stage set was done on a huge stage-size piece of photographer's paper upon which I painted from top to bottom a row of brick tenements complete with fire escapes. A window at the top was cut out so that I, as the mother, could lean out and call down to the street below. The front door to the tenement was cut out also, so that a neighboring character could run into it from the street with the terrible news of the murdered boy.

The paper set rumbled during the dramatic action which leant an ominous excitement to the production. I was pleased with how the set came out, happy with the dramatic part I played in it, and the fact I could skip all those hours away from school work to live in this theater world.

That spring there was a graduation of the eighth grade class. Mother made me a white organdy dress with lace shirring at the top. My skirt was full, like a romantic length tutu. It was all I could do to keep from spinning so that the skirt would stand out.

While parents, teachers, and friends were all filing into the plain wood auditorium, I was to sit at the upright piano and play my compositions. My classmates sat up on the stage waiting for the ceremony to begin. As soon as everyone was finally seated, I went up on the stage also and sat with my classmates.

I could see Mother and Mana seated side by side. Mother didn't have that far away look she so often had. She seemed to be really present at this event. Mana looked proud and I felt happy to see them together.

During the spring, the boys in my class would go out with some of the girls. Giggling and secret meetings in the basement cloakroom took place and I felt very much left out of what seemed to be a part of growing up. A boy named Arthur took me to the movies at the Waverly Theatre a few times, but the anticipation of "goodbye time" during the date had an effect on me which took away the enjoyment of the movie.

I was always tense and afraid of doing something I could not tell my mother. It was difficult at the end of a date to refuse a boy a light goodnight kiss. In order not to hurt his feelings I would just say, "But I don't love you! I like you, but I don't love you."

Then when I went back to Mother, I could look her in the eye, my conscience clear.

I had an inkling of how babies were born, but the inkling was composed haphazardly of fragments from schoolmates and drawings one of the boys made in the school yard.

I tried asking Mother several times, but to even broach the subject caused a quiet tension. I began feeling guilty for wanting to know something that made her feel pain. Once when I attempted to ask she said, "A mother and father must really love each other very, very much in order for the baby to happen."

"What happened after that then?" I asked knowing something terrible must have happened between Mother and Mana causing their love to end. I thought then it was the "nice lady" who took Mana away.

"A man cannot love a woman when she is going to have a baby," Mother answered bitterly. Her whole expression changed. "Mana told me that," she said.

I knew then it was all my fault. If I hadn't been born, Mother and Mana would still be together. I decided then that I should do everything possible to make up for the terrible thing I did by being born. Mother noticed that what she had said had a devastating effect on me, and immediately attempted to make up for it.

"Oh no," she said. "Nothing could replace the wonderful life we now have together. To have you my dear child is more than anything I could have dreamed of. Now you are my breath of life! We are mother and daughter, sister to sister, we are pals. We have a whole life together and no one will ever take that away from us, no one. Two against the world, dear; two against the world."

Mother wept now, dramatic tears. She clung to me and made me feel needed and I began to feel better. Right then I knew my purpose was to make up for all the hurt I may have caused my mother by supporting her as soon as I could, and staying with her forever and ever.

Not only was I naive, and way behind my contemporaries in knowledge about life, I was also a late bloomer. All of my contemporaries were developing physically in various parts of their bodies, acting as if it were all some kind of great accomplishment. The boys were developing grotesque voices with a mixture of croaking and scraping. I had high hopes of avoiding this awkward period.

"Perhaps," I thought to myself, "I will become a dancer and make my body what I want it to be." I wasn't really ready to grow up yet. There was too much I wanted to do first. I knew that if I could stay as I was, Mother would be happy. The only change I welcomed was that which is earned through accomplishment.

That summer it was decided I would go to Washington Irving High school, where I could major in art for five periods a day. I was happy about this and I was pleased that school was within walking distance from home. My art portfolio passed the examination for entrance with no problem.

My fourteenth birthday was coming up the ninth of August. I knew that time was running short if I were ever to start real ballet lessons. The rhythms class was fine, but would never prepare me to make my life dance.

Mana was coming to take us to dinner for my birthday. But before he arrived, I saw on the Italian sofa a large box wrapped in tissue paper. I started to open it, half expecting a fall dress for starting school in September. Inside was the evening dress from the thrift shop I had so wanted. I burst into tears and hugged my mother. She knew after all how much I wanted that dress. She knew it and bought it, and saved it for my birthday. She was the only person in the world who knew.

Registration day for high school was held at the end of summer. Mother and I went the route on foot that I would be taking for the next several years. I chose to go on roller skates while Mother went on foot. When we arrived at the entrance, I removed my skates.

While Mother and I waited, I made the acquaintance of two girls. The one, very blond with blue, blue eyes, had the exotic name of Anzia. I remarked it would be a good name for a dancer.

"That's what I want to be," she exclaimed, "a dancer!"

"So do I! More than anything else in the world," I said.

We struck up a close friendship, not only because of our mutual love of ballet, but art. Both our mothers were divorced, and had little money. Our desire to dance was so strong that to grab any kind of ballet training, good or bad, was imperative to our survival. I had found a soul mate, and so had she.

The other girl was Jacqueline, who I had remembered from Greenwich House Music School, where she was a violin student. Although Jacqueline took the academic course, we became good friends and often walked home together. Anzia had an aunt who lived on Greenwich Avenue and she would walk home with me once a week to visit her aunt.

I attended the school session from eight o'clock in the morning to four o'clock in the afternoon. The art course was wonderful; five periods a day. There was still life, drawing, tempera and watercolor, and even a life class in which our teacher, Miss Meras, would smuggle in a local washer woman to pose nude if we all contributed fifty cents for a modeling fee. Nude models weren't allowed, so the model usually had a small wrap tucked under the stool to quickly cover up in the event a school official suddenly turned up.

Other subjects were English, civics, and home economics which I found to be perfectly useless. With Mother's help, I finally got out of home economics and into biology class. We were just about to learn about the "birds and the bees." The snickering among the girls made it uncomfortable, so Mother again came to my rescue and I was switched to music appreciation.

A German woman named Miss Steibritz taught us two periods a week of climbing ropes, rolling on mats, and swinging on bars in the basement gym.

We were assigned middy blouses and black shorts complete with modesty cuff. Sneakers and tan socks were ordered. Mother didn't have the money to buy new shorts, blouse, and socks. She made the shorts from scratch, bought the middy at a thrift shop, and dipped a pair of my old white socks in coffee. The middy was big, so I pinned it. The modesty cuff in the shorts didn't suit Miss Steibritz and she let me know it by screaming, "Scourge to crucify me, your shorts are too big for decency." The socks were never noticed. Mother dipped them in coffee after every washing.

Assembly was held twice a week, in the huge auditorium on the main floor. It had a balcony and a huge stage with footlights. Anzia and I decided to present a ballet at assembly. We asked Miss Hamilton, the drama teacher, for permission and she agreed to let us perform the next Tuesday. She opened up her ledger and wrote down our booking.

"Was it that easy to obtain a booking?" we asked each other at the same time. We had a lot to do to get ready for our performance. Here I was, with limited dance education, and Anzia, a few lessons with a Margaret Severn, booked to perform before an audience.

I couldn't wait to tell Mother the news. I hoped she would be able to stay away from the shop to see my performance.

Anzia and I decided to do our own solos for the first time, and then after we proved a success, collaborate on a production together. I decided on Chopin's *Prelude in A Major*. As I listened to it play once again I felt the same magic I felt when I improvised to it years ago. It would be short enough to create a dance in one week. As the record played, I got out the box with my evening dress. I put on the dress. Then I took my shoes off, put the needle on the record again, and composed my dance for my first public appearance.

When Mother returned from the thrift shop and saw me dancing, she showed no surprise. However, she was alarmed by my wearing the beautiful evening dress to improvise.

"Oh no," I explained. "I am not just improvising. I am having a dress rehearsal. I am booked to dance next Tuesday morning at assembly and I am wearing this. Will you come and see me Mother?"

"Of course I'll come," Mother answered. "I'll even put the record on for you. You know I'll come."

The morning of the assembly it seemed the clouds parted and a morning sunbeam made a spotlight on my bedroom wall. I got out of bed with a purpose and that special feeling that had never left me.

When Miss Hamilton announced my name over the microphone, I went out where the overhead lights hit me, and the footlights spread before me at my feet. At center stage I took a pose to start. I could see my rose-petaled skirt out of the corner of my eye as the light hit it. I could hear the gramophone needle set on the groove of the Chopin record and I knew my mother was out there and was going to see me dance.

The prelude started. I slowly began to dance and as I bent over or turned so that the rose petals stood out, I could see my feet with the pink socks I wore, point here, point there, and then disappear again behind another rose petal. At the close of my little solo, I bowed deeply and the audience responded in a rainstorm of applause. I bowed again and exited, which was a little more difficult, because I instinctively knew I should still face the audience as long as I was in the lights.

Now I had the experience of theatrical light shining on me dancing. I was addicted.

As I stood in the shadowy wing and watched Anzia dance to *Dance of the Hours*, I felt the same excitement for her as she experienced her first performance on a stage creating theatrical magic.

We were both called out for a curtain call. As we stood there holding hands, applause came out of the dark before us and over the footlights. We bowed together, and for the first time, I felt confident and deliriously happy.

This event was the first of countless assembly ballets Anzia and I presented; twice, sometimes three times in a day. Soon we had so many bookings we were permitted to stay in our costumes as we attended classes between performances. Our repertoire grew vast. We did ballets for Halloween, Valentine's Day, Easter and, of course, Christmas, in which I danced the role of a melting icicle to a Chopin's *Nocturne*. For the Halloween ballet, I was a large black cat that sprang to life as a human while Anzia, as Goldilocks, read from a huge book about a black cat that grew to human proportions. I had a black cat costume left from a discard at Hedgerow Theatre, and it was too good a thing to overlook.

Mother always came to put on our records for us. I don't know what happened to the job she had at the thrift shop. It just seemed to fade out.

Marta poses in her Strauss costume at age 17. Photo by Gradys Rice.

Lessons Finally Begin

In the fall of 1938, at the end of my rhythms class when everyone was packing to leave, two ladies watching the class called me over. One was tall, wearing a cartwheel hat, manicured nails with silver polish, and elegant dark hair.

"Why aren't you in a regular ballet class?" she asked. "Your talent is in ballet, not interpretative dance."

"Ballet lessons are too expensive and besides, Mother can't even afford dancing slippers like everyone else," I said, pointing my pink socked foot out.

"Suppose I were able to obtain a scholarship for you in a real ballet class?" she asked.

"Oh, that's what I would like more than anything else in the world," I answered.

"I'll speak to this teacher who, for me, will audition you one week from Saturday. His name is Gluck-Sandor. Find some kind of costume to wear for your audition, and make up a dance or routine that will show your talent in ballet style as well as your creativity. My name is Frances Mann."

I was ecstatic! This door had been closed to me and I was determined to slip through it as fast as possible and never go back out.

"Mother!" I cried, after I got home. "I was offered a chance to try for a scholarship at a real ballet school and I'm to audition a week from Saturday!"

"Yes," mother responded, studying her stocks.

"Mother," I said. "Mother, will you please make me a ballet skirt for me to audition in, please?"

"Of course, my dear," she said. "Of course I'll make you a costume."

She put down her stock papers and we both concentrated the rest of that week on making some kind of tutu for my audition for Gluck-Sandor.

I couldn't wait to tell Anzia. She was excited and expressed the hope that perhaps in time, she might audition for Mr. Sandor, too.

After school, Mother and I met in Union Square to spend the afternoon looking for material for my costume. The closest thing to skirt material Mother could afford was curtain yardage. At Woolworth's we found a whole selection of bolts ranging from dotted Swiss on gauze, flocked checks on net, and plain rayon silk netting. None seemed stiff enough, so we went to Hearn's and settled on mosquito netting. It was stiff, strong, and at a distance, looked like the real ballet material of tarlatan.

Mother rooted about in an old suitcase for discarded costume bits from her Hedgerow days. She found a faded pink satin bodice, pointed at the center in an Elizabethan style. I tried it and it fit perfectly. It had once been used for one of the pages in *Twelfth Night*.

Mother worked diligently on my tutu. By Wednesday it was finished. The costume fit fine. It was a strange combination with its stiff, full skirt standing out like a shelf.

Thursday night came, and there was Frances Mann at rhythms class. She told me Mr. Sandor would be expecting me at eleven o'clock, Saturday morning.

At the end of rhythms class I lingered, wanting to say goodbye to Ingaborg Tarrup. I wanted to thank her for her inspiration, but didn't know how. I stood in the doorway gazing into that large room that had been a happy part of my life.

Frances Mann stopped by, squeezed my arm and said. "The very best for you on Saturday, my dear."

I knew nothing about ballet life, but what I did know was that it was the only beautiful life that existed. If there were pitfalls, disappointments, more lows than highs, so be it. The worst pitfall in the world had been the closed door, now it was opened. I was going inside at last, and I would accept whatever this magic world had to offer.

When I returned home, I spoke to Mother about it.

"Mother," I said. I made a point of standing while I made my speech.

"Yes?" she said, looking up from the tiny stove where she was fixing supper.

"Mother, if I get this scholarship, I'm going to take it and never give it up. I don't care if I don't have enough to eat. I'm fourteen, and it's already late. Now that I have this opportunity to dance, I will hold on to it forever! I will never give it up, not even for you. Not for Mana."

"All right," Mother answered, "We'll do the best we can, won't we dear? Mother understands. We'll be in this together, you and I, two against the world."

We agreed not to say a word to Mana. As far as mother was concerned, to have secrets with me from Mana simply strengthened her position.

Friday night I dreamed of being bathed in the blue spot light of a Swan Lake performance. I wanted to immerse myself in this world of ethereal beauty, and never come out.

Saturday morning arrived. The anticipation of my audition for Gluck-Sandor created a sense of purpose to everything I did that day. After a breakfast of cocoa with floating marshmallows and toast, Mother and I prepared for the trip to Gluck-Sandor's studio.

My costume was stuffed into a cardboard suitcase along with my pink dancing socks.

We passed Guttenbergs Costumes. From behind a tall plate glass window I could see the display. It included everything from Wagnerian armor to Elizabethan dress; lush velvet capes to one side and then a columbine tutu standing right out next to a Pierrot and harlequin clown suit, framed by masks staring out into the street through the glass. Out on the sidewalk was a cardboard box full of second hand tights of all colors; ten to twenty five cents a pair.

Mr. Sandor's studio was up one flight of stairs, over a restaurant called the Excellent Goodie Shop. As we ascended the stairs, I could hear a piano playing the Brahms *Dances*. Inside, little girls in pink tutus, some dancing and some standing along the side, made the studio resemble a Degas painting come to life. Some of the students wore toe shoes, some soft ballet slippers.

Mother and I stood in the doorway, watching and waiting for the combination to finish. A man, slightly bald, with dark hair around the ears and temples was seated on a small bench in front of the mirror, facing the students. He had a mesmerizing personality that made you want to become a disciple of what ever he stood for, which for me was ballet.

When the combination was over, he turned his head in our direction. "Yes?" he asked, with a charming curve of his voice. "Can I help you?"

"My name is Martha Beckett. I'm to audition for Gluck-Sandor, at eleven this morning. Miss Frances Mann spoke to Mr. Sandor about me."

"Oh yes, I'm prepared for you," he said. "Please go into the dressing room and get dressed. When you're ready, come right on out." he smiled at me and resumed teaching.

Mother came in to help me dress. The walls were hung with street clothes the students had worn to the studio. A few pairs of old toe shoes hung from tired worn ribbons, looped over wall hooks. Boxes of lamb's wool were scattered about on the bench, and a bottle of rubbing alcohol stood on the dressing table.

I stepped into my tutu. While mother hooked my bodice, I studied my reflection. I seemed taller than the little girls in the class, and thin. My tutu looked as if it could carry me off if a sudden wind came up.

As I put my pink socks on I felt a sense of embarrassment at going out there to dance for a famous ballet teacher in front of those little girls who were wearing real pink satin toe shoes and tarlatan tutus. I went out in to the big studio, part way.

"All right," Mr. Sandor said, clapping his hands. "Everyone, take a break for a moment." He beckoned for me to come out. "What would you like to improvise to?"

"I would like a Chopin *Nocturne*," I answered.

Mr. Sandor nodded to the accompanist. Suddenly, music filled the room. As I improvised, I retreated into my own world. Nothing else mattered; my too thin legs, my height, my tutu, not even my audience of little ballet students who were ever so advanced compared to me.

I felt alive, really alive. I was not only performing, I was one with the music. My improvisation ended in a dying swan pose on the floor. There was a round of applause from the little girls. All of a sudden, I was back in the real world. I must have been all right; they applauded. Perhaps that meant I could become one of them now.

"That's fine," Mr. Sandor said. "Classes are every Saturday, and if you would like, because you live nearby, you can come in the middle of the week and practice. I will help you if I'm here."

I knew I would come every day. I was advised to get ballet slippers for my first lesson the following week.

We tried Guttenbergs Costumes box. We rooted among old tights and tap shoes, but no ballet slippers could be found. Mother told me she could give me two dollars for ballet slippers, but that was all.

When I told Anzia about my scholarship she was excited for me, and we agreed to spend Tuesday, after school, walking up Broadway to find a store that might sell second-hand ballet slippers.

After blocks of wading through the garment district we found Mrs. Spark's theatrical thrift shop. Costumes, feathers, plumes, hats, satins and velvets were pressed against the dirty store windows. A white-haired lady sat at the window looking out. We decided this was the place. So to the tinkling of a cow bell tied to the door, we entered.

It was obvious the lady had been dozing and as we stepped in; she blinked her eyes. Our entrance startled a dirty, nervous poodle that barked and jumped about the store.

"Well hello," said the lady. "Can I help you?"

"We're looking for second-hand ballet slippers," I said, trying not to breathe the dog-filled air.

"Back there," the lady answered. "They're back on the rear shelf. We have all kinds of dancing slippers."

"A gold-mine," I mused, as I studied the row of ballet slippers. I found a pair that fit. Anzia found a pair for herself, too. They were fifty cents a pair. My eyes hungrily scanned the shelf further and there they rested on a row of toe shoes. There was one pair that looked like my size. I tried them on. They were not comfortable, but they were only sixty-five cents. I decided to buy both the ballet slippers and the toe shoes.

The following months, I became immersed in the world of Sandor's studio. To my amazement I was told to get toe shoes after only my third week. The shoes had to be bought new because the second hand slippers from the thrift shop were too big.

Because I was told to get toe shoes so soon after starting ballet lessons, Ellen quit Mrs. Van Dyke to study with Mr. Sandor too. She was still in soft ballet slippers while I was ready to work on toe, so Ellen decided that Mr. Sandor must be a better teacher since I was advancing so quickly.

Ellen started with Mr. Sandor about a month after I did, then Anzia came and auditioned and was admitted on a scholarship. The three of us came every Saturday, regularly. I would go and practice after school three times a week.

My feet became strong, and it wasn't long after I started toe that I was able to do pas de bourrees, pique turns, and triple pirouettes. I was under the impression that this was where technical learning ended and from there on expression took over.

Mother finally made me a pink tarlatan ballet skirt like the others wore, but I continued to wear the faded pink bodice.

Because I performed everything I learned with panache, Mr. Sandor had me demonstrate in front. Frances Mann would come each Saturday and watch. I always had the feeling that she was infatuated with Gluck-Sandor.

The rows of ballet mothers sat on a bench to watch their little darlings, but I noticed that one eye was always on Mr. Sandor. They were all infatuated with his magnetic personality. Mother was not affected by Mr. Sandor's charismatic personality. She continued to spend her Saturdays, until noon, watching her tape in the board room. At the closing however, she would race across Union Square to Mr. Sandor's studio to watch the classes which carried on until the day ended at five thirty p.m.

I was now demonstrating at all of his classes. He would buy me my lunch, ending in a fancy chocolate torte at the Excellent Goodie Shop downstairs. After lunch, I would go back upstairs where I would dance and demonstrate all afternoon. My feet were bloody from wearing toe shoes all day long. I didn't even feel it. I was almost drunk with the happiness that comes from fulfillment.

Frances Mann started taking me to dance and ballet performances. She took me to the dance series at Washington Irving High School. I remember the famous Ballet Joos performed on the very stage I performed on at assembly. We went to the Ballet Russe where I saw *Le Coq d'Or*, *Fantastic Toy Shop*, *Petrushka* and *Swan Lake*.

It felt strange to have this elegant lady come into my life and take over, shepherding me into the world of ballet. I felt as if I had patrons who cared and fostered my talents.

My mother was being left behind. Frances Mann never invited Mother to go with us. I was too busy being swept into this new and wonderful world to notice.

On dance days, I would not get home until six or seven p.m. Mother must have known what she was talking about when she said that dancing lessons would give me too expensive an appetite. Not only did I eat a huge lunch at the Excellent Goodie Shop, I was ravenous at supper.

When Mother would come to pick me up at Mr. Sandors, she must have used this opportunity to play on the sympathy of the ballet mothers who started bringing us cartons of eggs, packages of bacon, and oranges. If I had known, I would have been embarrassed to tears.

"Martha will have to give up her ballet lessons because she's not getting enough to eat," Mother would probably say.

Mother made it a point to look poor to everyone, especially when going to the dentist. Mana was again starting to make comments about Mother not looking for a job. At this point, out of desperation, she took a job at Orbach's selling children's coats. she worked there six weeks and sold so many coats that they put her name at the top of a list on the store bulletin board. Because of this, she thought she would get a raise in salary, and proceeded to tell them so. The job didn't last, after those six weeks, so mother went back to the thrift shop two days a week.

I gave up piano lessons because my teacher tried to discourage my composing. Besides, giving up music left me more inspiration for dancing.

When Mana finally found out about my scholarship, he was distressed.

"You are indulging Martha too much with her art and music lessons," he chided Mother, sourly. "She shouldn't even be taking art course in high school. She should be taking the academic course to prepare her for the business world, and I'll even foot the bill for a secretarial course which will enable her to earn a living right away."

"Don't dancers in ballet companies earn a living?" I cried.

"No, that's different. Besides, how do you know that you have any talent?" Mana said.

Mother and I felt that Mana should come to the studio. We both felt if Mana could be exposed to Mr. Sandor's charismatic personality and feel the magic in his studio, he might be a little more positive. It was decided Mana should come to Mr. Sandor's and pick me up.

I wanted Mana to approve of this world I wanted. After the class was over, a few of the students remained. Mr. Sandor was surrounded by a bevy of ballet mothers.

A dancer friend of Mr. Sandor's named Leon Varkas was working on some steps in front of the mirror and I felt confident that the stage was set for Mana's arrival. Mother was seated beside me on the bench, and although the scene seemed ideal to influence Mana favorably, I was apprehensive.

I glanced toward the dark stairs and saw Mana coming up; first his head, his shoulders, and then the rest of him. Suddenly I realized he was out of place in this studio devoted to spinning fantasy.

"Hello. Are we ready to go?" he asked, looking uncomfortable.

"I want you to meet Gluck-Sandor, my teacher," I said anxiously.

I took Mana by the hand and pulled him over to Mr. Sandor. I was amazed at myself for taking the initiative of taking Mana's hand. Somehow, I had never really done that with him, nor he with me.

"So this is Martha's father. I'm pleased to meet you," Mr. Sandor said. "You have a very talented daughter, very talented. Are you aware of that?"

"Oh," Mana said. "Well, I really don't know about those things. I don't really believe she should..."

"Talented children need encouragement, not discouragement, Mr. Beckett," Mr. Sandor said.

"Well, I think we'd better get going," Mana said.

I was shattered. I couldn't believe how ungracious Mana was to this ballet teacher, who was giving me free lessons.

"Shall we go to Schrafts?" Mana broke the silence once we were outside.

I asked, "Don't you like my ballet studio? Isn't Gluck-Sandor fascinating? Doesn't it feel theatrical, up there? Isn't it wonderful?"

I hoped for a glimmer from Mana's face, a reflection of my enthusiasm.

"To be frank, no," Mana said.

My heart sank. Mother didn't say a word.

"What's wrong with it?" I pleaded.

"The whole place is unwholesome; black drapes, scary masks, and that man dancing in the back. I don't want you to have anything to do with those people."

"What's wrong with those people?" I pleaded.

"They're all sick, not normal, and the room doesn't even have windows. Black, dark. I don't want you to go up there anymore."

"Inside a theatre, it's dark," I said. "The only window on the world is the stage."

"I don't want you to go there. I don't like it at all. That teacher; there's something creepy about him...like Rasputin," Mana continued.

I now was aware that it would always be hopeless to expect Mana's approval of my artistic pursuits. As I sat at Schraft's picking on my chicken fricassee, I wondered how Mana could possibly think I would not be affected by those unforgettable performances which had become the very fiber of my inspiration. I felt sadness more than anger. It was almost as if inwardly he regretted having sown the seeds of my inspiration. But it was too late now. I was thankful to Mana for planting them back in those early years. I remember looking up into his face and silently thanking him. I knew it would do no good to say it. I would never give up dance. Perhaps in time, I thought, I will do something to make Mana glad that I am what I am.

I was so concerned about Mana I experienced a sickness inside until I practiced after school the following Tuesday. I rushed upstairs with an idea I had. Perhaps it would make up for everything and show my appreciation for what Mr. Sandor was doing for me.

Mr. Sandor was in the back where he had a kitchen, and lived with two other dancers.

"I want to paint murals on your walls." I said. "I want to paint scenes from *Le Coq d'Or*, and *Les Sylphides*.

"Wonderful!" answered Mr. Sandor. "When would you like to start?"

I can paint Monday, Wednesday, and Friday. Practice on Tuesday and Thursday. Have class and demonstrate on Saturday."

Mr. Sandor agreed and I wasted no time getting started. The black velvet drapes were removed, and the exposed walls were maroon. I was given white oil paint with which I created my scenes. I was inspired. I felt honored that he allowed my art to become a part of his world.

Mr. Sandor began to choreograph a ballet for me and a young man named Charles Lowery who lived in the rear apartment with him. The ballet was about a man, and death. Charles was the death figure and I was the nun who struggles in the dance to survive death and temptation in a passionate pas de deux.

The music was Saint-Saens *Danse Macabre*. I still remember when the final four chimes of dawn signaled the close of the ballet, I retreated to my monastic life after the tempestuous performance.

Charles was tall and handsome. He was very pale, and his thin face was surrounded by black hair. His penetrating blue eyes made him look like a prince from some unworldly royal family that may have existed only in the art of Aubrey Beardsley or the literature of Oscar Wilde.

Working with Mr. Sandor on this ballet, and dancing with a male partner for the first time was an invigorating experience. Mr. Sandor actually created with us, choreographing and arranging movement the same way a painter moves color around on his canvas until the arrangement is just right.

I actually "became" the nun, as if I had put on the habit, and suddenly, from the first step, I was in another place and another time. When rehearsals were over, it was a shock to return to myself.

Charles became enamored with me and wanted to take me out for an evening. At first I declined. I liked Charles. I liked him in the studio. He was a good strong partner and we certainly complimented each other when we danced.

However, I was afraid of a relationship. He insisted on calling one spring evening and so, reluctantly, I dressed up in my organdy graduation dress. The doorbell rang and there was Charles Lowery in a dark suit, holding a single long-stemmed red rose in one hand and a container of spumoni in the other.

Mother was fluttering about nervously, and got some bowls from the cupboard for the ice cream. I put the rose in a vase, and then sat down.

We sat, hands in laps, my eyes looking down at the hem of my dress. His intense gaze unnerved me. I knew he was hoping I would look up, for even a short moment, and reflect back the message he was sending me.

The only sound was the tapping of spoons dipping into the china bowls, followed by the nervous scraping to scoop up every last bit. I had handled childhood so well. Why couldn't I just stay a child? I envied Peter Pan.

I don't remember much else about that evening, except that it was short and tense.

I remember getting dressed for bed in my little room off the porch. I looked in the mirror and I could see that I was no longer a child. I was starting to succumb to adolescence. Perhaps I wasn't working hard enough. I went to sleep thinking of ways to hide the various parts of my body which were beginning to blossom.

Anzia and I continued giving our assembly performances which occasionally included some of our classmates who studied ballet as well. However, we directed and took the major parts. We collaborated on scenarios we wrote together to music from the overtures of *The Merry Wives of Windsor* and *La Traviata*, and also an orchestral arrangement of *Over the Waves* to which I danced a mechanical doll.

We also presented a tragedy to *Valse Triste* in which we were two sisters in love with the same man. We agreed that one of us would go under a gypsy's spell and dream she marries the young man. The other actually marries him. Naturally, the dream is the happier marriage. The real one turns into a tragedy.

Anzia and I became the art teacher's favorite students. She occasionally slipped us presents such as boxes of tempera colors, crayons, and lithograph sticks.

Aside from the four to five periods a day of art, I was admitted to the creative writing class conducted by a Mrs. Avery. We were guided through the construction of everything from short stories to novels. I remember filling in scribble-in books mother bought me at Woolworth's. On many occasions I illustrated my stories, and I would hand-print some of my philosophical ideas.

One day after school, I took Anzia to Mr. Sandor's hoping that she too would be given a chance at a scholarship. To our delight, she was admitted.

That following summer, Mr. Sandor taught out at Manhattan Beach in Brooklyn. Most of his young students lived in Brooklyn, and many of the ballet mothers tried to get him to establish his school out there during the winter so they wouldn't have to commute. Overhearing talk of this move behind closed doors made me feel uneasy. I loved the studio and could not imagine getting the same inspiration in Brooklyn. Also, my thoughts wandered to concern for my murals. They were a gift from me to Mr. Sandor; an unmovable gift. I had given them life, but now their destiny was apart from mine. I realized that on an inspirational impulse, I had done a very serious thing. It made me think that next time I must be more careful about where I spread my dreams.

The schedule out at Manhattan Beach occupied six days a week from dawn to dusk. I commuted on the subway. Mr. Sandor was preparing his own version of *Les Sylphides*, and, happily, I was given one dance sequence after another. We presented the work at the end of summer. Mother made me a romantic length pink tarlatan for this grand performance. Anzia and Ellen danced in the ballet, and the whole event was a grand finale to the happiest summer. I was dancing, it seemed, twenty-four hours a day.

I would come home sometimes around midnight on those hot summer nights, exhausted. Morning would come a few hours later, and I would bolt out of bed and get myself aboard the subway to Brooklyn so I'd be ready for the first class at 10 o'clock.

The smell of the salt air and the Chopin music amplified from loud speakers on each side of our dance space was intoxicating. We danced on a cement floor, the worst possible thing for pointe or any kind of dancing. We were all so deliriously enthusiastic we were oblivious.

The space was about the size of an opera house stage, surrounded by bleachers. They were full most of the time. The *Sylphides* music soared from the speakers, and when Sandor directed us, his voice had that charm that made passers-by take notice and stick around to watch. I wore out toe shoes as fast as we used tissue to wipe up perspiration from the terrific heat and exertion. Frances Mann must have supplied my pointe shoes; certainly Mother could not have been able to keep up. I was now able to perform triple turns and double pique turns in a circle. I was developing a lyric style too, and my elevation was fairly good.

Mr. Sandor's one complaint about me was that I commanded complete attention from an audience once I stepped on stage, but off-stage I acted like a nobody. He tried to make me a stage personality off as well as on. It just didn't work.

At the end of summer it was finally announced that Mr. Sandor would be moving his studio to Brooklyn. I was crestfallen. However, I did follow him and his flock out to his new studio. I took class and demonstrated on Saturdays, but only one other day a week could I travel that distance for private coaching. The copious lunches at the Excellent Goodie Shop were through, and there was nothing in Brooklyn to take it's place. The new studio had nothing of the atmosphere of the former Fifth Avenue loft.

I remember moving day from Sandor's Fifth Avenue studio. There were boxes of old costumes, shoes, tights, memoirs, and half a dozen huge life-size stuffed dolls leaning against a steamer trunk waiting to be picked up and carried to a new life in Brooklyn. There also were some photos of Mr. Sandor's ex-wife, Felicia Sorels. As the boxes were carried out, my murals remained affixed to the walls, staring hopelessly down at me, as if to say "You gave us life. Is this all you can do for us now, say goodbye and leave?"

"Come dear," I felt Mother's arm around my shoulders. "We'll go home now and have some supper." Even today I cannot look back without a measure of pain.

By now I was fifteen years old. I had been taking ballet from Mr. Sandor for a year and, although I was far ahead of where I had been a year ago, the enthusiasm I had gotten from his Fifth Avenue studio was just not there in Brooklyn.

When I looked in the ballet class mirror, I could see that my legs were beginning to look very strange. They were always toothpick thin, but my knees were becoming knobby. In my effort to turn out, they simply refused. My feet turned out and were very strong, and willingly took a lot of abuse, while my knees remained facing forward, and, when relaxed, actually turned in. Mother was noticing something strange and finally asked Mr. Sandor why this happened. All Mr. Sandor said was that it would be easy to remedy the situation by wearing padded tights.

Mother wasn't convinced, so she decided to take me on a tour around other ballet schools in New York. We must have gone to three dozen ballet schools in and around the Fifty-Seventh Street area, not to mention the School of American Ballet. We sat in on a Vilzak-Schollar class, and about four or five others in Carnegie Hall, including the Ballet Arts Studio 61, and a few smaller ones on Fifty-Sixth Street. The variety of French ballet terms in these studios was staggering! I had never heard them before, and when I would get home, after these sessions, I would attempt a few of the steps I had seen, the results of which were absolutely devastating to my self-confidence.

When watching some of the classes at the School of American Ballet and Ballet Arts Studio, some of the well-known contemporary ballerinas would be there taking class. Right there in front of me, close enough to touch were

Alicia Alonsa, Annabelle Lyon, Mary Ellen Moylan, and Marie Jeanne. When they would do grande jets or fast turns across the room I could feel drops of sweat flick across my face as they sped by. I was obsessed with the world of ballet, so much so I kept a scrapbook filled with photos of contemporary dancers.

The American Ballet Theatre was just being established, and magazines with full-page color photographs would appear. I would clip them out and add them to my scrapbook.

Mother and I watched every class we could find. Whenever we detected the sound of ballet music pouring out of a window or down a hall, we would follow it to the source and watch.

For the first time I saw ballet was not just free, lyric expression; a medium of the muse to express joy or sadness, or an escape from earth to air. It was a constant struggle to overcome the physical problems we were born with; make a new instrument free from the encumbrance of nature.

When I returned to Mr. Sandor's after having visited some of these ballet classes, I could see the mistakes he was making in his teaching. I could see that some of his students would probably end up alright because they were naturally turned out so that not too much damage had been done. However, some of the others were headed the way I was headed without knowing it. I wanted to say something, but they were happy in their ignorance.

Even Anzia could not understand my disloyalty to Mr. Sandor.

When I would practice some adagio of the leg, front, side, and back, which I had observed were being taught in most of the ballet studios, Mr. Sandor would see me and say something about control work which he said was unnecessary.

Mother and I continued looking for a teacher. Around the corner from the Ziegfeld Theatre was a small walk-up. We could hear recorded ballet music and a stick beating time. We saw a small sign hanging over the doorway that read, "Madame Duval Classical Ballet Ceccetti Method." Mother and I were drawn up the narrow flight of stairs and through a doorway at the tiny landing which led into a large loft that had a stage at one end with a huge skylight overhead bathing the studio in daylight. There was a variety of students, all shapes and sizes, taking class. Down below in the darkened area sat Madame Duval. The students were performing simple exercises. It seemed they all had exaggerated turn outs. I detected strange stick-like apparatuses on their backs. Some had straps around their knees and around their rib cage. All of them had zombie-like expressions, as if concentrating on something going on in another world.

There was one member in the class who did not wear any of these sticks, straps, or belts. She was in the front row and taking directions from Madame Duval as if there was a connection between them more than student and teacher. Her name was Joze and she was exquisite. It wasn't long before I could see Madame Duval and Joze were mother and daughter.

As the class progressed, I realized that Madame Duval was the teacher for me. Afterward, we inquired about classes.

Madame Duval told us it was sixty dollars for three classes a week, for three months.

She asked where I had been studying and when I told her Gluck-Sandor, she retorted in a disapproving voice, "Why Gluck-Sandor's not a ballet teacher. He knows nothing of ballet! He's a modern dancer! How dare he!"

When I told Anzia she lit into me. "How can you leave this man who has given you everything he knows, free? Where is your loyalty? Where will you go? You'll have to pay, and I know your mother could never afford that. Free lessons are better than none."

I tried to explain to Mr. Sandor that I needed a teacher who specialized in dance therapy, to straighten out my legs. He still insisted the problem could be remedied with padded tights.

Frances Mann was devastated. Neither she nor anyone else at Mr. Sandor's understood.

When Mana found out, he looked pleased. However when he learned that I would have to pay for new lessons, he balked. He called me flighty for changing teachers, and told me I should start to grow up and learn a practical occupation.

At my audition for Madame Duval, I performed to *Swan Lake* ending in the slow dying movements of a swan as I sank to the floor. I stayed in that pose for minutes it seemed. I finally rose to my feet and stood, dejected.

"Would you mind doing it again?" Madame Duval asked.

"No, of course not," I answered.

"I want my daughter Joze to come out and see you. Just a moment." Madame Duval went into their apartment and asked her Joze to watch my improvisation. She entered and sat down gracefully on the couch. *Swan Lake* played again and I danced with more emotion than I ever had before, as if my very life depended on it. At the finish, when I again sank down into the dying swan pose, there was silence.

"Well Joze, what do you think?" asked Madame Duval.

"I think that Martha dances with a great deal of feeling and expression," answered Joze. Then she rose went back into the apartment.

"Come over to me at the foot of the stage, Martha," said Madame Duval.

"There is no question that you have talent," she said. "However, so much damage has been done to your legs through bad training that I don't know if I can help you."

"I want to try," I pleaded. "I'll do anything! I'll work hard...harder than hard!"

"Yes, I know you would work hard," Madame Duval answered. "In the one year that you had this bad training you worked so hard that you managed to hasten the damage. If you do decide to come to me I will have to take you off pointe for several years, and ask that you put your body through only the training I give you. No more improvising. No more just dancing around; just good old plain therapy for two to three years. You not only have to get rid of your bad habits and correct your alignment, you'll have to build the correct instrument from scratch, which may not be for a few years."

There was a pause, a pained pause. When Mother asked Madame when she thought I would be able to earn a living as a dancer, Madame retorted. "Not until a dancer is perfectly trained should she be paid for a performance. Ballet is an art not a barter."

Mother asked Madame if she would consider a scholarship. Madame Duval told Mother that classes paid her rent, and she could not afford to give any scholarships.

"I will be coming to your classes somehow," I told her.

"We will find the money somehow for Martha's lessons," Mother said. Then she pulled a ten dollar bill from her purse and gave it to Madame as a deposit.

"I'll do what I can for you," Madame Duval assured me. "I know you will work hard, but whether you are willing to give up dancing the way you have been dancing in order to weed out your garden is a different matter." She smiled and we departed.

When school started, Anzia was cold to me. No plans were made for the coming season's assembly performances. Meanwhile, Mother had paid a visit to my well-to-do aunt to ask her to pay for a year's tuition at Madame Duval's. Approaching Mana on the subject would be useless. Mother did skimp enough money from groceries to get me started. However, when the drama teachers at high school inquired when Anzia and I had planned to present our ballets again at assembly, it all spilled out about my need to change teachers because of what Sandor's training had done to my legs. I had to explain that my new teacher said it would be bad for my new dance therapy to perform right now.

Later, Mrs. Eltzner who was principal at the time, called me into her office. "We have a scholarship fund here at Washington Irving," she said, "Left by a very young and gifted gymnastics teacher who died some years ago. On behalf of myself and the faculty, we wish to draw from this fund and give you enough to study ballet. A check for sixty dollars will be given to you for the first three months."

I didn't know what to say.

"Only one thing," continued Mrs. Eltzner. "We here at Washington Irving have enjoyed your performances at assembly. We look forward to you resuming these performances as soon as you feel they wouldn't be injurious to your new training." She cared, they all cared.

"Oh, I want to perform as soon as possible," I said to Mrs. Eltzner. "I thank you from the bottom of my heart for your gift."

My daily schedule consisted of attending the school, then taking the subway to Madame Duval's every day for the hour and a half, five o'clock class. Sometimes it wouldn't finish until seven o'clock, then home again for a quiet supper with mother, after which there was homework and then finally to bed. On Saturday, my ballet classes were at ten a.m., as well as three and five p.m.

On Sundays, Mother and I would often go to the Whitney Museum. We'd take long walks, or sometimes I'd paint at home if the weather was bad.

One such painting done in red and blues with an umber patina over the whole surface was my favorite. The faces glowed from the painting; perhaps self portraits of myself and Mother, from a former life.

The younger of the two was in the foreground, holding a sprig of bluebells. I titled the painting, *Withered Bells*. Mother found an antique gold frame in a junk store which fit perfectly.

I was pouring my imagination and ideas into my paintings now, probably because I was not allowed to do it in my dancing. I was confined to therapy in my dancing.

In about two months, I ventured for my first return assembly performance. I performed a solo to *Jewels of the Madonna*. Mother made a classical length tarlatan of three layers of skirts from deep purple ending in pale lavender. The bodice was deep purple velvet. I danced in soft ballet slippers.

The teachers noticed an "upness" in my dancing now; a more formal style, and how classical my arms were. Before, I seemed to wave them about with much emotion and flamboyancy. I was dancing with more elevation than I had before, and using steps I had not heard of at Mr. Sandor's.

I never told Madame I had danced at assembly. She did know that the gift from the scholarship fund at Washington Irving High School helped me to continue my lessons with her.

In the meantime, I started planning my next assembly performance. This time Anzia joined me in a solo of her own. We did not collaborate on any more ballets. Our styles were growing further and further apart. However, our friendship grew strong again.

That spring, Madame planned a recital, and I was gratified she gave me quite a bit to perform. Naturally, Joze was the featured ballerina.

Madame prepared the ballet, *La Source* to music by Leo Delibes. Joze designed the costumes, and a seamstress named Mrs. O'Rourke was picked to sew them. Mother made my costume herself. To everyone's amazement, Mother made me a costume as beautiful as the other three girls' in the ballet. I felt very proud of her, and relieved I fit in.

Joze was a pure vision in white, and did an exquisite pas de deux with Igor, an older student who was an excellent partner. We gave the recital in Madame's studio. An audience member loved the show so much, arrangements were made to give *La Source* at the Astor Hotel ballroom. There was to be a dance convention there, and our group was to appear in the evening.

Mana showed up at the Hotel Astor performance. Surprisingly he liked my dancing this time. He wasn't overly exuberant, but I was pleased that he wasn't adamantly against it either.

Madame was pleased with my progress, and even hinted that I might go back en pointe that summer.

Madame had a photographer come to her studio and take pictures of *La Source*. The photographer, Michael Kidd, became a very well known choreographer. Mother bought one photo from the set because I had the central position in the picture.

When school was out in the spring, I accelerated my ballet classes to three a day. At this point, I don't know where the money came from to pay for these additional lessons. The scholarship money had about run out. During the winter, Mother did visit my well-to-do aunt from whom a new winter coat was coaxed; possibly another series of ballet lessons as well.

The following summer Madame put me en pointe again, and my legs were showing signs of looking more normal. I practically lived the entire day at her studio. With the light filtering down from the skylight, the studio resembled a garden. All of Madame's students were there "weeding their gardens" in order to make as perfect an instrument as possible.

Joze was always my idol. But then there was Dorothy and Katherine, sisters. Katherine, who was the older of the two, had just joined the Ballet Russe de Monte Carlo. Madame claimed Katherine was not perfect yet.

Dorothy, the younger sister, was a very good dancer and was extraordinarily beautiful. Their mother was an ex-Ziegfeld showgirl. I learned my mother, too, had a career in the theater. All I could get out of her was that she had toured the Keith circuit in a vaudeville show called *Models Abroad*.

"Your father didn't want me to work after we were married for fear the family in Hamilton would think he couldn't afford to support a wife and family." This made me resent Mana all the more. He was so anxious for Mother to work now, but then, he wouldn't allow it.

There were other fascinating people in class. Igor was Joze's official partner, but during interludes waiting in the studio for the next class to begin, we practiced lifts and finger turns, when Madame wasn't looking.

His father had been a gardener for the Czar, in pre-revolutionary Russia. He and Igor escaped to Finland, then finally to America. With no money they managed to settle down in Harlem. Igor described how he and his father had lived on raw fish.

Then there was Karla; tall, blonde and very beautiful, with an Austrian accent. She aspired to Middle and Far East dance. Her mother, Mrs. Priest was a photographer. She took many lovely portrait photographs of Joze during that time, which Karla later gave to me. Karla was always given boys roles in Madame's recitals. More than once, she was my boy partner.

Then there were was Isabel Mirrow and Rosalind Taubman. Rosalind was tall and thin, and she had a perfect turnout. However, she kept growing taller and taller and finally was too tall for ballet. Isabel later joined the American Ballet Theatre, and married a dancer in the same company named Kelly Brown. They had a daughter, whose name is Leslie Browne. She played opposite Baryshnikov in the film *The Turning Point*.

Then there was Greenwillow, a Japanese fellow who was polite and reserved to an extreme.

Summertime came and faded into fall. I was now sixteen, back en pointe, and already planning new assembly ballets.

Mother continued to go out with Mr. Marquis and Mr. Bernstein. A Mr. Morrison, who owned a Mexican shop specializing in pottery piggy banks and blue bubble glassware, called on Mother several times.

I was beginning to feel uncomfortable when gentleman came calling, because they looked at me differently than they used to. I couldn't understand why friends of Mother's would eye me up and down like some tasty morsel. I worried there was something about me now that caused these men to regard me this way. The worst blow came when I had my first period, automatically turning me into a woman. I resented this new role. I wasn't ready for it, and I could see that Mother wasn't ready either.

She made me uncomfortable clothing to wear which made four days out of every month shear torture. I felt suddenly like some kind of prisoner, punished for something I didn't want to do in the first place, the sin of becoming a woman.

At the same time, there were rumblings of war in Europe. Mana came one evening to take Mother and me to dinner and was very upset because Russia had just invaded Finland. The war was all far away, however, and when the 1939 World's Fair opened in Flushing Meadows, New York, the festiveness of all the countries displaying their cultures together made life appear optimistic. Even the Russian and Italian pavilions were there, but represented a very austere picture compared to the other pavilions. There was no German pavilion, but my memory of the beautiful Hungarian and Czechoslovakia pavilions were, as the last brilliance of autumn, the last gasp of their native display.

After the bombing of Pearl Harbor, the United States was pulled into the war. At this time there were many American communists in New York who were "drum-beaters" for the working man. They would distribute leaflets and even had their own newspaper, *The Daily Worker*.

There were dissenters who filled Union Square, listening to speeches on soap boxes. Many of them were with the WPA arts groups. Drossie's Russian Restaurant was filled nightly with crowds of socialists. Greenwich Village was openly a haven for rebels and freethinkers.

The skylight over our daily classes was painted black. Greenwillow disappeared and a week later, Madame received a book of photographs of gardens and waterfalls from Japan.

Every young available man was drafted, and the streets were crowded with soldiers and sailors. Those who were not drafted enlisted. Even conscientious objectors offered themselves, in ways other than fighting on the battlefield.

Mana, who was almost fifty, told us one evening that he had enlisted and would be sent to Oregon to Camp Adair to write on an Army newspaper there. He had hopes of going to Europe to fight in the front lines. He informed us that there would be no more food and rent money from now on and suggested Mother find a job and go to work. This announcement laid a "bomb" in the middle of the living room floor. Mother was frantic. When I inquired about her office and the work she did there, she said as she had before.

"Oh no, dear. We don't touch Mother's stocks. Those are for our old age."

As soon as Mana had gone to Oregon, Mother announced that this was to be my final year at high school. I was going to quit and go to work.

"This summer you'll make up some dances for a nightclub act, and then we'll find an agent who will book you. Madame will help us. She has many contacts. I'll make your costumes. From nightclubs you'll sail straight into vaudeville as a headliner. You'll be booked all over the country. Mother will travel along with you and wash your tights, and mend your costumes. It will be two against the world dear."

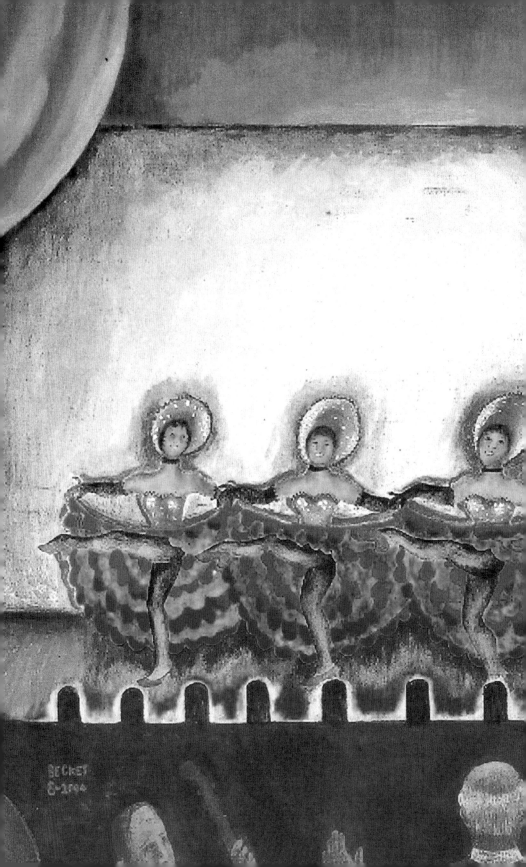

ACT TWO: *Pursuing Art as Occupation*

SCENE ONE

The Night Club Era

My teachers were devastated when I dropped out. Miss Meras had hopes of my getting a scholarship at the Pratt Institute.

I directed my thinking toward being positive. After all, I was now going to dance professionally.

I took ballet classes all summer. Whenever I had any quiet time, I made pastel ballet drawings which Mother framed in plaster of Paris frames and sold at Milo's gallery across the street. We made enough money to buy costume material for the act, as Mother called it.

On Saturdays after class, we would sample selections for the act in an airtight music store listening booth. I selected two Strauss waltzes, *Serenade* by Drigo, *Slavonic Dance in E Minor*, and *Shon Rosmarin* and *Caprice Viennois*, by Fritz Kreisler.

Mother put my pastels on consignment in Jenson's, on Fifth Avenue, and at the Fifth Avenue Cinema when the Ballet Russe films were scheduled to be shown.

She borrowed a sewing machine from Mrs. Meyerson upstairs and worked on my costumes. Mother asked Madame to see my dances and recommend theatrical agents to book my act.

Madame was positive in her criticism, and coached me in a manner that made me feel better than I had expected.

"You'll need to get some glossies; photographs to hand around to the agents," she said.

I posed for Richard Kollmar in four different costumes, and then had glossies made up at Moss Photography.

Madame gave Mother a list of theatrical agents, and told me I could audition in her studio as long as it didn't interfere with classes. Madame also said I would need to get orchestrations for my dances from Schirmer's or Carl Fischer's.

We bought the complete small orchestra scores for all my selections. Every one of my dances was available, and was less expensive than we had thought. We did not skimp on the number of parts, especially the strings.

After supper, I would listen to my records and match what I heard on the score sheets. With my small knowledge of marking directions for each instrument, I wrote my changes, repeats, or acceleration marks for each instrument.

The thought of auditioning for theatrical agents, did not sound inviting to me. When Mother finally took me by the hand, with my envelopes of glossies, on the grand tour of agent's offices, I was a little disillusioned.

The Roseland, the famous Brill Building, the Strand Theatre with offices upstairs, and the Palace Theatre were filled with an endless array of agent's offices. They were drab with old brown desks and telephones that seldom rang. The agent himself would sit staring out the window at the remains of a Broadway he once knew.

At my first audition, the agent was late. My feet were sore from waiting for him in toe shoes, but he came. All he said was that my act was "awfully high class" for his clubs, but to come to see him at his office the following Monday.

He gave me a contract for a weekend on New Year's Eve, at the Hula Hut in the Bronx. I was to be paid eighteen dollars and fifty cents, ten percent of which was his.

At home, there were still remnants of my childhood. It was warm enough outside so that we could open the French doors.

Some neighborhood cats would wander in and out from the rooftops. We sort of adopted one, a big black cat. It was Mother who named him Chimney. I loved to have him look up at me with those big yellow eyes which seemed to say he loved me, too.

In my frustration, I would hug and stroke Chimney. Sometimes I would cry softly to myself and hug an old curtain which hung as a closet door in my bedroom.

There were two more auditions at Madame's studio, and from these we obtained two more contracts; The Old Homestead, and Feltzman's.

Christmas of 1942 wasn't the happiest Christmas for me. This was the first Christmas when childhood was distinctly a thing of the past. New Year's Eve was coming up, and I felt as if I were going to be thrown to the lions, and from then on would have to fend for myself.

Getting a work permit, thumb print and Social Security Card was an ordeal with Mother dragging me from one desk to the next. Once we were done, we went to Woolworth's for make-up. Mother picked out blue eye shadow, liner, rouge and lipstick, and a box of face powder.

The morning of New Year's Eve was cold. Mother packed my makeup in a tin tool box. I pasted a label on the lid: "Tania Mavinska-Martha Beckett." The Russian name was to be my stage name, but never got any further than the lid.

The Hula Hut was a Bronx brownstone converted into a nightclub. Inside, one small neon sign blinked, reassuring that there was draft beer on hand.

A man held the door open for Mother and me to get in with all our cargo. A stiff wind almost swept us off our feet. The large cardboard boxes were like sails which either assisted or hindered our navigation.

Inside, the air was stagnant. Artificial palm leaves hung from the ceiling. The only visible light came from the two spotlights over the dance floor, blue and fuchsia.

I could see a tiny platform with an undersized piano, trap drums, and a saxophone leaning against the wall. There were no violins, but I was hopeful that maybe the violinist would come. Chairs were up on table tops, allowing the cleaning man to get underneath. A man with a half apron asked if we were entertainers for the show.

He took us toward the kitchen. I was horrified at how slippery the floor was. Going through the kitchen door, I was overwhelmed by the smell of fried potatoes and old chicken fat.

"Downstairs is the dressing room," the man said. "The band will be here at six."

The dressing room was long and narrow, with mirrors over a dressing counter on one side, and a clothes rack on the wall opposite.

"We'd better hang up the costumes," Mother said. The wrinkles weren't too bad, but the costumes looked so out of place. I could see they occupied over half the clothes rack. I knew my Strauss costume would fill the entire dance floor.

"Hi," said a short redheaded woman. "Looks like we made it before the band tonight."

She pulled a pair of striped pajamas with ball fringes out of her suitcase, turned to hang them on the rack, and said, "Wow, what gorgeous costumes. Yours?"

I nodded.

"You're new in this business, ain't cha?"

"It's my first club," I answered.

Suddenly I heard the sounds of feet upstairs, a roll from the trap drums and the opening phrase from *Moonlight Becomes You* on the saxophone.

"My name's Ellie. What's yours?"

"Martha is her name. I'm her mother," Mother answered.

"Well, Martha, I'll go upstairs and rehearse with the band first. I'll tell 'em about you, and that you're new and ta help ya out a little, okay?"

As Ellie rehearsed, several performers made their way down into the dressing room. A tall blond song stylist was joined by a subdued brunette, who turned out to be the female half of a dance team.

I felt out of place, so I let each act go up first to rehearse with the band before me. When there was no one left to rehearse, I gingerly walked up the stairs with my new orchestrations under my arm.

"You're the new one, aren't you?" asked the piano player.

I nodded.

The musicians looked over their parts.

"This score is for an orchestra, not a band," said the saxophone player. "Neither tenor nor alto carry the melody here. The only parts that play the melody in this arrangement are the violins. We got no violins here. This is a band!"

"We'll have to fake it," said the piano player. "Here, take the first violin and transpose from that."

"Boy, the last time I had to transpose like this during the show was ten years ago." The saxophone player said.

"C'mon," said the piano player. "Let's get with it. The show goes on in half an hour. We have no time to putz around. We'll do the best we can, okay?"

The first attempt at the Strauss was made. It was a fiasco. Each of the three instruments played separately. The snare drum tried in vain to keep the piano and saxophone together, but would fade out four bars after the others. My other pieces didn't sound much better.

"You'll do okay honey," said the piano player. "We'll do the best we can for ya and you just go out there and pretend we sound great, and you'll do your best too," he winked.

"Okay, clear the floor. Show starts in ten minutes," a voice from beyond called.

My name was third and fifth on the call list. There were six acts on the evening's bill. As I prepared, I was nervous. And Mother at my back, hooking me up and prodding me didn't help. Upstairs, the emcee's voice nearly blasted the microphone. I couldn't understand what he was saying.

After Ellie's act, she made her way to the dressing room, "Happy New Year, everybody!" she called.

All during Kristine Marlowe's song, I knew I was next. The song ended. My heart thumped. While Kristine walked past me back through the kitchen door, a waft of perfume followed her. This, mixed with the aroma of alcohol and cigarette smoke, made me nauseous.

"Now we have a cute little tippy-toe dancer who's gonna dance to a waltz number for us. Martha Beckett is her name. New to Hula Hut. Let's give Martha a nice big hand. C'mon Martha," the emcee said.

I came out onto the floor as gracefully as I could. The emcee clutched the microphone as if it was his lover. I took my place at the upper left of the tiny dance floor and smiled.

The band struck up the intro. They were not together. The snare drums finally took over with a monotonous rhythm. The spotlight was blinding. However, I proceeded to go through my paces in the cramped space. The audience surrounding me was absorbed in eating and drinking. I moved through a veil of cigarette smoke that made a sort of illusionary veil encapsulating me. Finally the dance ended and the band actually stopped with me. The now familiar chord, "dah dah dahhh" was followed by a smattering of applause.

I walked off as gracefully as I could.

"Thank you, thank you little Martha Beckett. Now that was great, wasn't it? Let's give Martha a great big hand."

Mother was waiting in the darkness with a towel. The dance team of Nadine and Leandro was up next.

I went downstairs, followed by Mother.

"How'd it go honey?" Ellie asked in a confidential whisper.

"Okay, I guess," I answered. "I could have been better and I don't know what to do about my music. Anyway, I survived. I'm still in one piece."

"Don't forget, you follow me after my second number. I'm going up now, and at the end of *Tea for Two*, you be ready," she said.

"Okay," I answered.

I was upstairs and waiting while Ellie was busy hoofing away in the same costume she wore before, only with a sequin feathered head piece instead of the Mexican sombrero.

"Thank you, thank you, Ellie Kelly. That was just wonderful, wasn't it?" the emcee said.

"Break a leg honey," Ellie said in passing.

"And now we have our little twinkle-toes here again to perform another toe dance for us. C'mon Martha Beckett."

The round of applause sounded good until I got out on the dance floor in my pink and black tutu. Suddenly catcalls came from the rear of the room. I wanted to melt into the floor. The band went into their slow rendition of the *Serenade*. Sometimes the saxophone would skip a bar, but the drums and the "oom pah pah" of the piano would carry on. The final twenty-four bars were my circle of pique shine turns. I raised en pointe, arms in fifth position over the head, while the band at the same moment struck up their finish chord.

I bowed quickly and got to the stairway as fast as I could to be out of sight.

"Come on upstairs honey, after ya put somethin' on. We're gonna eat. The next show is eleven o'clock. After midnight we do the first show again. That'll be next year, 1943." Ellie laughed.

We were served hamburgers, french fries, Cokes, and coffee. Our supper was part of our pay. Mother ate right along with us.

After our supper, Mother and I went down into the dressing room and waited for the next show.

"I made it," I thought as I sat with my feet propped up on a chair. This was the first hurdle. It was the most terrifying experience of my life up until now. While I was performing *Slavonic Dance*, a drunk walked across the dance floor. I almost kicked him with my foot. I assumed he was taking a short-cut to the men's room.

The celebrating reached a climax at the stroke of midnight. I thought the floor overhead would fall in. Ellie quietly cleaned her face with cold cream and said, "Ya know, it's always good luck if you can work through New Year's, honey. Just remember that. I've worked steady for the past eight years. I've been lucky. Most of my friends haven't worked steady through New Year's Eve since 1935. Don't worry about the last show, honey. By one in the morning everybody out there's bombed. That's why I'm taking off my makeup. We only do half a show anyhow."

She put on a flowered wrap, fixed four unoccupied chairs, lay down on them and took a nap.

The last show was uneventful. I danced the Strauss waltz again. I didn't want to go through the *Serenade* with the catcalls over my tutu. I danced *Slavonic Dance* for the middle show.

The floor shows the next night were uneventful. Either the band sounded a little better, or else I had resigned myself to it. I learned to be satisfied with what I had.

As the band thumped out the dance music upstairs I knew I had more going for me than I had five years ago. I was dancing. At seventeen I was a professional. Perhaps one day I would get good enough to dance on a real stage.

After the final show, the saxophone player had some advice.

"Get some good parts written for the sax, so the sax can carry the tune. Every club has a sax," he said. "Then you can count on the sax to carry the melody for you no matter what club you're in."

He told me to go to Francis Pauly in the Roseland Building.

Ellie had some advice, too. She said I should crumple and fray the edges of my sheet music so it would look as if I'd been around for awhile.

It was 1:40 a.m. by the time we were dressed to go home. Following midnight, everyone was tired and it seemed that standing in line to be paid for was the last straw.

When it was my turn, the proprietor's wife handed me an envelope. Mother took it from my hand almost immediately. She counted the money, her lips moving nervously at the passing of each dollar bill. She took care of washing, cleaning, cooking, and now I saw she was going to take care of my earnings, too. I really didn't care. I was absorbed in giving the best performances I could.

After awhile, because of my nightclub schedule and money running out, my daily classes were paired down to two a week. I gave a few more auditions at Madame's, but soon started renting a studio for fifty to seventy five cents an hour at Goldfarb's and Malin Studios. Most of these studios were bare rooms lined with a barre, an out of tune piano, resin box, and wavy mirrors. There was no way to escape the sounds of people in studios around you.

The waiting room at Goldfarb's led off into two dressing rooms, one for men and one for women. The people waiting to rehearse were older, or they were children accompanied by mothers.

One day, a pair of six year-old twins waited to audition. The girl had blond, curly hair, and wore a hoop skirt with pink ruffles, a bonnet, and toe shoes tied with big bows. The boy wore a tuxedo complete with top hat and cane. Both children looked stiff in their tight apparel, like an unhappy pair of dolls on a shelf. Both wore bright-red lipstick. The little girl had overly-rouged cheeks.

I realized I had been lucky. At least I had a childhood. Six years old was a bit young to be toted around like a product. I wondered if they supported their mother too, and if they had a father.

There was one studio I liked. It was down in the Forties between Sixth and Seventh Avenue. It was a special room that Malin Studios would let me use if nothing else was going on. The ceilings were high, and even though there were no mirrors or practice barre, it had an elegance that made up for it. There were never sounds of other people rehearsing. It was apart from the rest of Malin Studios. I guessed it was used for meetings and dramatic rehearsals.

It was at Goldfarb's I did most of my rehearsing. A large alarm would ring five minutes before your hour was up, to warn you to pack and get out so that the next occupant, who was impatiently waiting outside, could burst in and start. Whatever creative idea you had would quickly dissolve. When the bell rang again signaling the start of the new hour, you suddenly found yourself out in the waiting room, bag and baggage, with a wad of sweaty rehearsal clothes and a cloud of unfinished ideas.

At the Old Homestead, in the Bronx, I was to perform for five days. The family dinner club had a dance floor about fifteen feet in length, and only five feet wide.

I had to alter my choreography on the spot. I couldn't do *Slavonic Dance* at all because my foot would hit customers sitting along the sidelines. I did do Strauss and Drigo's *Serenade* at each show.

There were five acts on the bill. The only familiar face was Ellie. The band played my music a little better, too, although I didn't have a written part yet for the saxophone.

The following week, I went to see Francis Pauly about arranging saxophone leads for my music. The remainder of the afternoon was spent making the rounds of agents' offices. You were more likely to get bookings if you went to the agent's office to visit, make small talk, and butter up his ego. Sometimes the telephone would ring and the agent would spring into action.

"Harry Stone Productions," he would answer. "Yes, yes, okay. I have it. You want seven acts at the Groveland. Second week in February. You got it!"

Suddenly the whole office was alive with acts signing contracts. We were all there at the right time. Actually, we had all been there every afternoon that week, but you didn't think of that at a time like this.

I was now starting to work pretty steadily. I felt so happy and inspired that I started dreaming of new dances.

My booking at Feltzman's was for seven consecutive nights. I had heard that if they liked you, you'd be asked back. The pay was only twenty-five dollars for the week, which wasn't very much for three shows a night. However, the minute I walked into the club I liked it. The dance floor was eighteen feet square.

A few of the musicians had already arrived and I could see that this band was larger than the ones at the Hula Hut and the Old Homestead. There was a trumpet, two saxophone, snare drums with a set of symbols, and a full-size upright piano. As I heard them warming up before band rehearsal, I could tell that they were far better than the bands at the Hula Hut and the Old Homestead.

In the dressing room a blond lady midget was putting on her makeup as she sat in the star's place at the counter.

"Hello sweetie. Just find yourself a place and make yourself at home. I'm Sheila. I'm a permanent fixture here," she laughed. "I do the emceeing, sing, and play the accordion."

I introduced myself and she added my name to a list for the evening's entertainment. I could not help but think how happy Mother would have been if I had not ever grown any taller than Sheila.

The dressing room door opened and two girls burst in, followed by their mother. Beautiful red hair fell down their backs. They unpacked their costumes; chiffon Grecian tunics of different colors. The Graham Sisters seemed more experienced than I, but were about my age.

When Sheila asked them where their unicycles were, they answered, "Downstairs," at the same time.

They unpacked several pairs of slippers, Grecian sandals, toe shoes, tap shoes, and a bugle and violin for each girl. I wondered if they managed to perform with both instruments at the same time.

They spread open some sheet music and started to sing *Der Valkyrie* by Wagner.

"Hi everybody! Hi Martha!" Ellie came in smiling.

The door opened again and in walked Nadine.

The call for band rehearsal came. The musicians all delved into my Strauss waltz which, compared to Hula Hut's rendition, sounded like a full Viennese band playing *Voices of Spring, Slavonic Dance,* and Drigo's *Serenade* also sounded better.

I peaked through a crack in the door to watch the Graham Sisters go through their paces. Their mother directed the band on how to play. The two girls looked as if they had stepped out of a Titian painting. They rode their unicycles to *The Flight of the Bumble Bee*, and ended their sequence by playing the same selection on their violins. This led into a jazzed up version of *Der Valkyrie*, where they continued to ride their unicycles and then coast, bursting into a pair of glorious Wagnerian voices, singing along with the band, which then broke into a Sousa march, where the girls threw away their unicycles and strutted around the floor on toe, waving American flags. This was followed by their mother handing each of them a bugle upon which they joined the band tooting along with a roll of the drums and crashing symbols.

Sheila was indeed a fixture at Feltzman's. She played her accordion and sang her songs. She announced the acts and was familiar with everyone. She had an admirer who came every night and sat at a table at the bottom of the stairs. Without fail, he would order a monstrous mug of beer and spit in it so no one would ask him for a swig. He had come every night for the past five years.

The booking that followed Feltzman's was at the Groveland, in Brooklyn. It was like a beer garden, with colored lights strung around the dance floor, a nice size for performing. The band was good, and they played my music well. I even put *Shon Rosmarin* back into the act. By now, I was beginning to feel almost like a seasoned performer.

Then there was the Hi Hat Club in Bayonne, New Jersey. The best thing about the Hi Hat was its dressing room, with a makeup shelf that went clear around the room. At this particular club a man recruited me as a member of the American Guild of Variety Artists.

I did not like the Hi Hat's collapsible stage. At show time, a platform rolled out over the dance floor, and was high above the heads of the crowd below. It shook when I danced too close to the edge, and there was fear of falling off.

During my few idle nights, I offered to perform in Army hospitals and found myself dancing at the Stage Door Canteen several times.

The hospital engagements always made me sad. Entertainers were picked up by an Army vehicle and carried to one of the Army hospitals. One was out in Brooklyn, the other in the Bronx.

Wounded soldiers wheeled into the auditorium for the occasion were in no condition to react to our entertainment. My *Serenade* went over pretty well because of the tutu. In this case, I didn't mind.

At dance class, there was a notice pinned on the wall, sent by an artist named Louis Kromberg. He needed dancers to pose for oil paintings. I obtained posing engagements at seventy-five cents an hour, for five to six hours at a time.

Because I had many costumes in which to pose, Mr. Kromberg used me quite a bit. I felt contemplative, and even inspired, as I stood on a podium in a typical Degas like pose.

There was one booking I had, at the Fulton, a Chinese restaurant and nightclub. They had a big dance floor shaped like an oval. It would have been perfect except there was a pole in the middle of the floor with a decoration of lotus leaves around the top where it met the ceiling. All of my dances suffered from this except the *Serenade* which managed to get applause when I did my turns around the pole.

There was an unusual dance team there. Byron and Byron dressed in costumes depicting Egyptian slave and master. The man was the master and I remember him stalking his tunic-attired slave around the pole with a giant scimitar, grabbing her by the hair at the finale.

The man was marvelous for the role which he designed for himself. He had a prominent nose, and a pair of high cheek bones. His lips were full and sensuous.

As I headed for my dressing room to change, he stopped me. "My name is Frank Byron. I'm retiring my act after this engagement and opening my own agency. Come and see me, I think I can get a lot of work for you."

One of the other acts on the bill was a soprano, who sang arias from operettas. She wasn't the best soprano I had ever heard, but she was so sincere, I felt sad for her.

Her manager husband accompanied her and coached her. Her high notes were painful, but her husband would watch her with as sincere an expression as she had in her presentation.

He loved her, and heard something in her singing that wasn't there. She tried to please him. The result was a beautiful soprano voice only the two of them heard.

At the end of the engagement her husband handed me his card. It read "Arturo Pascani. Vocal coach-opera-operetta-concert-impresario-concert manager. European tours arranged."

There was another club with a collapsible stage called La Casa Seville. It was supposed to be a higher class club than many of the ones I'd danced in before. There was a glass display window out front with glossies of the weekend's entertainers. There I was, in my tutu.

Between shows, in the dressing room, we often made idle talk. I remember mentioning to Nadine that I hoped one day to be able to dance on a real stage, in a real theatre.

"I know an agent who books theaters," she said too fast.

"Burlesque theaters is what we book here," Solly Shaw said when I went to see him. "Lets see your glossies," he said as he held out his hand which resembled a clump of small balloons, to receive one.

I timidly went up to him and pulled out a glossy of me in my tutu. I cringed. He looked at my photograph with that same smile and moved his tongue around his lips in a way that sent shudders through me.

"Very cute," he said. "Now at the end of your act can you take it off?"

I didn't even take the glossy back from him. I turned and ran. I can still hear them laughing.

At a more reputable agent's office, I got a booking for the Gay Vienna. I was told to be there for orchestra rehearsal. I was sure to bring all the string sections with me this time. Orchestra rehearsal to me meant one thing. There might be violins.

We arrived at the front door of the Gay Vienna, a grey brownstone with no indication of anything going on inside, except the sounds of a string quartet tuning up. We rang a buzzer, and waited. Soon a monocled eye peered out through the hole, and a German voice asked who we were.

"The entertainer for tonight, Martha Beckett," Mother answered. The door opened. The gentleman, dressed in a tuxedo, ushered us into the main room. It was darkly lit, soft and plush. A string quartet sat on a platform, and the dance floor stretched out in a full rectangle.

A few guests, in formal attire, sat at the surrounding tables. The string quartet orchestra went into a series of Viennese waltzes. Not a word of English could be heard. I felt as if I had stepped into a scene from a pre-war movie about old Vienna.

The head waiter ushered us to the dressing room, a room about big enough for two people.

I was called upstairs to rehearse my show music. The musicians played my music as if they were getting much pleasure from it. They would smile and observed the markings so perfectly. The selections only had to be played through once. After they had gotten through *Shon Rosmarin* to perfection, I handed them *Caprice Viennois*.

"Ah," the first violinist said. He took the music, put it on his stand, and played the opening solo passage. The rest followed. For the first time I would be able to dance *Caprice Viennois*. No nightclub musicians could play it before this.

The audience filled up with more formally attired guests, all German. Was Mother right about this club being run by the American-German Blond?

There was another act on the bill. A black tenor named Billy Banks. I expected him to sing something from *Porgy and Bess*. Instead he sang German lieder songs to perfection.

I returned to the Gay Vienna several times. I guess they liked my act. They liked Billy Banks too, because he was always there.

During this time, I met a magician named Zoro who convinced me to act as his dancing assistant. It didn't really matter what I did when to the music. What mattered was that I brought Zoro his props on time, and fetched them immediately when he was through.

It was fun rehearsing, and being part of something unusual like this. However, I had hoped we were going to actually create a ballet for the combination of magic and dance, some kind of fantasy fairy tale type of story. I could see now that all I did was replace the dumb blond Zoro usually had as an assistant.

He promised to pay me after we started working. One afternoon I came ready to rehearse and I found him sitting on the steamer trunk, dejected.

"My agent says I have to go back to the dumb blond," he said. "My agent says a ballerina assistant would kill my act. Everybody would be looking at her. I'm supposed to be the headliner, Zoro the Great. I'm sorry."

He really did look sorry. He handed me a five dollar bill.

"Here's for your time," he said. "I appreciate it, and I want you to have this."

"Thanks," I said. "I'm sorry too. It was fun rehearsing with you." I turned to go, and as I went out he called after me.

"Martha, you were born too late. With your talent, your personality, you could've been a headliner. You could've been a star about thirty years ago."

"Thanks," I said. As I left, the elevator door opened and out walked a buxom blond.

Billie Banks had suggested I go up and see Frank Lewis. Frank booked high-class acts like miniature opera companies and classical dancers. He didn't make any money from booking such attractions, but he made up for it by holding a job as a chief plumber for the Roseland Building.

"Something is always going wrong in that old building," Billie said.

Frank Lewis was holding auditions in two weeks at Nola Studios for acts he was going to book into Bouche's Villa Venice for a summer-long engagement. If I passed the auditions, I would audition for Papa Bouche himself.

Meanwhile, I had to go and scrounge up a booking for the following week. I didn't have anything except a weekend at Murphy's, in three weeks. What I remembered about Murphy's was that the elderly proprietor himself turned the color wheel on the floor show. The walls were lighted fish bowls that stretched from floor to ceiling. The pay was twenty-five dollars for Friday, Saturday, and Sunday. The only food provided the entertainers were layer cake, pie, and coffee.

I went to see Frank Byron, the Greek, who said he was retiring his act to become an agent.

"What took you so long?" Frank Byron smiled. "I have a club out of town, not too far from here," he said. "A week in Bridgeport, Connecticut. They want two acts for six nights. Includes room and board for sixty-five dollars. Will you take it?"

He pulled a contract out of his desk drawer, wrote a few lines on it, and then handed it to me to sign.

As I went to leave, he stopped me, "I think I can get a lot of work for you, but I think you need a Gypsy number in your act, with a tambourine and all."

We could only afford one railroad ticket, so the following week I had my first booking out of town, away from Mother.

When I arrived at Bridgeport Depot, there was a taxi waiting. I took it without any hesitation.

"Okay, here we are," said the cabby as he screeched to a halt in front of Club Hollywood.

The cabby helped me with my costume boxes by setting them out on the dirt sidewalk for me. I paid him, and he sped away.

There was a cow in the yard on the next block, and chickens were scrounging around my feet for food.

Inside, a man in an apron was sweeping and throwing sawdust on the floor. A fat woman sat at a table in the rear.

In the center of the room, out of the rear wall, was a small stage resembling a shelf.

"You one of the entertainers?" asked the fat lady.

"Yes," I said meekly.

"Dressing room's over there," she said.

Inside it was the tiniest dressing room I'd been in. There were only two mirrored places. The costume rack could hardly accommodate my large wardrobe.

As I was hanging up my costumes and wondering where to store the cardboard boxes, a woman of about forty came in with a suitcase. She had the mousey look of Nadine, but with pitch black hair in curls that fell to her shoulders.

The fat lady poked her head in and told us that supper was on the table. She said we'd have some time to check in at the hotel and clean up, in time for band practice.

"Don't we each get our own room at the hotel?" I asked the other entertainer.

"You kidding?" she said. "Me and you share one room at the hotel around the block."

We were fed spaghetti and tomato sauce. The meal looked as if it had come out of a can. The other entertainer's name was Valerie Vale.

"I was formerly of Vale and Vale, dance team," she said. "Me and my partner broke up, so I decided to do a single."

After we finished, Valerie suggested we go to the hotel and check in. The clerk gave us keys and we went up in a small elevator to the second floor. The door opened onto a very small room with one double bed, a sink, a closet, a chest of drawers, and two chairs.

Methodically, Valerie went about arranging her things from a cardboard suitcase as if she'd been there at least a half dozen times. I stood gaping at the situation holding a brown paper sack filled with my pajamas, tooth brush, tooth paste, hair brush, and some clean underwear.

"Do we both sleep in the same bed?" I asked.

"What do ya think we got here, a room at the Waldorf Astoria?" Valerie clipped.

I unpacked and we went back to the club. I could see that the place was jumping with sailors. Valerie rehearsed her number first, and I afterwards. I was not happy with the band's attempt at my musical selections. I decided not to do Drigo's *Serenade* in my short tutu. Besides, there was hardly any room at all for my turns. A very squeezed in version of Strauss and *Shon Rosmarin* was all I could settle for.

The emcee opened the show with a few off-color jokes; not too bad, but bad enough. I realized Strauss and Kriesler would be out of place.

When my turn came, I was horrified to see the audience of sailors massed clear up to the edge of the tiny stage. Their chins could rest on the apron. I could hardly move on this shelf. All I could do was simply mark the dance.

The lights remained on, so I could see sailors grinning, drinking, and talking all during my number. A shout of "take it off" came from out front.

The next morning, I got up at about ten a.m. I wanted to get something to eat and perhaps go over to the club and find a small space to stretch. Valerie was still in bed by the time I was up and out of the hotel.

The man in the white apron brought me a cup of coffee and a plate with two donuts. Donuts were not exactly the breakfast to have, but I ate them anyway because I was hungry.

I noticed the proprietress sitting at her usual table, leafing through some glossies. She looked up at me and beckoned. I got up and went over to her. She flipped the glossy of me in my tutu to the top of the pile.

"How come ya didn't wear this outfit last night?" she asked.

"Well, when I saw all those sailors out front, I didn't want to wear something so revealing," I answered.

"Honey," the fat lady said, "I don't think this is the place for you, I think you'd best take the next train home."

I realized I could not be all things to all people. Frank Byron should have known better than to book me into a club that preferred a girlie show to classical entertainment.

I wondered if Mother would be upset because I had been fired? When I arrived at the station, I called her.

"Mother," I said. "Mother, I'm at Grand Central Station. I'm home. Club Hollywood was terrible. There were so many rough sailors I couldn't wear my tutu, so they fired me. Are you mad at me Mother? Please, can you meet me and take me home with all my boxes?"

There was a pause.

"Please say it's all right, please Mother." I pleaded.

"It's all right dear, and I'm not angry with you. I understand. I'll be right over to help you home with the costumes. Before we go home though, we'll have a nice supper at Child's Restaurant there in the station, and you can tell me all about it."

I was so happy to see her that I wept and literally fell into her arms.

The following week I went to audition for Frank Lewis, at Nola Studios. This was the first time an agent had rented the studio for my audition. Up to now I always had to do it. Nola studio took the whole second floor of the Brill building. All the big-time bands rehearsed and recorded there. My audition was set for Studio Two. Studio One, right next door, was where Vincent Lopez was rehearsing his orchestra.

There was a bench along the wall where acts waited. On my way to the dressing room I noticed a Spanish dancer, an Italian tenor, and an East Indian dancer, all in costume, waiting for Frank Lewis to arrive.

My audition went well and I was asked to return to audition for Papa Bouche.

All through the preparations for the audition, Mother talked about how she would be able to find an office in Chicago, when I would be booked into Papa Bouche's theatre restaurant.

During the two weeks of preparation, I had a very interesting two evenings at a place called The Viking Cabaret, up in Harlem. An agent, who wanted to try my act out, said this booking would only pay seven dollars and fifty cents. He told me there would be only two shows a night, one number for each. As I neared the entrance which opened up onto a flight of stairs, I could hear a band playing polkas.

An enormous dance floor occupied the central position, seven couples dancing happily to polkas.

It was my turn to rehearse with the band. The music for Strauss and Dvorak went very well except the band played my music the same way they played their polkas; a sure and steady tempo all the way through.

The other performer was called Twisto the Great. He was a contortionist. His musical accompaniment, *Queen of the Nile*, was repeated over and over again as he proceeded to bend himself into a pretzel.

My appearances at Feltzman's and Murphy's the following weeks had nostalgia about them. Somehow I knew it was the end of an era, the start of a new one for me. I had been fortunate to have shared the metamorphosis of vaudeville, which found its only survival in nightclubs, as I was ascending the ladder into a theater world.

I had been in Steinway Hall many times to watch ballet classes. Now, only two years later, I was in Steinway Hall to audition for Papa Bouche.

It was obvious who Papa Bouche was. He was a huge man with a head of white hair and a broad smile.

"This is Martha Beckett, our ballerina," Frank Lewis said.

Papa Bouche, nodded. "What will you dance for me today, Martha?" he asked. His gravely voice had a fatherly warmth to it that made me feel comfortable.

My dances went well, and at the finish everyone in the room applauded which was the first time I had received applause at an audition.

We were told to be up at the Park Sheraton Hotel to sign contracts with Bouche the following Monday afternoon. The prospect of dancing all summer without worrying over where the next booking was coming from gave me a feeling of financial security.

One of the ballet mothers at Madame's claimed that the only reason I got this job was because I was pretty. I took the entire lesson with a lump in my throat. I felt guilty for not being perfect, for exhibiting myself professionally before I was technically ready, for being accused of my beauty passing me through doors which were closed to others who were probably more deserving.

It was Mother who made me go to work dancing professionally before I was ready. No, it was Mana's fault. If he hadn't enlisted again, we'd have had enough to eat and pay the rent, and I could have finished school and continued my ballet training.

When I left Madame Duval's that afternoon, I decided never to go back.

When I went to sign my contract, Papa Bouche greeted me with that warm gravely voice. "I want you to meet Miss Lorraine. She will be staging the shows and doing the costumes for the line girls," he said.

Papa Bouche's Villa Venice was on the outskirts of Chicago, near a small town called Des Plains. It was a leftover resort from the days of prohibition and gambling. Papa Bouche had been a brother-in-law of Al Capone. Miss Lorraine was Bouche's mistress, and had staged and costumed his floor show for many years.

At the Villa Venice there would be two bands. One was the rumba band for dancing and the other was the show band. There would be a line of girls to back up the acts which would number about ten. We were to get our room and board as part of our salary. There would be three shows a night for six nights a week. I would be paid sixty-five dollars per week, and Mother could share my room and have meals. Our transportation to Chicago, and then to Des Plains, was provided. Frank Lewis impressed upon us that for Bouche to include Mother meant that he really wanted me.

The big new show at Bouche's Villa Venice was to open the middle of June. All the acts were to be there by the first of June and the line girls by the middle of May.

Mother and I had a few weeks to prepare. As I shut up the apartment, I could see Chimney through the French glass door. I wanted to run back and take him. We had made arrangements for a friend of Mother's to feed him regularly, but that wasn't enough.

"Come dear, we'll be late." Mother said.

"Will Laird really come and feed Chimney every day?" I asked.

"Yes, dear," Mother answered. "And if she should be unable to sometimes, Chimney can fend for himself, that's what we've had to do."

"Yes," I said, "but Chimney doesn't understand why we will be gone, and not be here to feed him. When we're hungry we know the reason. A cat doesn't."

Papa Bouche's Villa Venice was a sprawling two-story Spanish building. Giant trees and a front lawn spanned the entrance of the palatial grounds like an apron of green and shade. It was Hollywood-like, resembling the rambling mansions of movie stars I had seen in magazines.

Inside, we were ushered through a lobby and past several large rooms. One was filled with costumes, large feathered head pieces, a roulette wheel, two large card tables, and another table for blackjack. Slot machines were lined up along the window.

We walked on through to the main showroom. The stage was way up at the far end, with an alcove for the orchestra to the right. The dance floor was immense. French windows lined the sides, looking out onto lush gardens and a winding river in the back. I could see what looked like a gondola banked along the edge.

We were told to sit and wait for someone to come and show us to our rooms. Mother and I were in room 5. There were two single beds on each side of the window looking out onto the garden below.

After we settled in, we went downstairs and mingled with the other entertainers. By the time all of the rest of the acts had arrived, the line girls were rehearsing a cancan to *Orpheus in the Underworld*.

During dress rehearsal for the girls, I watched them practice a slow number to *Love for Sale* wearing what looked to me like sheer black negligees. My favorite number was their cancan. Their grand finale was simply parading around the dance floor wearing nothing but g-strings, sequin pasties, and feathered head pieces.

Now that the acts had all arrived, I could see some of them practicing, others mending their costumes, and generally milling about the casino. I struck up an acquaintance with Jean Guilles and Velena because ballet was what we had in common. They rehearsed some charming pas de deux, in which Jean usually finished with his spectacular series of batterie and multiple pirouettes. Otero practiced her castanets. Napoli could be heard vocalizing, while members of the orchestra tried out their instruments as they arrived.

Amid all these preparations for the big opening, vacuum cleaners moved about ruthlessly interrupting.

The show band had an entire violin section. The leader played first violin.

There were two cellos and a bass, plus all the other instruments, and an actual baby grand piano. They blasted the casino with excitement.

Miss Lorraine asked if I would participate in the finale. I was fitted for a costume and I practiced twenty-four fouette turns, ending in a split.

Papa Bouche's new review, which he called *Caprice Oriental*, opened the third week of June, 1944.

The summer season saw acts coming and leaving. Later there were new production numbers and old ones changed. Some of the headliners were asked to parade around wearing a g-string and pasties.

"If they didn't," Bouche said, "They could take the next train back to New York." Bouche did not ask this of me. Perhaps it was because Mother was with me.

Jean and Velena stayed only a few weeks. Jean was called back to France to join the fighting forces against the German invasion. Their team was replaced by a ballroom act in which the couple fought constantly. Often after the shows, we met Bouche's Chicago associates. Champagne flowed freely. Those who didn't imbibe could dump their champagne into a bucket under the table.

Mother took the commuter bus to Chicago three times a week. She was able to get a lift to the bus stop from a waiter named Chico. Many times she took me, although I was exhausted from the three shows the night before. We'd go to her office at Hornblower and Weeks. After a lunch at a downtown beanery, we'd get on the bus in time to meet Chico who would take us back to the Villa Venice.

This schedule brought on some pretty bad stomach aches which didn't leave by show time. Our dinners at Bouche's alternated between spaghetti and meat balls and Irish stew.

Between shows, Mother and I often would take a walk down the country road. Down that road we could hear the rumba band in the distance. We could see the thousands of colored lights from the big trees surrounding the Villa. It looked like fairyland.

Our vantage point was a farm house with a pig pen with five pigs rooting about in the dark mud. To gaze down at that fairyland, no one would dream that it was rumored bodies lay in the Des Plains River, right behind Bouche's Villa Venice, or that occasional prostitution went on upstairs over the casino, and that gambling went on in there, even though it had been outlawed years ago.

I made friends with some of the acts, and one very good friend with one of the showgirls. The East Indian dancer, Litia Namora and I established a friendship which lasted until this day. She unfortunately left the Villa before the season was over and was replaced by a Princess Vanessa, who boasted of being engaged to Sabu, the elephant boy of Hollywood.

Toward the end of the season, Bouche was to throw a huge party for the performers and his friends from Chicago. My act was the only one that had remained the entire season, so Bouche wanted me there. He always referred to me as the class act of the show.

Mother returned from one of her Chicago jaunts, with a contract from General Amusements for me to appear in Cincinnati.

"You don't get paid for going to that party," she said. "We're going to Cincinnati where you will perform at one of the biggest hotels in Ohio. You will be paid $125 a week. If they like you, the contract can be extended. This can be the start of big things for us," she said.

"But I'm tired, Mother," I pleaded. "I would like to stay for Bouche's party and then go home."

My pleading did no good. Mother packed so we'd be ready to leave the morning after the last show.

Bouche was displeased, but he knew it was Mother's fault. On closing night he gave a speech. With his arm around me he said, "Martha and I were the only ones who were up before noon every day. Martha was in here practicing and doing her dance of perspiration, and I was out in my garden tending my flowers, doing *my* dance of perspiration."

Everybody laughed. Bouche squeezed my hand and bid me goodbye.

That night, preparing to leave the next morning, I was alone with one of the showgirls. As I sat there wishing I could stay, she whipped her beautiful blonde wig off to reveal a perfectly bald head!

"Honey, you're lucky you still have your mother. I lost mine nine years ago. Don't you ever forget, your mother's your best friend. The best friend you'll ever have."

She dropped her head down on the dressing table and sobbed, "Oh God, I wish I had it to do over again."

We left Bouche's Villa Venice early. Chico gave us a ride to the depot in Des Plains.

There was a chill in the air as the train pulled into Cincinnati. Fall was challenging the last days of summer, and winning. The Sherry Netherlands Hotel was a tall building with a marquee advertising an elaborate ice show upstairs, dining and dancing,with dinner and entertainment in the patio room downstairs.

We were met by Esther Silsby from General Amusement. The patio room was small, had an imitation marble floor for dancing, and a three piece band. There was only one other performer on the bill, a blond male crooner.

Some relatives on my father's side unexpectedly turned up for the Saturday matinee luncheon. They saw a picture of me in the Cincinnati Post announcing my appearance. The visit afterward, over a sandwich and coffee, was heavy with tension.

Between Mother's daily visits to her office to watch the tape, she would drag me down to the cafeteria nearby to lunch with Esther Silsby. Esther was having an affair and Mother was addicted to hearing of its progress.

By the time the third night came, my legs felt as if they would fall apart from dancing on the hard floor. I told Mother I could not stand another week of it, so reluctantly she agreed to let me leave after the first week.

When we arrived home, I ran over to the glass French doors and unlocked them to go out onto the porch. Everything was covered with a layer of soot and dirt. The geraniums were dead. I called for Chimney. He never came. I called again. Time had passed and taken my best friend with it.

Mother's friend Laird fed Chimney. But one day he just didn't show up. "He was very old," Mother said. "He just probably went away to die."

I wanted Chimney. The comfort a cat can give is deeper than all the elegant words exchanged between humans.

Frank Lewis was glad to see me, and said he had heard I was quite a hit at Bouche's Villa Venice. He told me he had a booking for me at a Russian restaurant in Montréal called The Samovar, for a whole month, and then another after that called The Old Romanian down on the lower east side.

To fill in the next few blank weeks with smaller bookings, I went to visit Harry Stone and Frank Byron.

I was shocked to see that Frank Byron was no longer in business, and Harry Stone was in the process of closing for good. When I walked into his office, he looked surprised to see me.

"Thought you were caught up in the 'big time,'" he said.

"I was. I still am," I replied.

"Good for you," he quipped. "You'd better get what you can, young lady. Vaudeville died twenty years ago, and now the nightclubs are closing. The ones that aren't closing are cutting out floor shows. Singers and bands, that's what they want now. I'm closing up and moving out."

"Where are you going?" I asked.

"I'm quit'n show business, been in it too long. I'm going to join my brother and his wife on their farm in New Jersey."

Upon returning home, Mother announced that we were going to have to move. "They're raising our rent, and we have to stay within our budget," she said.

Mother and I agreed on one thing, we should look for a loft that could be lived in and used for a studio. The next week was spent hunting for a loft and preparing for the month's engagement in Montreal.

"You know," said Frank Lewis when I was signing the contract, "your meals and room are provided as part of your salary, but not for your mother. She will have to pay for her own room and meals. You know that you can't have your mother tagging along after you forever, don't you?

"Bouche would like you back at the Villa Venice next summer, without your mother," He added. "Think about it."

My contract was ninety dollars a week. There would be plenty of money for Mother's room and meals.

Mother didn't seem as upset as I had expected. As long as my loyalty was ever present, she was satisfied. Arrangements were made to stay at a rooming house within a short distance from the Samovar on Queen Street.

Our rooming house looked something like an illustration from Charles Adams, with high ceilings inside, a huge square staircase and dark wood paneling everywhere. Dim, electrified gas lights illuminated the dark brown hallways. I was dismayed to see that there was only one bed.

"This job doesn't pay for two beds, dear. We'll save the money by sleeping together," Mother said sternly.

I was anxious to get to the Samovar, hang up my costumes and look at myself in the dressing room mirror. I hoped that I would see my reflection, not Mother's.

We got to the Samovar in time for dinner. The Samovar was exquisite, a remnant of old Russia. Paintings lined the walls and pillars surrounding the dance floor. There was a show orchestra and a balalaika orchestra.

A man came forward and introduced himself as Mr. Carl Grauer. It certainly wasn't a Russian name, but he was the owner and manager of the establishment.

We were ushered to the dressing room where I was surprised to see Litia Namora, the East Indian dancer from Bouche's.

Dinner was being served to us out in the dining room. When Litia and I walked in, a male tap dancer with red hair and a beard sat at the table already dining. His name was Eric Victor. Mother was talking to Mr. Grauer, and then came over to me.

"I'm going down the street to the cafeteria for dinner," Mother said. "The meals are too expensive for me here. Don't worry about me. I'll be back in a little while and then we can go to our room."

Like a whisk, she was gone. Litia broke the spell Mother left me in.

"Here's the food. My, doesn't it smell good?"

I turned, and in front of me were a hot bowl of borscht and a large plate of purutchki, a small pastry filled with meat. This was certainly some of the best food I had ever had. For a moment, I wished Mother was there to enjoy it too. And then the conversation and the exotic food broke my train of thought, and for one full hour I did not think of Mother at all.

A few doors from the Samovar was a ballet school and rehearsal hall. I was there the next morning to practice my barre. After that, Mother and I went for a short lunch at the cafeteria and took a look-in at her office. Mother wanted to take in some early afternoon sightseeing before going to the Samovar for band rehearsal. I was not too enthusiastic about the idea. Mother insisted, so we went.

We decided to take in St. Peter's Cathedral. While wandering about gazing up at the great central dome, marveling at the light which filtered from the tiny openings, I heard a scream and turned. There was Mother, flat on the marble floor by a stone step she must have missed.

"Help me, help me!" she cried. The few tourists ran to help her up. I felt it must have been my fault. If I had been beside her, holding her hand instead of gaping at the dome, she would not have fallen.

We took a cab to Victoria hospital. I was shocked to learn that I had to put down a deposit before Mother could be admitted.

Mother had broken her wrist. It cost ninety dollars for the deposit, my first week's salary at the Samovar. The whole thing! I wondered if Mr. Grauer would give me an advance.

I hurried down the hill on Queen Street by foot, all the way to the Samovar. I had no money left for a cab and I was embarrassed at having to request an advance on my salary from Mr. Grauer. I had made a good impression, and now I feared that this favor I was asking was not going to be good for my opening night.

When I reached Mr. Grauer, he smiled, until I made my request. He had already had words with my mother concerning her meals. I could see that Mother was a bigger factor in my presence here than I was.

"How much do they require at the hospital?" he asked.

"Exactly ninety dollars. My whole week's salary will go toward Mother's deposit. They said they'd wait for the rest." I stood paralyzed with embarrassment.

"It's strange that they want exactly ninety dollars," Mr. Grauer said. "I'll give it to you. But you'd better live up to the praise I've been hearing about you. The critics will be here tonight, you know."

I paid the full ninety dollars to the cashier at hospital. I was told to return next morning when Mother would be released.

I left the hospital feeling as if I had been through a steamroller. I got back to the Samovar in time to rehearse with the orchestra before supper.

Somehow, the anticipation of being without Mother for a full twenty-four hours in itself was comforting. Because of an unexpected accident that whisked her out of my life for a short time, I was given space to think for myself.

After orchestra rehearsal, I sat down at my dressing table and, staring back at me, was my own face. I put on my makeup and, for the first time, Mother was not reflected in the background of the dressing room mirror.

Opening night came and went. I could tell by the reaction of the audience that my act went over well. Later I had a chance to sleep in a room by myself in a strange city. The exhilaration of that first opening night without Mother was a time I savored.

When I arrived at the Samovar the next day, Mr. Grauer was all smiles. He held up a French newspaper and said, "You did well. You made a fine impression. I'll read it to you and then translate it."

There was one line that said, "Marta Becket personifies the dance itself." This stuck in my memory for years. Also, I kind of liked the way they misspelled my name. I stored this in my memory.

The review in English had a line about my "performing able toe work indeed." Perhaps my performance and the good review would make up for the request I'd made the day before.

When I went to pick Mother up, she was sitting in a stuffed chair waiting for me. She greeted me with a forlorn smile and muttered something about my being late. She had a cast on her left arm which hung in a sling around her neck.

"Take me to the board room dear. I've already missed the opening prices," Mother said.

I took Mother down to her office and left her there in the front row. Her eyes immediately glued themselves to the tape.

For the rest of the month I made up my mind to enjoy my engagement. It was particularly difficult at night, in that one small bed, trying to sleep, and Mother's cast hitting me as she turned.

Two weeks after returning to New York, I was booked into the Old

Romanian. The Old Romanian had a line of girls, and a big woman who sang bawdy songs in Yiddish, cracked jokes and announced the acts. Her name was Sadie Banks. She was known as the Sophie Tucker of the East Side.

During the two weeks prior to this engagement, Mother and I looked for a new place to live. We walked around the loft districts and finally found one on Seventeenth Street, between Fifth and Sixth avenues. The loft was huge, sixty-five feet long and about thirty-five feet wide. It contained two rooms with a doorway in the middle; so large that it felt like one large room. The floor was wood and not in very good condition, but suitable enough for dancing. The rear was dark; no light could come in because it backed up to a factory that manufactured camouflage cloth for the Army. All night long, great spindles went round and round without ever stopping.

There was no bathroom; just a men's and women's toilet, and a big sink. Mother bought a small gas stove for cooking. Taking baths was difficult, especially in winter. The sink was big enough to sit in and take a sponge bath. However, to get into it, one had to step onto a chair first. Soaking in a hot tub was a luxury of the past.

I did have space to work on new numbers and practice. Our rent was a little more than the old rent, sixty dollars a month. But our old place was jumping from forty to seventy-five dollars a month. So we were still ahead.

The walls in this loft were like large blank canvases. It wasn't long before I started painting murals, gradually making the loft look like a Russian village with dancing peasants in colorful costumes.

The engagement at the Old Romanian provided me with more ideas for a painting than it did for a satisfying place to perform. The management wanted the entertainers to mix with the costumers between shows. Because I preferred staying in the dressing room with a cup of tea, I did not fare too well.

I was nearing the end of the job, with nothing else in store. Mother said something about taking me to the unemployment insurance office. But I wanted to work for my money, to dance, to do what I loved.

"Everybody collects one time or another," Mother said. We didn't have a Christmas tree that year. We couldn't afford it. Besides, we weren't in the mood. We hung some Christmas tree lights up in the front room of the loft.

After the engagement was over, Mother took me to the unemployment office. Many of my co-performers were there, some already collecting. It was depressing.

Between the visits to the unemployment office, Mother began taking me in earnest to the agent's offices again, but this time, the top ones. The small ten percent men were being edged out by the bigger agents.

Mother and I never got past the receptionist, but the effort made her feel she was doing her utmost. Mother even took me to see Sam Rausch, producer of the stage shows at the Roxy Theatre. The chance that there might be a production number using a ballet dancer had occurred to her. Mr. Rausch was friendly and didn't close the door on us.

Mother then suggested that I go up and see Esther Silsby, who had moved from the General Amusement's office in Cincinnati to the one in New York. I really didn't think I knew Esther that well, but Mother did, and this time I felt it would have helped if Mother went along. However, she said it was important for her to watch the tape, so I went alone.

"Hi Martha," Esther said, as I stepped into her office.

She sat back in her office chair looking me up and down. "Martha, I think it would be good for you to go out and have an affair." I stared back, dumbfounded.

"That wasn't what I came to see you about," I said hesitatingly.

"I still think you ought to go out and have an affair," she repeated. "Find some guy and go to bed with him. You work too hard. You can only get just so good, and no better. What's more, there's going to be less and less work. It's a dead end. Go out and find some guy and have an affair. That's what you need now. Take it from me," she leaned over and stared at me.

I never told Mother what Esther had said. She may not have believed me.

I finally received my first weekly unemployment check. It was so small, and fluctuated from one amount to another. The effort didn't seem to be worth it. The ordeal put me through such depression that I could hardly do my work. I did manage to turn out some very depressing paintings. They were good, in fact they were quite good.

Mother would rise early each morning and go to her office and I would wake up alone, later each day, because I had nothing to get up for.

I would go through my daily barre, sometimes review some of my dances, and then spend the afternoon making contacts which, time after time, were fruitless. Unlike my paintings, my dances were now becoming an ordeal rather than a joy. I could do a hundred paintings, and if they were not sold, store them in a closet for a better time. After many years, I could get them out and they could be as fresh as the day they were painted. However, my dances could not be stored.

I began feeling guilty because I spent so much time each day on my dreams, while my dancing was not earning a cent. Oh, if only I could put my dances in storage like my paintings, and get them out at a better time.

One day I decided to go back and see Sam Rausch at the Roxy. "Come with me," he said as he led me backstage. We ended up in a large rehearsal room filled with props, feathered head pieces, and huge balloons standing at the ready, waiting for the Roxyettes to return after the second show and rehearse.

"Sit down," he said and gestured to a huge painted drum while he sat down on an identical one alongside it.

"Martha, I want to tell you something. Even if I had a star part for you in my next production, where would you go from there? Nothing lasts in this business any more. You can't live on a three-week engagement here, and a two-week engagement there. That doesn't pay the bills, does it?"

I nodded meekly.

"Where and how are you and your mother living now?" he asked.

"We live in a loft that is big enough for me to work on new dances and practice," I answered.

"Do you have heat and hot water? Do you have a decent bathroom and kitchen?" Mr. Rausch asked.

"Well no, but that's not important. A regular apartment doesn't have studio space like a loft has, and that's what I need."

"What are you going to do with all your dances, perform them for yourself in your cold loft the rest of your life? The day of the stage show is over, Martha. Vaudeville has been dead for over twenty years. I'm going to make a phone call on your behalf, Martha. You probably won't like it."

Sam Rausch got up from the drum. Back in the office, he sat down at his desk and dialed his phone.

"Hi, Nick, this is Sam here. Is that you? I have a young dancer who would like to audition for the Corps. When are your auditions held? Right, Tuesday and Friday at three o'clock. Okay. Her name is Martha Beckett, and she'll be up Friday. Thanks, Nick."

"You go to the Fiftieth Street stage door at Radio City Music Hall this Friday to audition for the Corps de Ballet, three sharp," he said. "I just spoke with Nicolas Daks, and he says, right now they're looking for dancers. If you get the job, it'll be steady. You'll have enough money to eat right, move into a warm apartment, hot baths and a decent kitchen. Forget your act. There's no place for it anymore. Quit starving for a lost cause."

When I told Mother about the audition she said, "It'll just be temporary. You'll get a solo spot, you'll be discovered. Mother's making some money in her office now, and one of these days you'll not have to worry ever again. You'll be touring all over again soon, and Mother will be right there backing you up all the way. Remember, Mother's with you all the way."

Christmas and New Year's went by unnoticed. I had managed to work through New Year's 1944 at the Old Romanian. But now, several weeks had passed. I was collecting unemployment insurance, and on and off danced at a few more hospitals and the Stage Door Canteen. At the same time, I was anticipating my audition. Mother suggested that if I did get the job, we move into a smaller and cheaper apartment near the big theater. This way, she said, I could come home between shows and eat my meals with her.

The appointed Friday arrived. Inside the small lobby were about eleven other girls waiting with their practice clothes. Soon, we were told to go up in the elevator to the rehearsal hall which was on the top floor. We stopped at the third floor which was the dressing room for the ballet. I saw two large rooms lined with rows of mirrors, hanging ballet skirts, and piles of toe shoes.

The room we dressed in was very small and it was all we could do to squeeze all twelve of us in. Once dressed, we went into a big room and stretched, warmed up, and exercised at the barre.

Then Florence Rogge, the ballet mistress and choreographer for the troupe, who had been associated with the hall since 1932, came into the room. We were then introduced to the ballet captain, Mignon Dallet.

Miss Rogge waited for a few minutes for us to warm up and then she clapped her hands to start the audition.

The audition started, and all went well. Double pirouettes were asked for, and to end, sixteen foutte turns and a circle of pique turns. The best part was when we were asked to improvise.

While a piano player named Oscar played a Chopin waltz, we were each asked to improvise some sort of solo to exhibit what we felt to the music.

The others found it difficult to create a routine on the spot. Years later, I learned that it was very unusual for Florence Rogge to ask for improvisation. Fortunately for me she asked for it this time. It was the improvisation which won me a position in the Corps.

Mignon Dallet singled three girls out after the audition; Virginia, Marie, and me. We would be on call she said.

I thought back to when I was a child and how I wanted to be like one of those many beautiful ballerinas I had seen at the Ballet Russe and at the Roxy. Now it was really going to happen.

The contract read forty-five dollars a week; four shows a day, early morning rehearsals, five shows a day on holidays, and a midnight show New Year's Eve. After six months, I would get a raise of five dollars a week. Then that's it, until we can dance no more. All costumes and one pair of pointe shoes a week would be provided.

Because it was fairly warm afternoon, I decided to walk and then catch the bus.

"Martha!" a familiar voice called. I turned. It was Mana!

"Why," I said surprised, "I thought you were in Oregon." I wasn't too happy about seeing Mana back, but I knew that news of my new steady job at Radio City Music Hall would please him.

"I've been back for several days. They wouldn't send me to Europe, so I decided to come back. I'm on the *Post*. I'm on an assignment. How about you?"

"I just got a job with the Corps de Ballet at Radio City Music Hall."

"Wonderful, wonderful," he said. "A steady job at last. I was distressed when I heard your mother took you out of school to dance in nightclubs. Are you considering finishing high school and getting your diploma?"

I told him dancing jobs do not require high school diplomas, or college degrees. The conversation drifted and Mana said he would meet Mother and me for dinner soon.

When I got home, I saw all of the costumes from my night club act strewn about the loft never to be worn again. A pang of sadness went through me like a knife. It was good-bye to a very colorful part of my life which would eventually become a part of my history.

Classical pose at age 24 Photo by Gradys Rice. Rice, a teenager at the time, was the daughter of a well-known fashion photographer.

Radio City Music Hall to Broadway

After we signed our Radio City Music Hall contracts, we were each told to watch the part of the girl we were to replace in the present show. That week was *Rhapsody in Blue*. The three replaced girls would be taking their three days off which came every four weeks.

We were given passes to go out front and watch the dancer for as many shows as was necessary. Later we were taken upstairs to the third floor dressing room to meet the girl we would be replacing and then up for a costume fitting.

We were led through a side door into the vast cavern of Radio City Music Hall. We scrambled to get front row seats so that we could get a good view of the stage.

At the end of the overture there was a smattering of applause, and then the opening strains of *Rhapsody in Blue.*

The orchestra pit lowered, the great contour curtain went up, scrolling itself into folds which seemed to devour each other, revealing the great stage. On the stage floor was a huge tilted mirror. The entire Corps and all the Rockettes were headed by a pair of soloists who were followed by a huge spotlight. It was difficult to locate the dancer I was to replace. They all looked alike in their silver gowns and robot helmets. What's more, they were all bathed in a blue light, and with the reflection of the entire *Rhapsody in Blue* cast, there were twice as many images.

To make matters worse, the great mirror on the stage began to turn on cue. During the grand finale, even the giant Wurlitzer joined the frenzy. I sat in my plush seat feeling as if the whole Music Hall, more a "concrete mixer" than a theater, was about to collapse around me.

While the rest of the stage show and then the movie went on, I decided to find the nearest telephone and call Mother to let her know I'd be home late.

I joined Marie and Virginia in the Music Hall cafeteria for a supper of spaghetti. The cafeteria was a hot, white tiled, steamy place bustling with stagehands, ballet girls, Rockettes, musicians, and even a few ushers.

After the nine fifteen final show, I had quite enough of *Rhapsody in Blue*. I felt as if my mind had been laundered with Clorox.

I went home to the loft, and Mother was waiting with supper ready, just as I knew she'd be.

Rehearsals were a creativity killer. The worst was at six in the morning. The first dress rehearsal, following this run through, was slated for the next morning. Everyone in the production was now wearing the long silver gowns and helmets; thirty-two ballet girls and thirty-six Rockettes. Finding the girl with the blond hair, or the red scarf, I was to kneel beside was impossible.

"Beckett!" was called constantly. "You're all wet. You knelt in the wrong place and you're off count."

I was trying my hardest to conform to an uninspiring world. I was lost in this world of hundreds of silver clad bodies in a shuffle reflected a thousand times on this slanted mirror under our feet. When the giant turntable began to turn for the grand finale it was a scramble to survive. "Keep counting. Go where directed. Land on the knee the correct count, 236."

No one said anything to me after that first show. I didn't know whether I did well or not. I supposed as long as no one said anything, and as long as my name was not called, I was alright.

In the middle of the first week's employment, we were doing four shows a day and already rehearsing for the next show.

Between the last two shows, we were free to do as we pleased for a blessed two hours. There was a preview room where all employees were encouraged to go to see the films which were being screened. Survey forms were distributed. The big question was, "Was this a Music Hall picture?"

I needed to heal during these final two hours between shows, so one night after the third show I took a walk down one of the corridors on the seventh floor. No one was there.

I came upon a huge double door left slightly ajar. I pushed it a bit, and it swung open. Inside, I saw the huge broadcasting room where the orchestra rehearsed and recorded. It was deserted. Two concert grand pianos stood back to back. Only two pin spotlights from the ceiling were on. I ventured in. I was in the middle of a forest of silence and space, alone.

There were the pianos, one with its lid up. It seemed to beckon to me. I sat down and began to play a Spanish rhapsody I had composed. It sounded magnificent on that concert grand compared to my out-of-tune Hamlin at home.

I played and played, and soon forgot where I was. I played almost all of the pieces I had ever composed, and slowly began to remember who I was. Suddenly, looking up from the keyboard at a large wall clock over the door, I saw it was eight thirty p.m. I was horrified! The next show was nine fifteen! There was barely time to make the performance. As I turned to leave, I noticed a stage hand sitting against the wall. I don't know how long he had been sitting there.

"That was beautiful," he said. "What are you doing working in the Corps when you can play like that?"

"Thank you," I answered. "I'm afraid I only play my own compositions now. I couldn't make a living doing that. Do you think I could come here and play again? Would they mind?"

"Mind? No, kid. You can use any piano here you like. We have four concert grands on this floor, and they're never in use all at the same time."

The seventh floor would be my sanctuary.

I was drawn to the broadcasting room at preview time each day; almost every night, too. The stagehand would sit in the back and quietly listen.

Rehearsing the next show was not bad at all. The setting was in a ballet studio. We were all to be students. Nicholas Daks donned the costume of a 19th century ballet master, complete with cravat, whiskers, mustache, and beating stick. We were fitted into white tutus. Black velvet bows sat on the top of our heads and, happily, our own hair was visible so I had no trouble following the dancer ahead.

By now I had received my first paycheck of forty-five dollars. Mother took the check and opened a joint savings account. Her name was at the top.

After awhile I began to feel like one of the girls. I realized I was now in a company of dancers who had at least twice as many years of training as I. Many were from out of town, and quite a few from Canada. Many were foreign and had been with one of the Ballet Russe companies.

Then there were dancers who were not very good at all, but could catch on quickly. Quick studies were important because of the constant change in the stage productions.

There was one dancer in the company who could do anything. Her name was Bettina Rosay. In the ballet school number she was asked to do sixty-four foutte turns during each of the four shows. The company supplied her with one extra shoe a week for the foot she turned on. The other foot never touched the floor during this feat, so an extra shoe for that foot was unnecessary.

Bettina was brought out front in the spotlight many times to perform technical solos. She never became excited over a special solo spot, and never was disappointed when she went back into the Corps. It was all a job. An additional ten dollars a week was paid for a solo spot.

While performing the ballet class number, we rehearsed a hula number, a playing card number, a black light number where we were flowers growing out of pots, and a tea cup number. The following summer we did an undersea ballet. We were mermaids with long cellophane hair which blew in an artificial breeze emanating from the wings.

I had made some good friends. For fun, we bought hideous rubber masks on Times Square and hung out the window of our dressing room wearing the cellophane wigs on our heads. We would look down on the line of tourists queued around Fiftieth Street and laugh like witches, which I'm sure made those waiting downstairs wonder what the show was inside.

Even with all the trouble I had catching on, I was made a steady in just a few weeks. Virginia was still on call. I never really understood that. Her name was never mentioned for mistakes. She blended into the Corps beautifully. The secret of a successful career in Radio City Music Hall was not to be noticed at all.

When I became steady, my salary was raised five dollars per week. I decided that I should be able to afford to take class again, even if it was between shows. Mother consented, and made an allowance for me to take two classes a week up at the Ballet Arts Studio in Carnegie Hall.

Mother found a cold-water flat on Forty-sixth Street off Sixth Avenue. It was a walk up of three flights and much smaller than the loft. It had been a lace factory. The frosted glass window in the door, leading into what later became my small bedroom, still had the letters "Lace Factory" in bold black print. Our rent was forty-five dollars a month. The bathtub was in the kitchen. Aside from the gas stove, there was a hot water boiler to heat our water. The toilet was out in the hall closet.

Mother hoped the move would allow me to come home more often. She would complain about being left alone evening after evening to sit in Bryant Park behind the library while I would be dancing at the Music Hall.

"The park is full of the lonely," she would say, "who live in nearby rooming houses, and now I guess my time has come to join them."

I felt sad for her. But then, I had to earn the money for us to live on. The biggest factor that made me different from other girls in the Corps was my home life. The girls had a roommate, had their own apartments or were engaged. Even a few were married.

I dreamed up excuses to stay late at the big theater. Extra rehearsals, I would say. Any spare moments were spent in the broadcasting room composing on a grand piano. I bought manuscript paper and compositions poured out.

I also spent time in the dressing room between shows doing pastels of ballet subjects. Many of the girls in the Corps bought them. I got some on display in the window of the Kamin Dance Book Shop.

There were idle moments up in the rehearsal hall when I would take five minute breaks, sit down at the piano, and give short concerts of my compositions. Florence Rogge and Mignon Dallet stayed to listen.

In November, we began rehearsing the Christmas show which traditionally featured the famed nativity scene including live animals. That year, there were camels, sheep, some donkeys, and a huge elephant named Juno. Juno also performed an act of her own, wearing huge spangled bracelets.

I was shocked to hear my name cast as the Virgin Mary in the big finale of the nativity scene. Up until then, all they had used was a dummy dressed as Mary with a spotlight on her face. She would be set in a leaning position over the Christ child, a doll. Now they had cast me to replace the dummy. Everyone teased me about my angelic face.

When the final chords reached their peak and the soprano made it to the top, the barn doors of the crèche opened. The floodlight from below hit my face and the spot from above bathed me in blue. From out of the darkness came a long stream of animals, Corps de Ballet dressed in biblical attire, along with the Rockettes and members of the Glee Club. Slowly, they formed themselves around the crèche.

I felt strange. I was trying so hard to be like everyone else. I thought I was almost succeeding when rehearsing the circus ballet. I was one of the thirty-two tigers complete with striped leotard and tights, tail, and skin hat with ears which made me look like one of the girls so that you couldn't really tell us apart. It was en pointe, and my name had been called only three times during rehearsal. Now I was cast as the Virgin Mary. All she did was kneel, looking pious. I decided as long as I was stuck with this role, I'd better play it for all it was worth.

Mana was overjoyed at my Music Hall assignment.

"Oh, what an honor to portray the Virgin Mary in the biggest show place in the world," he said.

He even went to tell them at the *New York Post* about it. A photographer was sent to photograph me in the famous scene. The next day a photograph of me in the nativity pose was in the paper, which embarrassed me to tears. Not only was I unhappy to be singled out to play a part that took absolutely no skill, but I even got my picture in the paper for it. Mana thought this was the best thing I had done.

There were many mob scenes in which we dancers had to participate. The Rockettes did their share, too, standing on stage set balconies in hoop skirts, or lounging on beach chairs around a real swimming pool especially rigged for a high diving act, or standing up on the deck of a big ship in sailor's uniforms during one of the Rockettes numbers.

For one scene, a group was assembled to listen to a violinist play *Kiss Me Again*. There was a piano on the set, and for two dollars and fifty cents extra each week, I was assigned to sit at the piano and simulate accompanying the violinist. The soloist was first violinist in the orchestra. He appeared in his tuxedo with tails. I was wearing a red satin gown. The whole scene reminded me of one of those romantic paintings in perfume advertisements.

When the great contour curtain rose, the spotlight hit the violinist. He picked up his violin and began to play. He was the most handsome, romantic man I had ever seen, and the music he made was exquisite. He was not tall, five feet, eight inches perhaps, with curly brown hair and the largest brown eyes. He was pale, and his face stood out startlingly sensitive from the dark space around it. For the first time in my life, I was falling in love.

When the curtain fell and the illusion of the stage lights disappeared, he noticed me staring at him. He nodded, and then swiftly left. I was swept off stage by an army of stage hands, to clear the way for the next act.

I found a copy of the current Music Hall program and scanned it anxiously to find his name, Zelak Kaufman.

The anticipation of meeting him four times a day in that drawing room, with his exquisite rendering of *Kiss Me Again*, wove a spell which I wished could go on forever.

The show ran for several weeks. I knew I had to do something to let him know how I felt. Whether he would respond was unimportant. He was unobtainable, destined for great things. My art was the only way I knew to express how I felt. Words would be too blunt.

I bought black India ink, crow quill pen points, a holder, and a tablet of white paper. Between the second and third shows I rendered in pen and ink the visions I imagined when hearing great musical selections. They were painstakingly done with cross hatch technique and fine lines with surrealism and symbolism.

The series I called *The Violinist and the Ballerina* depicted an endless studio space disappearing into a forest, a grand piano floating off into the distance, and a ballerina dancing with a partner resembling a huge violin.

I was embarrassed to reveal my secret. However, the girls in the Corps finally caught on when one of them saw me slip a drawing under Zelak's violin.

The first time Zelak lifted his violin to play and saw a drawing there, he looked confused. Then he looked at me. I remember blushing, my face grew hot. I forced a smile, shyly. He smiled back, turned his face to the audience and the spotlight, and played.

After the curtain went down, he turned and faced in my direction. "For me?" he asked, with his charming European accent. His large brown eyes told me he hoped it was.

"Oh yes," I answered. "There will be more Just wait and see."

In a split second, Zelak disappeared into the darkness of the great stage toward the elevator.

"Martha's in love," the girls teased as I would pour over each drawing to be placed under Zelak's violin. Then they made bets that if Zelak proposed to me, I would say "Yes," and give everything up.

Zelak hadn't even asked me out for a cup of coffee, and by now, he had twelve drawings. By the time the show's run was over, he might possibly have fifty drawings. "Marriage," I thought. "Oh no. I wouldn't want everything that goes with it."

No, I just wanted love, romance, and the inspiration that I had just from knowing Zelak to go on forever. Perhaps I could inspire him, too.

Then a dark cloud passed over my dreams. How would Mother fit in? I realized Mother must never know about Zelak.

Nevertheless, I continued to turn out pen and ink sketches by the dozens. Zelak always accepted them, with that warm, gracious smile and then vanished. It got to a point where he expected them. He would lift his violin, just knowing another one of my artistic love messages was waiting for him.

One day, when I was in the dressing room readying myself for the next show, the girls called me to look out the window. Down on the street corner was Zelak, talking to a short, heavy blond woman, his arm hooked around hers. "Maybe she's his wife," I thought to myself.

"We didn't want you to know, but you might as well, Martha," one of the girls said. "Better now than too late. We just found out that Zelak and Marie have been engaged for some time."

"Her name is Marie? Is she a musician?" I asked. I knew she couldn't be a dancer. She just didn't seem to fit the mold.

"No, she's neither a musician nor a dancer," another girl answered.

"Maybe she's an artist, a painter?" I asked hopefully.

"No, she's a secretary in some office nearby," said another girl.

I couldn't believe that Zelak would fall in love with any woman who wasn't an artist of some kind. Two people, to share their life and artistic vocation, was to me, the ideal, inspirational love.

After the drawing room scene was over, we were all left in the drab grey of work lights. As we disbanded, for the next scene, Zelak smiled at me, took his newest drawing and vanished, as if nothing had happened. Nothing *had* happened, really; not to him.

As I blended in with the Corps de Ballet, we were swept out onto the great stage and everything I knew. No one could see inside me that there was a change. I was in love, and my heart had been broken for the first time.

Up in the dressing room, I thought about what had happened. "Perhaps it's all for the better," I mused. "It wouldn't have worked out anyway because of Mother, and besides, Zelak was looking for a wife and found one." I certainly was not looking for a husband. I just fell in love, that's all.

I was compelled to get out my white tablet, pen and ink, and start working on another sketch for Zelak. Soon the lump in my throat began to disappear, and as I became more involved in the drawing, the lump disappeared altogether.

That August, I turned twenty-one. I quit the Music Hall job and began going to Broadway show auditions. Helen Tamiris and Daniel Negrin were holding auditions for a revival of *Show Boat*, to be produced by Richard Rodgers and Oscar Hammerstein.

After my class at Carnegie Hall, at Ballet Arts Studio, I ventured to the Ziegfeld, which was already crowded with dancers.

Sets and props stood around for *The Red Mill*, also a Hammerstein production. Work lights were shining down on the bare stage and from out front, somewhere in the dark theater, a voice called out and told us all to line up, twelve at a time. On Broadway, your appearance is more important than your talent, at least in the chorus.

I passed the appearance test and after a short dance tryout, we were shown a few choreographic inventions based on the type of dancing done around the 1800s; soft shoe and bouncy footwork with a coy style. I rather enjoyed the audition, but felt nervous waiting for the verdict. Seven dancers were thanked and sent away.

Then after a short wait with five of us remaining, a voice called again. "Thank you very much. Equity call is next Thursday. It will be twice as crowded then."

At the call, many of them seemed to know one another like a family that lives from one show to the next. There was a sportsman-like attitude, each wishing the other well.

Again, I passed the examination for looks. After we danced, those who were asked to step forward were thanked and told, "That will be all."

The rest, including myself, were left standing. At last we were told to leave our names, addresses, and phone numbers. There were 125 dancers left. I overheard someone say that all they needed were eight dancers. Including the open and equity call, at least 2,000 had shown up to audition. We were thanked and told, "Don't call us, we'll call you."

A tired smile and a nod from the choreographer's assistant, Daniel Nagrin, gave me hope indirectly, but reminded me that nothing in this life is for sure.

That evening, we had dinner with Mana. He announced he had endowed a seat at his community church for Arturo Toscanini. I had an opinion on this, but wisely kept it to myself. Mana, on the other hand, never ceased to voice his opinions on the decisions I made.

In two weeks, I received a phone call. Assistant stage manager for *Show Boat* Reggie Hammerstein's voice was on the other end. "Can you come up right now? We're replacing two dancers who didn't work out, and we need to settle on the girl dancers today."

"I'll be right there," I answered. I felt a twinge over the fact I had not been called. I was working on a painting at the time, so I quickly put down my brushes, gathered my practice bag, and hurried to the Ziegfeld.

We were put through the rigors of the audition we had done before.

"Betty Jane Geiskoff and Martha Beckett stay. The rest, thank you very much," Daniel Nagrin's voice came from out front, in the darkness. My heart pounded.

Betty Jane and I went up in an elevator to an office where we signed our contracts. Our salary was to be sixty-five dollars a week. I was going to be a member of chorus equity. I had now joined the world of the Broadway gypsy.

Marta dances in a gypsy costume in Wonderful Town, *1954.*

SCENE THREE

Broadway Gypsy

how Boat opened on the 14th of January, 1946, starring Jan Clayton as Magnolia, Charles Fredericks as Gaylord Ravenal, Ralph Dumpke as Captain Andy and Ethel Owen as Parthy Ann Hawks. It also had Buddy Ebsen and Colette Lyons as Frank and Ellie. The role of Julie was played by Carol Bruce whose sultry voice brought tears to my eyes each time I stood in the wings to listen to her sing, *My Bill*. Even with my lack of experience concerning love, the effect of her singing on me was so overwhelming I could hardly pull myself together for the dancers' entrance.

Kenneth Spencer played the part of Joe, and although he sang *Ole Man River* magnificently, memories of Paul Robeson from childhood days had influenced me permanently in thinking he was the only one to sing this song.

Pearl Primus played Sal, and headed a bevy of black dancers in Helen Tamiris' choreography that far outshone anything we Caucasians performed.

In the World's Fair scene, I was the English beauty in the congress of beauties. Each one of the eight beauties had eight bars of music to back up a solo. I cherished these eight bars and made the most of my solo. For that small moment I had the spotlight, and in my blue and white tulle skirt and gold scaled bodice, I represented England with all the flare and projection I could muster. Even though it was just eight bars, it was all mine.

Upon opening the program, I noticed my name was spelled Marta Becket. "That's me." I realized. "That was me all along, and now the truth is uncovered in the playbill." From then on I was Marta Becket. This change did something for me. I was now the person I felt I really was. No longer Mana's daughter named for a grandmother I never knew; no longer Mother's little Martha. I always disliked the name Martha. I suddenly was happy with myself.

Of course, Mana was so upset about this that he couldn't even be happy about my being employed in a hit show.

Once *Show Boat* had run for almost a year, there was no talk of it closing yet, but Jan Clayton was slated to leave the cast to go west to Hollywood. All who tried out for her part could never measure up to her.

A farewell party was held on the stage of the Ziegfeld. I had been talking with a group of dancers down by the apron of the stage, when someone tapped me on the back and told me Jan Clayton wanted to see me. I couldn't imagine what she would want with me. I was a chorus dancer, one of many in the cast, and she, a leading lady. Shyly, I went to where she was surrounded by other leading members of the cast. When I stood in front of her she took me aside so that what she had to say would be confidential.

"I don't know who you are, what your name is, where you came from, or where you go from here. But I've noticed you from the very first day the show opened. You're going to do something special, important in the theater someday. You may have a long wait, but honey, stick with it. That's all I have to say. Whatever your destiny is, it's up to you." She patted me on the shoulder and said, "Good luck honey."

No one before had ever said anything like this to me. In a way, I was on cloud nine, and then again, I realized that whatever Jan Clayton saw was not something everyone saw. However, something must be there.

There was no one I could share this wonderful moment with. I tried telling Mother, but all she said was, "I told you that you were special all along, dear. I always knew you were special." Every mother thinks her daughter is special, and I realized I shouldn't have told her.

Show Boat finally did close, and the cast disbanded, some went into *Annie Get Your Gun*. I started going to auditions again. I continued taking classes at Studio 61, and although I didn't have to worry about money just yet, I felt buffeted by the competition of hungry dancers all looking for their place in the sun. I had managed to save some money, although Mother had frequently taken out sums for her "investments" for our old age.

Every visit from Mana was an occasion to remind me that I should look for steady work that would be lasting. He would have been relieved if I had shown signs of wanting to leave show business and make some effort to enter the job market. At Mother's insistence I sought unemployment insurance.

Photographer Fernand Fonssagrieves took this modeling test shot in 1948.

SCENE FOUR

The World of Fashion

Collecting weekly checks and telling lies about looking for work while continuing to take class twice a day was just not for me. One day, while Mother was at her office, I went to the Trapphagen School of Fashion and inquired about modeling for art classes.

"Seventy five cents an hour, one dollar an hour for costume poses, and one dollar and a half for life class," the lady at the desk said.

"I have costumes," I answered.

"That's fine," the lady at the desk said. She hired me for the following week. I enjoyed one full week of being employed, wearing my beloved costumes once more.

When mother heard that Trapphagen had my Social Security number, she knew I could not collect unemployment and make modeling money at the same time. She ordered me to call and cancel my bookings from that week on. I did, against my will, and then went into my little bedroom off the hall and cried my heart out.

This was the first time I discovered a person can make more money being useless. I began to despair about life and paint depressing subjects, in ocher and browns, and sepia with a wash of blue. I painted the unemployed sleeping on park benches, bag ladies feeding pigeons, the unwanted out cold in a spot of sunlight with an empty bottle at their feet. They made good models. They were still, and didn't require model's fees.

While at Trapphagen, I was encouraged to make the rounds of high fashion photographers. So, during the daytime I pursued this advice. I was told there was a lot of money in fashion modeling for top magazines and that once you were in demand, you could make as much as sixty dollars an hour. All this led to a sitting with Louise Dahl Wolff, a photographer with *Harper's Bazaar*. This was the first of a series of fashion shots I did for magazines such as *Vogue*, *Mademoiselle*, and for special ads such as Saks Fifth Avenue evening wear and lingerie. I was swept into the fashion world which kept strange hours and required me to be on call at almost any time.

All the time, I was squeezing auditions in between, but if a photo session turned up when an audition was scheduled, the photo session won out. There was money in that. The auditions became less frequent, and my dancing began to suffer from too many other activities. I ceased to take classes. They were eating up my savings.

The sweat and tears wasted over attempt after attempt to obtain a place in a chorus line simply wasn't worth it. To find yourself in a ballet company, yes, but not the chorus. My dream of becoming a classical dancer faded as my modeling career burgeoned.

Evenings were spent by my easel, painting. I was accumulating quite a bit of art work to make a portfolio. When not modeling or making rounds, I made the tour of galleries to see if there was one that would show my work. Many were interested, but when they'd find out I was a dancer who was modeling to make ends meet, they lost interest and advised me to concentrate on one thing.

That Christmas, I made my own greeting cards. For some reason I sent one to the publicity director at Radio City Music Hall. He called me on the phone and told me he had shown the card to his father who was then drama editor of the *New York Herald Tribune*. His father, Arthur Folwell, called me to his office and said he liked the card so much he wanted to try me doing cartoons for Broadway openings, along with Al Hirschfield. Life was whipping along, like a yo-yo. I was going from dancing, to posing, to modeling, now to cartooning. They hardly had anything in common.

I even got caught up with the Equity Library Theatre and managed to act in a few plays. I made rounds for readings from *Casting News* and performed monologues at Chamberlain Brown's open readings. I tried everything using almost every talent I possessed. However, most of the money I made during this time was from fashion modeling.

My slim figure, long legs and arms and long neck, topped with what many considered a pretty face, got me more than enough jobs modeling graceful evening dresses, negligees, nightgowns and long slips. I was used quite a bit modeling hats, especially for *Vogue.*

I gave up dancing. Strangely, I didn't miss it. I would wake up in the morning relieved that I had decided to no longer put myself through the ritual of class or practice. At first, I thought about my "garden" drying up. Then I would reason that I no longer needed my "garden" I was becoming a well sought after model for fashion photography. I joined the Hartford Modeling Agency.

I was now attending Broadway show openings as well, and doing cartoons for the drama page. Neal Folwell and I would go to dinner at some of the finest restaurants on and off Broadway, and then attend opening night of the show I was assigned to cover.

While acting in the lower depths for Equity Library Theatre, I met a young playwright named Jack Rote. On Sundays, we would go on picnics to Fort Tryon Park. I would take my sketch book, and he would write. These were carefree times. No day was the same as another. No schedule to meet.

Mother and I would go on picnics, usually Saturday afternoons. We'd go to Central Park where I would sketch all afternoon, while she would study her market charts.

One evening, Neal took Mother and me out to dinner which was the beginning of a succession of evenings that had nothing to do with sketching cartoons for Broadway openings. After dinner, he took us to the Music Hall and showed us the publicity office at night which consisted of several desks piled with unfinished work to be resumed the next day.

"How about going to the broadcasting room and giving us some music?" Neal asked.

"How did you know I played?"

"Everyone here at the Music Hall has heard about your compositions," he answered. "Even Florence Rogge was impressed. She said if you hadn't left, she was planning a production number featuring you and all of your talents."

I was stunned. Neal led Mother and me up in the elevator and through the familiar hallway to the broadcasting room. There was no feeling of nostalgia as I walked through the halls. We could hear the sound track from the movie being shown in the preview room. I was glad. I did not care to bump into anyone I knew.

There was the interior of the huge, dark broadcasting room and the pin spot on the piano. Neal went over and uncovered it, opened the lid, and gestured for me to give him and my mother a concert. As I caressed the keys

I realized how much I had forgotten, how much I had let slip through my fingers. I was out of practice as well.

The piano in the broadcasting room was inspiring, and as I played, my music improved. Neal insisted we all go out to dinner twice a week, followed by a piano concert by me in the broadcasting room. These were fulfilling sessions. I not only had the chance to compose on this grandiose piano, I had a devoted audience as well.

There was one particular modeling session that was the beginning of a turning point for me. I was to meet the fashion editor of *Vogue* to go to Lexington Avenue for a hat sitting. Mrs. Montgomery and I met at *Vogue* and we took a taxi to the shoot.

"My dear," she said during the drive. "We have used you for lingerie, gowns, evening dresses and hats. We can never use you for anything that reveals your legs. We would like to make you a permanent *Vogue* model if you would agree to do something that would enable us to use you for daytime wear, dresses, shorts, and even bathing suits."

"What would that be?" I asked timidly.

"Well my dear," Mrs. Montgomery paused for a moment. "Surgery, of course. I might as well come right out with it. Even though you're not dancing anymore, you've got dancer's legs. They're too strong looking for our clientele."

The silence in the taxi was tense.

"If I had this done, would I ever be able to dance again?" I asked.

Mrs. Montgomery laughed. "Of course not, but you've stopped dancing anyway, and think of the prestige of being a *Vogue* model."

Nothing more was said. I was horrified! I had stopped dancing, but I was not going to make a physical commitment like surgery to prove it. I was nothing but a mannequin. My talents had been buried two years now, unused, and probably dried up.

The hat sitting with Mrs. Montgomery came to an end late that afternoon. All during the sitting while they were fussing over me with pins, hair spray, makeup touch ups, and hat changes, I felt like nothing more than a store window dummy. But my mind was spinning. I was angered because I had given two years of my life to a phony world, while the inside of me dried up.

That evening, when I got home, there was a free-lance cartooning job waiting for me. Mana had a friend on the *Ladies Home Journal*, who with the art editor there, assigned some sort of political cartoon to illustrate a story. The idea did not particularly excite me, but there was money in it. The fact that I had gotten it through Mana and not my own efforts made it even less interesting.

The radio was playing softly. Chopin floated through the air. My thought and concentration were interrupted as the Chopin, like perfume, was inhaled with each breath I took.

Work on the cartoon stopped. I began to sketch impulsively. I shook all over as I continued to sketch. The sketch was that of a ballet dancer in repose with a wistful expression. Tears rolled down my cheeks. It was as if my entire body was a house, and my best and only friend had returned from an absence and told whoever was living inside to leave. I tried opening my mouth to say something, and my throat was tight.

"I must go back to dancing," I finally got out. Mother had to ask several times what I had said. After the third attempt I finally made myself understood.

"Anything you want to do is all right with Mother," was her answer.

That evening was the turning point in my life. I promised myself that if I ever recaptured my dancing, I would never give it up again. The sketch, I have to this day.

Marta dances with Andre Van Damme in the Charleston Ballet, 1957.

SCENE FIVE

Back To Radio City and on To Television

The next morning, I phoned Mrs. Bass at the *Ladies Home Journal*, and told her that they would have to find someone else to do the political cartoon. There were many objections, plus the threat to tell Mana. I didn't care.

I continued my modeling rounds because the few remaining jobs I would take would help pay the bills. When I returned home I was excited, as well as apprehensive. I was planning to spend evenings reacquainting my body with the rudiments of ballet. I was worried that perhaps it was too late. But I would work and work until my body responded.

I got out my old tights and ballet shoes, and put on one of my old flowered silk tunics that Mother had made me years ago. I dressed as if I were going to take a complete class. I stood in front of the mirror. Yes, I was still thin, but my legs had grown soft from disuse. My muscles sagged and even trying to pull my knee up made my legs tremble. With effort, I reached for the strength that was no longer there. I worked away at my stiffness.

After an hour, I stared at my reflection in the mirror. This instrument I had willfully abandoned was now useless. It didn't even deserve to wear the tights and the tunic any more. I was no longer a dancer.

I was painfully stiff the next day. Doing the modeling rounds didn't help much. After supper that evening I put on my tights, tunic, and ballet shoes again. This time, I not only went through what I had the day before, but added more.

Night after night I went through the same ritual. My body began to respond, almost as if it were now remembering a former life. It took only one week of this ritual to discover that my body would not take as long as I had feared it would to dance again.

After six weeks on this nightly ritual, I finally realized if I were to go any further, I'd have to either take class or rent a studio uptown somewhere and practice jumps and pointe work. The apartment wasn't large enough, nor was the floor right. I decided to rent a studio and work at my own speed.

I continued this ritual for four more weeks and suddenly, I was a dancer again. It took all of twelve weeks of hard work.

I had regained my instrument. The problem was, what to do with it. I had lost all of my contacts. I hadn't been to an audition in years. I knew no one. I wondered if I might get my old job back at the Music Hall. It was humiliating to go back. Florence Rogge never treated dancers very well who returned to the fold.

I began to develop a strange lump in my neck. It was painful. I continued to work out daily in spite of the lump, but after a few weeks when it showed no sign of leaving, Mother decided to take me to St. Claire's Hospital where there was a clinic for poor people. Mother always considered us poor; abandoned mother and daughter.

The doctor took an x-ray and told me that he was going to prescribe some drugs that would diminish my drive. He seemed to think that it was my drive causing the lump and my anemia.

"But I want to be underweight," I said. "I'm a dancer."

"You're working too hard; you're driving yourself so hard you haven't allowed your body to mature. You still have the body of a child."

His German accent was annoying, and his monocle shook and trembled as he emphasized his point. I do not trust anyone who wants to remove my drive.

I left the clinic and I decided that I would never go back. The lump remained in my neck for some time. I didn't care about that anymore.

I continued to work out each day, and even took a few classes at Studio 61. I desperately needed to find a job dancing. I phoned Neal at Radio City and asked him what he thought. He was disappointed there would be no more cartoons for the *Tribune*. He was also disappointed there would be no more dinners out, but he understood my need to earn money. He wished me well and said he'd tell Florence Rogge I would be calling to see her about returning to the Corps.

My visit with Florence Rogge was encouraging. "Of course you may come back," she said. "I want Alexander Smallens to hear your music. I have an idea for a production number based on the story of Tribly and Svengali. Instead of just singing as she did, Svengali will hypnotize you into doing a painting on stage, dancing, playing the piano with the orchestra and the whole number will be to your music."

I couldn't believe her plan. I certainly didn't believe my music would be as good as all that.

At the Music Hall it seemed that I had never left. I was to rehearse for Florence Rogge's version of *Swan Lake*. The lake was the tilted mirror. This time I made two very good friends from the start; Viola Crucil and Grace Thomas. We practiced together and shared our hopes.

Because I was the tallest, I was nicknamed the "Sultan." Grace was the "Emissary," and Viola, because she was tiny, was the "Molecular." The three of us named our little clan the "Kingdom of Mah Poo Kahn," and from then on we would exchange messages in a sort of Oriental code backstage.

The lump in my neck was painful for the first few weeks after starting work at the Music Hall. The head pieces we wore with chin straps drawn tightly from ear to ear pressing those tender glands under the chin deep into our necks were extremely painful to me because of the lump. However, one day after three weeks of suffering, the lump became soft, the tension around my throat lessened, and it looked as if the lump was gone. I think that lump was born from anxiety over finding a dancing job. Now that I was dancing, I no longer had the stress.

I was happier than the first time I was at the Music Hall. I didn't think about where dancing would lead me. I was just doing what I loved most, and that was enough.

I was now twenty-four and the kind of happiness I felt would be like that of someone who had an almost incurable illness for two years and by some miracle was cured.

I began working between shows on my music. The audition for Alexander Smallens, then conductor of the Music Hall Symphony Orchestra was to be in two weeks. I chose my *Spanish Rhapsody* to play for him, and *Capriccioso*, a heavy, serious piece I thought would impress Mr. Smallens.

Viola and Grace would come practice while I played.

Once, I was alone playing *Capriccioso* when someone walked in. I looked up, and with my poor eyesight and the dim lighting, it looked like Zelak in his tuxedo. He came closer and it *was* Zelak. I stopped playing. I was frozen.

"I hadn't seen you. Have you been working here long?" Zelak asked.

"No." I swallowed nervously. "I just came back to work a month ago."

"So did I," Zelak said. "I came back just a month ago, too. Is this some of your music you were playing?"

"Yes," I answered. "I'm supposed to audition for Alexander Smallens. Florence Rogge wants to use my music in a big ballet in which I am supposed to paint, dance, and then join the orchestra for the finale."

"Your music is beautiful, exceptional. I had heard much about it." Zelak pulled up a chair beside me.

"Years ago, I'd ask around about you. Everyone said you were crazy, nuts, you know." he laughed nervously. "Your music tells me that you think deeper and more profoundly than anyone here. You have a gift."

I knew my face had become flushed.

He continued, "As for Florence Rogge and her idea, I wouldn't bank on it, even with Alexander Smallens. Words mean little. Big dreams for someone who works at the Music Hall usually turn into a two minute skit, if you're lucky. I know. I was to play the final movement of a violin concerto, which inevitably turned into *Kiss Me Again*."

We stared at each other until Zelak broke the silence.

"If this big production doesn't happen for you, don't let that discourage you. Keep on composing. Remember, the Music Hall is just a stop gap between things that are better. I just came back from a concert tour, and because nothing was waiting for me in the way of a job for the next few months, I work here. I need to make money you know. We all do."

There was a tense pause.

"I must tell you that since I was here before, I have married."

I tried hard to keep my expression the same as it was before he had made this last statement. Seeing him again rekindled those romantic dreams I poured out on paper. I couldn't really imagine Zelak being a husband. To me, he was a violinist, a great artist.

"I would like you to meet my wife," he continued. "I want you to know what I need and want in a wife. When are your next days off?"

"Next week, starting Thursday until Monday," I answered

"I want you to have dinner with my wife. I can't be there. I will arrange to have her prepare dinner Friday evening for the two of you, alone."

He took a piece of paper out of his pocket and began writing his address.

He handed it to me, smiled, and left the room. His home was somewhere out on Long Island, in a place called Kew Gardens.

I was anxious over how I was going to break the news about my going out, alone on Friday evening. I knew I'd have to leave the flat about five p.m. in order to get out to Kew Gardens by six thirty. I decided to lie.

"Mother, guess what. One of the girls is getting married and there's to be a big shower party for her Friday night and I must go."

"Who's that?" Mother asked.

"Lisa," I said. "Her name is Lisa." There was no Lisa in the ballet.

"I don't know if I ever heard you mention her," Mother said. "Do you know her well?"

"Oh, I just forgot to mention her, Mother. I know her fairly well. Everybody who's off that week is going. It would look terrible if I was the only one who didn't."

"Are you going to have to take a wedding present?" Mother asked. "You know we can't afford trivials like that. I'm sure she would understand if you didn't."

"Oh," I answered quickly. I was getting good at alibis, on the double. "The girls all pitched in and we got Lisa one big present."

Then there was a cross examination. How much had I contributed to this frivolity! I was becoming annoyed and snapped at Mother, to which she responded with tears saying that my cold manner had hurt her. I tried to make up with her. But no matter how I apologized in situations like these, Mother always ended up on top.

I really didn't want to go and meet Zelak's wife, but Zelak wanted me to. As I rang the bell to his house, my heart was pounding. I could smell cooking coming from under the door. It smelled good. I couldn't cook at all.

Suddenly the door opened. There stood Marie, pretty much the same as she had looked standing down on the street. She was wearing a dark dress covered with an apron. Her face bore a look of anxiety and concern, covered by a forced smile.

"Come in," she said. "Dinner's almost ready." she ushered me into a dimly lit living room. I noticed Marie was much shorter than I. She watched every move I made. As my eyes got used to the comfortable light in the living room, I noticed about twelve of my pen and ink sketches beautifully framed, hanging on the walls in a row that stretched from one entrance to another.

"Oh," I exclaimed. "The drawings. You have framed them. I feel flattered that you wanted to hang them up."

"Yes," said Marie. "Zelak's idea, I think they're beautiful." Marie's forced smile made her cheeks quiver. My cheeks were quivering too.

Suddenly I heard the cry of a baby in the rear of the apartment.

"That's Raoul," Marie said. "He's just a few months old. Do you want to see him?"

"Oh yes," I answered, although I really didn't. The experience was almost too much for me.

As I was led into a rear room where the baby was, I thought to myself, "So this is what Zelak wanted me to see. He was trying to tell me but not in words."

"He should have been asleep by now," Marie said. "I guess it was our voices."

"He's adorable," I said.

We stood there a moment, and suddenly the silence was broken. "We'd better go and have our dinner," Marie said. "It will overcook."

Marie brought out the food and we started to eat. We made small talk. I could hear the baby crying softly once in a while. Then the crying finally ceased.

After dinner, Marie cleared the dishes away. I offered to help, but she refused, saying I was the guest and she the hostess. "The guest does not wash or dry the dishes," she said.

When I finally arrived home it was midnight. Mother was already in bed. She heard me come in, and her concern over how my evening went roused her curiosity enough to attempt a few questions in a rather feeble voice. Rising on one elbow she questioned me about the shower, when the wedding would be, how many were at the party, and then asked why I had come home so late.

Automatically I reeled off a barrage of lies, as if they were lines from a play.

When I returned to work at the Music Hall that week, Grace and Viola were excited over my audition as well as I.

I was to meet Florence Rogge at Alexander Smallens' office between the first two shows. Alexander Smallens was a tall, dark, imposing man with a mustache and a full head of hair. Miss Rogge introduced us, and he shook my hand warmly and made me feel at ease.

I sat down at his grand piano and played my *Spanish Rhapsody*. Mr. Smallens seemed duly impressed. However, he said he would like to hear something else, not with a Spanish flavor necessarily, but something lighter perhaps. I proceeded to play my waltz to which he displayed much more enthusiasm. Miss Rogge asked me to play my *Capriccioso*. Mr. Smallens expressed great interest in my music and seemed to be somewhat astounded that a ballet dancer could compose, especially such serious work.

"You should see her paintings," chirped Miss Rogge.

"I think we'll settle for the waltz," said Mr. Smallens. "Not the way it is, however. I want you to develop the finish, make it grander and grander as you approach the finale. Start it out the way you did, but keep developing the first theme, after you have established the second. Then intertwine the two melodies growing bigger and grander for a finale that announces, 'This is it!' Develop it to a twelve minute work at least."

Up until now, composing had been a sort of sanctuary, an art I absorbed myself in after my energies had been spent dancing. Now I must put equal energy into developing my music.

As Miss Rogge and I went down in the elevator, she chattered enthusiastically about our ballet, and said she was thinking of having Bob Devoie be my partner, playing the part of Svengali.

"Don't you think he would be ideal?" she asked. "He's tall. You'd look good together." She continued talking while my mind was busy sorting out all that had happened.

During the time I worked on developing the waltz, several months went by. The sessions with Alexander Smallens were exhilarating and the interest he and Florence Rogge showed in the project was encouraging. However, it all seemed to drag on and on.

Meanwhile the stage shows continued to change every few weeks. Patricia Bowman was a frequent guest now at the Music Hall. It was a thrill to watch her backstage from the wings, and to dance on the same stage with her at the same time.

We did one ballet to Rachmaninoff's *Piano Concerto*, which also starred Patsy Bowman. We had to make our entrance at the top of a forty-foot ramp, less than a foot wide, waving our huge chiffon sleeves that looked like wings. With my poor eyesight, it was a feat for me to do that number. Not only did we wave our arms to and fro, we boureed down the ramp en pointe which made it seem even higher.

Then there was the Fourth of July number, in which we all wore red tutus, with a firecracker headpiece. Before putting on the firecracker headpiece, I would study myself in the mirror and imagine myself as the doll in the red tutu. Florence Rogge had given me and another dancer, named Patricia Drylie, a small duet to Chopin's *Prelude in A Major*, the very music I danced to at assembly in high school.

I cherished this moment on stage and my dancing revealed it. The ballet captain was always telling me not to linger on my poses or retard, because she said, "It makes you stand out like a sore thumb."

One day, the news around the Music Hall was that Alexander Smallens would be leaving. There was some disagreement between him and the management. A new conductor, Raymond Paige, would be replacing him. Florence Rogge seemed to be absent, even from rehearsals for the next show. Our ballet captain was in charge for awhile.

Finally, after some time, I received a letter from Miss Rogge.

She wrote, "All this means we will have to wait on it. I will have to start all over again with Mr. Paige, and get his ear."

Time passed. The waltz had been developed. The girls in the ballet sympathized with me in my disappointment. Then we heard over half of the orchestra would be replaced with musicians Mr. Paige was bringing from Hollywood. My thoughts turned to Zelak. What would happen to him?

One evening, I was playing and working on my music in the broadcasting room between the last two shows. The stagehand came in, sat down, and listened. After I had stopped because it was time to go down and get ready for the last show, he said, "It must be a burden to carry so much talent inside you. You have so much, with your painting, your dancing, and your music. More of a burden than having a child. The child grows up and one day it is out on his own. But all of your children, your talents, depend on you. If you don't keep them alive who will?"

I wondered how this stage hand could be so wise. "As long as I'm alive, I guess I will," I answered.

By now, I had enough of Florence Rogge's promises. A month went by, then two months. Miss Rogge had not gotten Mr. Paige's ear yet. I decided that when I had my four days off, every five weeks, I would spend them trying to sell the idea to someone else; a production number built around my various talents.

Roy Raymond, a member of the glee club, had an Ampex tape recorder. He had asked if he could tape my work. I said I would agree if he would permit me to take the tape and have it copied. We turned out a very impressive recording.

There was a sense of relief when I first stepped out the door with my records, my resume, and my dance photographs to go to an interview that I had set up, all by myself, over the phone.

My first four days off were encouraging, but nothing definite happened. However, the next four days Ward Byron, of ABC television, was so impressed, he wanted to see me dance. We set up an audition. I danced, played my waltz, and he decided to give me a solo spot on the *Paul Whiteman Show*. The spot was to be two minutes. Now I had to cut the waltz down from the full twelve minute length Alexander Smallens wanted. When I returned to the Music Hall, after rehearsing for the show, I found it harder and harder to keep it all a secret. I didn't want Florence Rogge to find out about it.

I'd never been on television before, and I had never played the piano in front of an audience. The girls in the dressing room had finally found out, and I knew that by this time Florence Rogge had found out, too, and would be sure to watch.

My two-minute spot was not based on the story of Svengali. It was to take place at a garden party. Guests were seated, and Paul Whiteman's orchestra was up on a platform, behind the whole scene, but entirely visible. There were to be several entertainers, and I was one of them.

There was a regular group of dancers on the show, and a choreographer named Frank Westbrook. During rehearsals it was hard for me to get used to the fact I was a featured performer. I was so used to being referred to as "one of the kids" that when Frank Westbrook called, "Okay, c'mon kids. Try it again from the top," I'd wander over with the group, stand, and wait for directions. Everyone was amused by this. I was a soloist; a star for two minutes.

The choreography for my dance was Frank Westbrook's. This meant that the only part of the performance that was all mine was my music and the playing of my music.

I had arranged to have the whole show taped at Nola Studios from the airing. My mother wanted to be present in the studio when the show was aired, but I insisted I wanted her to see it at a friend's house so that she could relate how it looked on television. I really hadn't wanted her there at all. I wanted to experience this moment alone.

I felt that I was dancing well, but I was worried about playing the piano. Finally the moment came, dancing over to the piano and taking my seat, I joined the orchestra. Trying to contain my breathing from the exertion just spent and keep the fluidity of the waltz going smoothly was difficult. The actual performance was quite different than the rehearsals.

Soon the grand finale of the waltz got underway, with a crescendo to which, at the end of a series of arpeggio like chords, I rose from the piano seat, left my role as a pianist, and resumed my role as a dancer. With some grand jetes I danced to my waltz and finally finished the last triumphal chord in arabesque at the piano keyboard. There was applause from the surrounding tables.

I was relieved when it was over. Artistically, this was not the most rewarding performance of my short career. If I had gone through with Florence Rogge's plan, painting a picture as well, on camera, I would have felt like a three-ring circus.

Sometime later I saw a kinescope of this performance. To be honest, I had expected worse. Ward Byron was happy with it, and was looking forward to doing more things with my talents. However, I thought my performance just adequate.

On the Sunday afternoon following the show, Mother and I were walking down Broadway and we were stopped several times by people who had seen me on television. By the time we got home, I was beginning to feel like a celebrity.

Going back to rehearse my place in the Music Hall stage show was not something I looked forward to. Although the girls congratulated me on my television appearance, Florence Rogge said not a word.

Suddenly my name was called out over and over again. "Becket, you're all off!" "Becket" this and "Becket" that. I was becoming so nervous from all the hassling that I was making mistakes in counting measures. I was humiliated. A few days before, I was a star. Now I was being called on the mat because I couldn't fit into the Corp.

Grace told me that Florence quite often did this to girls who made a success of one of her ideas. To Florence Rogge, I was disloyal.

I made up my mind that I'd have to leave. I gave my two weeks notice. I lived through those two weeks, knowing the nightmare would soon be over. The ballet girls gave me a going away party in the dressing room, and for a gift, a plaster of Paris statue of a ballerina to remember them by.

By this time I managed to accumulate some wisdom along with the money I had put away. I continued to take ballet class with Cairol Leslie, and became involved with the choreographer's workshop, which was active at that time at the Ninety-second Street YWCA.

The Kaufman Auditorium had many concerts and dance events, and it was there that I became a member of a small experimental group directed by Herb Ross who presented one of his first ballets, *The Thief Who Loved a Ghost*. I was thrilled to have been given the part of the ghost, and to dance with Herb Ross himself, who played the part of the thief.

We would rehearse in his studio over the Fifty-fifth Street Playhouse.

Many an afternoon the manager of the theater would thump on his ceiling, our floor, because we were making too much noise.

When the performance was finally given, several of the ballet girls from the Music Hall came to see me and expressed surprise that I could do adagio and dramatic dancing. I tried convincing them that they could probably do it too, if they'd just quit the Music Hall, get out, and find out.

After the performance we continued to rehearse other ballets of Herb Ross, but when American Ballet Theatre bought *The Thief Who Loved a Ghost* from Herb, and put it in their repertoire featuring the well-known dancers on their roster, interest in his company dwindled.

Mother and I went to American Ballet Theatre performance and watched Ruth Ann Kosan play the ghost, and I felt an ache inside.

Marta models in an advertisement for Danskin Tights, 1957.

Scene Six

A Tree Grows in Brooklyn

I was as one of the four girl dancers cast in the new production of *A Tree Grows in Brooklyn*, directed by George Abbott. Herb Ross was choreographer so I was chosen right away at the auditions.

Mr. Abbott seemed to like me as well, so fortunately I found a home in another Broadway musical which was slated to open at the Alvin Theatre.

Our contracts were signed September, 1951.

A Tree Grows in Brooklyn was produced and directed by George Abbott, with music by Arthur Schwartz. It was to open April 19th, with New Haven, Connecticut and Philadelphia tryouts first.

We began rehearsals that fall in New York, and in January we prepared to open in New Haven, running there for two months and then on to Philadelphia for exposure to tougher critics and some drastic play doctoring.

The score was beautiful, and carried within its melodies that romantic nostalgia of the late 1800s. The sets were magnificent, designed by Jo Meilziner with costumes by Irene Sharaff.

There wasn't much dancing except for one ballet set in a summer evening on a rooftop. Skylights and chimneys punctuated the flatness of the roof providing entrances, exits, or a frame to surround a particular character singing a solo or acting out lines. Brooklyn Bridge stretched like an arc above the rooftop, painted on the backdrop to appear as if it had gradually become lost in the haze.

This was the big scene where Johnny Johnston sang to Kate, his wife, *I'll Buy You a Star*, which followed a rooftop ballet to *If You Haven't Got a Sweetheart*, danced to the accompaniment of the show's chorus and a romantic tenor by the name of James McCracken. James sat on a prop orange crate while we four couples danced atop the roof in a hazy blue stage light that I wished would last forever.

My dance partner was the most handsome, talented young man I had seen in ballet. From the moment he swept me in his arms and we waltzed together and then glided across stage to the final lift, to the exit on the other side, I was in seventh heaven. No matter that the glide on my right foot wore my shoe out in one place so that my bare toe scraped along the stage. That moment, in artificial moonlight, meant more to me than anything, and I could always take care of my bloody toe back in the dressing room. I never said a word about it, because I loved the glide step and was afraid Herb would change it, or give it to someone else.

My partner's name was Oleg Briansky. I heard that he had been engaged to someone back in Paris for sometime. Obviously, then, I could never expect anything more from this relationship. Perhaps it was for the best.

I remember my mother saying, "The unrequited love affair is the one that remains the most beautiful in one's memory. Anything else is a disappointment."

I was happy, living life on the road. I made friends easily and enjoyed the camaraderie of eating meals, traveling together and having a roommate with whom I could share experiences. Occasionally I thought of Mother, but not often. When I did there was no guilt attached.

During the end of our run in New Haven, Jerome Robbins was called in to do some play doctoring. There seemed to be some trouble with the beer garden scene, which was one of my favorites, although I wasn't in it. Johnny Johnston sang, "I'm like a new broom, I'm gonna sweep clean, I'm gonna sweep clean today." The lilting melody and lyrics indicated his vow to stop drinking and get a job. He played the piano in the local bawdy house, while his wife scrubbed floors, to keep their heads above water.

Harland Dixon, a vaudeville dancer, was hired to perform a charming tap number in the beer garden scene, his first theatrical engagement in years. The job inspired him to act and dance like a thirty year-old. He was full of energy spurred on by the fact he was not only working again, but performing in a legitimate Broadway musical. The cruel blow came when the beer garden scene was cut, for purposes of tightening the show. It was more than Harland Dixon could take. He was told, "Not to worry. We'll keep you on salary anyway."

He refused their offer as a matter of pride, walked out of the theater and was never heard from again.

After the show's three week run in New Haven, we moved on to Philadelphia where we opened at the Forrest Theatre. Rehearsals continued during the daytime while the performances went on each evening, with two matinees. Jerome Robbins was still doctoring the show, and we all wondered what he would cut next. The next blow was the cutting of the rooftop ballet. All there was left for Oleg and me was a slow waltz across the stage.

The rooftop scene was still in, since Johnny Johnston's number, *I'll Buy You a Star*, was a great hit.

I remember going to the ice cream parlor on Broad Street with Oleg and silently sipping ice cream sodas with lumps in our throats. I look back on that time, and I really believe that Oleg felt something special about our waltz, too, although he was careful never to say anything. The only contact we had now was that waltz, from one side of the stage to the other. I cherished it and held on to it more than ever.

On the road, the show was the only important thing. Nothing else mattered. But now the entire cast, which for the past two months had become a closely-knit family, would disband in New York. Each of us would return to the problems we had left.

I knew that once we were back in New York, Oleg and I would not be going out for ice cream sodas any more. I would be going back to Mother. I had a taste of freedom. Soon it would all come to an end.

However, with one week left, I made up my mind to enjoy it. I loved being near Oleg, and being with my friends. Now that I could see this final week in Philadelphia coming to an end, it was with heartbreaking reluctance I accepted the future. In my case it would almost be like returning to childhood.

I had a room in the St. James Hotel, right near the theater. At five o'clock we dancers would meet in the hotel dining room for dinner.

One evening we sat by the window for dinner. It was pouring rain outside. I was sitting across from Oleg and we were all talking and laughing. I was talking and happy, ignoring the rain streaming down the window pane. Suddenly one of the dancers exclaimed, "What's that face outside the window?" I looked up. It was Mother's face! Her expression was haunted and tragic. She was searching for me. She had come to Philadelphia, cutting short my final week of freedom.

I ran outside, and brought her in out of the rain. When I brought her into the dining room to introduce her to everyone, she held onto me tightly and embarrassed me.

I was annoyed with myself, for I was no longer the laughing, talking, independent girl who had been sitting across from Oleg. I withdrew because I knew if I didn't, Mother would become upset.

Arrangements were made for my roommate, Dorothy, to give up her bed in the room we shared so Mother would have a place to sleep during the last week in Philadelphia.

Mother would go to her old office on Broad Street and watch the tape during the day. In the evening, we had an early dinner together at a table by ourselves in the hotel dining room, while my friends ate by the window. I would glance over at them and gaze at Oleg seated across from Doris Wright, where I used to sit. I ached for the freedom I had enjoyed just a few days before.

Even waltzing with Oleg was not the same. I was not the Marta I had been a few days ago. I was Mother's little girl once more.

When the show opened at the Alvin Theatre, there was hardly anything left of the original. The new cut-down version with its fast pace and omitted dances and scenes left a shell of the musical I had learned to love.

The show ran for a year. Halfway through the run, Oleg had to return to France because his visa had expired. I felt a great emptiness inside when I heard the news.

We collected money from the entire cast for the unexpected expenses he was about to be faced with. I was the head collector because I was his partner in the show.

On our last night together, after our waltz crossover, Oleg and I went to Howard Johnson's for our final ice cream soda together. He was to embark for Europe from Pier 81 the next morning. We agreed that I should meet him to wish him "bon voyage."

When I finally arrived at the dock, the great ship was there with crowds thronging about. I went up the gangplank with the crowds, found the official in charge, and asked him where I could find Oleg Briansky.

After scanning the passenger list several times, the official looked up at me and said, "Sorry mademoiselle, sorry."

There wasn't an Oleg Briansky on the passenger list.

I descended the gangplank through the oncoming crowds. Had Oleg changed his name once on the ship? Had he not wanted to see me one last time? I was deeply pained to realize that not only was I never going to see or dance with Oleg again, but was also denied our final goodbye.

Three weeks later I received a letter from Oleg. He was back in France now. The letter was warm, but made no reference as to why he was not to be found on the ship.

I immediately wrote back to him at his address in Paris asking him why I could not find him. Two weeks later I received another letter from him saying that he had deliberately changed his name and somehow forgot to tell me. I did not understand this, but I continued to write him anyway. I even sent him a small recording I had made of a nocturne I wrote for a pas de deux, and also a few other pieces. Oleg intimated that he hoped to return to the states one day, and we could do something together. Then a few weeks later, I received a letter from Oleg telling me he had been married.

I began to believe it was not in the cards for me to experience love for a man in its full reality.

The show ran for another six months. Dressing room gossip about a two week notice to be put up on the call board, was indication of the end. My touring roommate, Dorothy, started going to auditions and got into a new show called *Paint Your Wagon*.

Whenever chorus members left our show, management did not bother to replace them. More and more vacancies became evident. The show was full of holes. We held a meeting with chorus equity on stage after one of the performances, to agree to a salary cut. Those left in the show wanted to keep it running as long as possible. Some of us felt that those who had auditioned and got into other shows were disloyal.

During this time I used to go to the theatre and work out. I would practice alone there in the dark, choreographing my dreams as if the stage were mine. Each morning, matinee days excluded, I would go there and have a sort of reverie with that part of myself that I was forced to subdue out in the real world. What I would experience there, alone on the darkened stage, was not unlike what I used to feel in the broadcasting studio at the Music Hall.

Often, the cleaning women would be banging their brooms against the backs of the seats up in the balcony. Occasionally, I could hear them talking, "Do ya remember the way Flossie used to brag on how many beaus she had?"

Another would say, "Mae used to brag on what big ideas Flo Ziegfeld had for her production number."

Another would add, "You should see Mae now, ya wouldn't know her."

These cleaning women had been chorus girls in the Ziegfeld follies. I had always heard that the Ziegfeld girls were the most beautiful girls in the world. And now they were cleaning women. As I practiced, I could not help but ponder my future.

Is this life's joke, life's penalty for the short precious years allotted to us, for peak performance? We are finally forced to give in. I looked down at my feet encased in their pink satin toe shoes and I realized I had years ahead of me and I should not be wasting them.

As I walked home that day, I promised I would dance forever. But then, I pondered, what is forever?

Marta appears as the king's daughter in The Mirror, the Carpet, and the Lemon, *1955.*

Universal Theatre Ballet and Dancing with Monica Lind Dancers

After *A Tree Grows in Brooklyn* closed, I was able to get quite a bit of work in television. The medium was still new. The airings were live, and in black and white.

George Abbott directed a new series which was sponsored by the *U.S. Royal Showcase*. I remember one big show called *Manhattan Towers*, and other shows on which I, again as a chorus dancer, worked under the direction of Herb Ross. I met and worked with such performers as Jeanette Macdonald, and heard Harpo Marx who played *Claire de Lune* exquisitely. I had some philosophic conversations with Harpo Marx while waiting for our part of the rehearsal to begin.

During this period, I would make the rounds of agents who handled talent for dramatic plays. I was at a point in my life when most dancers think about breaking into acting. It was on one of these rounds from a tip in *Casting News* that I chanced upon a small office on Seventh Avenue. One agent seemed to beckon to me from his desk as I started to pass his small cubicle going down the hall.

"Come on in," he said. "You are a dancer?" his accent was Yiddish, as he warmly motioned for me to sit down on the chair opposite. He was short, with curly brown hair.

"I'm looking for someone who can organize a company of, say, seventeen dancers to perform strictly Oriental style numbers for Greek clubs, Turkish clubs, conventions, weddings, and parties. Do you think you can do this for me?" he asked.

I was surprised with his faith in me as a choreographer, especially when he didn't even know who I was. "Oh yes," I answered. As I spoke, it seemed my voice came from a long tunnel, spilling enthusiasm and ideas. Someone had finally wished to tap my imagination. "Oh, yes. I can do it. I will create for you ballets based on the folk and fairy tales of many different Middle Eastern countries. I will even design the costumes, the scenery, and even make piano arrangements from ethnic recordings I will research."

"But I want you to be the star dancer, too," he continued. "I want the whole venture to be built around you, understand?"

"I'll do it all. I'll surprise you with a beautiful company, and beautiful ballets, sets and costumes, you wait and see."

The agent beamed at me across his desk. "My name is Sioma Glaser. What's yours?" he asked.

"Marta Becket," I answered.

"Well, Mata, we're in business." He rose and stretched out his hand. I stretched out mine, and we shook in one of the firmest handshakes I had ever felt.

"Mata, when you have something to show me, let me know. I'll come to see it and we'll make arrangements for our first booking. After that, there'll be tours. We'll do big things, you and I. From now on, just call me Sioma. May I then call you Mata?"

"Of course," I said. I left his office and walked down the hall. I could hear him go into another office and speak to his father. He mentioned something about needing money, for now his big dream was about to happen.

I wondered if Sioma Glaser had the money to back his dreams and mine. But I quickly shrugged off that worry and got caught up in his excitement. I would organize seventeen unemployed dancers, do research at the library on folk and ethnic fairy tales, go down to the Lower East Side and scrounge around for authentic Turkish, Indian, and Middle Eastern recordings and design the most beautiful costumes Sioma Glaser had ever seen.

The next day, I was slated to rehearse for thirteen weeks on the *Kate Smith Show*. Between rehearsals, I made phone calls to all the dancers I knew who were at liberty. Evenings, I went to the library and did research. Late at night, I would work on costume designs, and when there was one day off from television rehearsals, I went down to the Lower East Side and came home with at least seventy-five recordings of ethnic music, all authentic. I was drugged with enthusiasm with a purpose.

My high school friend, Anzia, found a free studio where I could rehearse to my heart's content. Seda's Studio, up on One-hundred-eighty-first Street, became the scene for some of the most fulfilling rehearsal sessions of my life.

I chose five folk and fairy tales. "*The Mirror, the Carpet, and the Lemon*" was one of my ballets, based on a Turkish fairy tale, in which three princes, each bearing a gift, seek the hand of the king's daughter. Within the magic mirror, one could see the four corners of the earth. Upon the magic carpet, one could fly to the four corners of the earth. The magic lemon, however, with its healing powers and promise of health, happiness, and a long life, wins over the king's daughter, resulting in a final wedding.

The Death of Kikos, was an Armenian folk tale in which even the trees mourn and weep, along with six peasant women, over the death of a village peasant boy.

Lost Talisman was based on an Egyptian fairy tale in which a bored pharaoh summons his wizard to conjure up some entertainment for him.

The entertainment consists of a barge filled with nine damsels playing small harps. One of the damsels loses her talisman which drops into the water. The wizard is ordered to retrieve her talisman. Upon being handed her talisman, she agrees to stay with the pharaoh. The whole ballet was danced in profile, as in an Egyptian frieze.

Then I did a ballet for only three characters based on the biblical tale of King Solomon, using strong angular gestures and sweeping arms. The costumes were long, circular skirts which helped accentuate the arc-like sweep of the legs.

Because I could not find an appropriate story for the Arabian ballet, I made one up to use the dancers I had recruited. The ballet I wrote was called, *Tent of Thieves*. A band of thieves return to their camp with a haul of stolen treasure. After a sensuous dance by Bedouin girls with ankle bells, each of the thieves empties his treasures onto the ground and re-enacts his conquest before the sheik and the crowd. Finally, the sheik's favorite thief steps forth, but before emptying his treasures, he requests a foil, a volunteer to act out the part of the victim. The sheik orders the favorite thief to choose his foil from the crowd.

The favorite thief points a finger at a man seated on one of the cushions. The thief then places a small stool center stage and orders the Arab to be seated. The two men glare at each other. The thief empties his treasures and begins his dance, acting out with pantomime his conquest, ending with a circle of air turns around the Arab. He stops just behind him, and pulls out a shining dagger. Lifting it up for a moment quickly, he stabs the Arab, who falls to the ground to gasps from the crowd.

Because murder within the tribe is an unspeakable crime, it is punished by death. Knowing this, the murderer thief stands beside his fallen victim, waiting for his execution. The sheik orders him to be chained and banished from the tent to await his sentence.

Before he is to leave, the sheik grants the thief one final request. The thief, without hesitation, points to one of the beautiful Bedouin women, his unfaithful wife; lover to the fallen victim. She must die with him. Because unfaithfulness is also a crime within the tent, the sheik wastes no time in ordering her to be chained to her murderer husband. Together, they await their execution.

As the thief and the unfaithful wife leave the tent, chained until their death, the lights fade and the curtain falls.

I could see materializing before me an exceptional dance company. Yet, dancers rebelled and more often than not, a dancer or two would arrive late. Usually it was one of my leading dancers playing prima donna.

Sioma Glaser would send people to audition for me. These people were not dancers, they were actors. There was one actor I kept. He was burly, dark, handsome, but slightly evil looking. I gave him the part of the murdered victim in *Tent of Thieves* and he was excellent.

For the first two months of rehearsal, things went wonderfully. But soon after, I noticed restlessness among the dancers. Sioma Glaser had not provided any financial backing up to this point; I knew I could not hold onto them much longer.

I was working in television, rehearsing during the day, with the shows on weekends. Weekday evenings were spent in the studio, desperately trying to create a miracle with a group of hungry, unemployed dancers.

Mr. Glaser would come up to rehearsals and look pleased. Each time he came, I thought, "This time, he'll say something about money." But, he never did. He would needle me about why I hadn't used that cute little blond he'd sent up, or that hefty woman who sang oriental love songs.

"But, this is a dance company," I would explain. Nothing I said seemed to sink in.

One day Mr. Glaser came to Seda's Studio grinning like a child who had inherited an amusement park.

I was hoping he was going to tell us he was about to pay the dancers. I had lost two of them to a summer job at Jones Beach Amphitheater. They were doing *Kismet* and needed a lot of dancers.

"I have great news," he said, "Our ballet company is bigger than I had ever expected; better and has more class than I had bargained for. Because it is such a good company, I have convinced my father to rent Carnegie Hall for our debut. Now what do you think of that?"

"What about money to pay the dancers?" I asked pleadingly.

"Money, money, money," he answered, his smile converted to a frown. "That's all you young people think of, money."

"What about costumes and an accompanist?" I continued. "We can't give a performance anywhere turning Victrola records and we've been at this for six months. We've done all the work and you've done nothing!" I was furious.

Glaser rose from his feet, "Carnegie Hall is rented, like it or not, for the evening of June 7th. The tickets are being printed now. It will be called Universal Theatre Ballet, starring Marta Becket, with guest artists presented by Broadway Artists."

"But this is May," I answered. "How can we be ready in less than a month?"

"You are ready now," he answered.

After he had gone, I stood frozen, surrounded by the fifteen dancers I had left.

"Marta," one of my best girl dancers came to me. "I didn't want to tell you this until I was really sure Mr. Glaser would not be able to pay us. But I've got to take that job out at Jones Beach too. I'm supposed to sign my contract tomorrow. I just can't keep on rehearsing like this without money to pay my rent. If ever things change, I'll come back, that is if you'll have me. Please don't be mad at me, please."

"No, I'm not mad. I thank you for staying with me as long as you did." I looked up. She squeezed my hand.

I then addressed the remaining group. "Look," I said. "You might as well all feel free to go. I can't present any one of these ballets without costumes and musical accompaniment. The big ballets we all rehearsed so hard will have to be eliminated. I will only do what I can afford to costume myself and pay for my own accompanist. I will keep *The Judgment of King Solomon*, but create a new one for a cast of only three."

"You mean you don't need us anymore? You don't want us?" one girl asked.

"I want you alright but I can't afford you," I answered, with a break in my voice. "I would like Charles Stuart to stay, Bob Marci, Bill Lamonica, and Jill Reynolds." I was about to collapse.

The remaining group, aside from those whose names I had mentioned, shuffled about, gathering their things. Without a word, they prepared to leave. Before doing so, each one personally assured me that he'd come back to me anytime things might improve.

Bill was the comedian of the group. Nothing ever got him down.

"I'll make the costumes," he said. "I love to sew and because I'm a hair-dresser, I have a feel for theatrics."

"Okay," I said. "That will be good. Maybe my mother can help, too."

I was holding the ticket in my hand. "Starring Marta Becket." My name was on that ticket bigger than life. I wanted to crawl inside myself.

When Mother learned about the turn of events, she said, "Everything will be just wonderful. I knew one day you would dance as a star in Carnegie Hall."

Mana, on the other hand, was furious. I was going to appear, with star Billing, in his sacred Carnegie Hall, under the sponsorship of a would be impresario who had nothing going for him. Broadway Artists was nothing but a cardboard front. The Universal Theatre Ballet was just a name for a dream that had never happened.

Charles did get me a good accompanist, and I devised a new story for a ballet that would need only three characters. The title of it was *Say it With Flowers!* The ballet involved a French soubrette who was being wooed by a willowy poet and a comic, well-to-do gentleman. To the music of Offenbach, the ballet was light, colorful, and filled with lots of action.

Bob Marci played the part of the poet, and insisted upon wearing some pale blue tights left him by his former teacher. Bill Lamonica, who was the rich gentleman, obtained a top hat from a local theatrical thrift shop. Each of the men tries to woo the soubrette's heart by bringing her larger and larger bouquets of flowers, until finally the stage was covered with them. In the end, she finally runs off with the poet, leaving the comic gentleman flat on his back amid a bevy of flowers.

Bill Lamonica made all the costumes for *Judgement of King Solomon*, and they were very striking.

June seventh was hot and muggy. It seemed hundreds of people were milling around backstage. I didn't know anybody except Bob, Charles, Bill, and Jill, and finally our accompanist, Jack. Of course Mother was there looking lost amid the confusion. Although my name was on the ticket as star, my presence was acknowledged with as much indifference as if I had not been there. Our dressing rooms were shared with a number of other people, and we had to be careful not to let our costumes and props get mixed up with those of the others on the bill.

I knew that Mana was going to be out front. He had bought some tickets for himself and a group of his friends.

The printed Carnegie Hall program did not have the participating performers listed in order. Mr. Glaser came back to tell us we would just have to wait in the wings and listen for our names.

Performers were listed in the program who hadn't even shown up. Others showed up who were not on the program, but who eventually performed. It was a surprise to see Mr. Glaser in a tuxedo. He looked good, but when he opened his mouth to speak, the irritating high pitch gravel to his voice reminded me of what a bag of wind he was.

I was not surprised to see *The Lost Talisman* listed in the program instead of *Say it With Flowers*. *The Judgment of King Solomon* was listed, so I reasoned I should be thankful for that.

Warming up backstage at Carnegie Hall was no easy matter, while straining our ears to hear the announcement of our names. When we finally did, we bounded out onto the stage and took our places. The grand piano was moved swiftly from the wings. Jack walked out elegantly dressed in a tuxedo, flipped his tails and sat down at the keyboard.

We danced not only if the stage was ours, but the whole world. This small fragment of a performance was what was left of a dream that has taken five long months of our lives.

As I danced the role of the soubrette, I decided to give it all I had. Carnegie Hall's stage was mine for twelve minutes.

As the ballet came to its finale, I performed circles of turns, ending with an aerial cartwheel partnered by Bill Lamonica. I then ran off stage with the poet, Bob Marci, to a round of applause. I returned with Bob as the three of us acknowledged the applause together.

Our poor little ballet was sandwiched in between opera arias, a rabbi's prayer, Hasidic dancers, a commemoration of concentration camp sufferers, the Barry Sisters singing *Where Can I Go*, and *Making Whoopee*.

When it was all over, amid performers, friends, relatives, and the five remaining dancers of the Universal Theatre Ballet, the scramble to collect our belongings was frantic. Mr. Glaser came back to congratulate everybody and say goodbye. For a moment, just before I was about to leave with Mother and the dancers, I could hear Mr. Glaser's high pitched voice above the crowd.

"Mata, call me Monday afternoon, vil ya? I have a great idea for something."

I pretended not to hear him.

"Mata! "Did you hear me?" He called again.

"Yes," I answered.

Through the years, Charles told me that those five months were the high point of his life. He and Bob Marci were the only ones who stayed in touch with me.

I continued to earn a living on television. It seemed a grind compared to the life I had hoped would eventually become my reality.

When Mana came to visit and take us to dinner, I was greeted by sour negativity.

"What a presumption, to think you are good enough to appear in the great Carnegie Hall," he said.

I informed him that anyone can rent Carnegie Hall, and that every spring, a tap dance teacher from Harlem rents the big hall for her class recital.

My father continued, "Fools step in where angels fear to tread."

Mother sat in the corner looking out the window, as if she had heard that line said to her long ago.

"The Offenbach ballet was all right, my friends liked that, but that *Judgment of King Solomon* was terrible," he said. "What an ugly story to present to the public and on the great Carnegie Hall stage, too."

"And that Glaser guy, whatever his name was, he had no right to pin your hopes on something he promised and couldn't deliver."

"I thank Sioma Glaser for his dream, for asking me to bring his dream to life, for his dream became my dream," I said in defense. "Just because it didn't turn out doesn't mean the dream is any less wonderful. I'm going to take the fragments of that dream and continue to hope. Perhaps I will find another outlet. I never asked you to help me become a dancer. I never will. I don't expect a pat on the back. Even if I starve pursuing my dream, I will never ask you for help. When you ask me to stop following my dream, you are asking me to die."

I don't, to this day, know how I managed to talk back that way to my father.

There was much talk at the time about the Straw Hat Circuit, which was a tour that went all through Brooklyn, the Bronx, Queens, Long Island, and even upper New York State. There were small troupes of actors, singers and a few dancers who managed to get these tours. I had hopes of saving all the work I had done on my little company, salvaging what I could remember and auditioning for agents, who, if they liked what I showed them, could offer me and my troupe a tour on the Straw Hat Circuit.

I found an interested party in an upstairs office of the Palace Theatre building. His name was Nat Jerome. He was very old, and I was surprised that he had interest in coming all the way up to Seda's Studio to see what I could show.

I had the studio ready to dance the entire *The Mirror, the Carpet, and the Lemon,* playing all the parts myself. The records were in a neat pile beside the gramophone. I waited for Mr. Jerome to arrive so that I could begin. The afternoon sun had about set, so a light bulb hanging from a cord above the rehearsal area was the only illumination. I greeted Mr. Jerome at the door and helped him in. Although he was breathing somewhat heavily, and the long subway trip showed on his face, there was a slight smile of anticipation. I sat him down and explained that I would dance all the parts myself and even change the records.

"If you like what you see, and think you could book it, I can get my group of dancers back in a minute. They'd much rather be touring in my company than performing in a large chorus at Jones Beach."

"Well, let's see what cha have. On with the show," he said.

I told him the story of the ballet, and then I began to dance. As the story unfolded, I detected a smile of amusement on Mr. Jerome's face. Going further, I pantomimed the wise sage whose wisdom influences the king's daughter to accept the hand of the third prince. Then came the wedding scene where all get to perform again in a sort of reprise. And finally there was the pose of the king's daughter shyly holding her fan in such a way that the magic lemon could balance perfectly on it, showing her acceptance of the third prince who had brought her the most precious gift of all. "That's wonderful; charming," Mr. Jerome said, finally. He even clapped.

"You like it enough to book it? I can get my dancers back tomorrow," I said, hopefully.

Nat Jerome shook his head. My heart fell. "You don't need all those dancers," he said. "You can dance the male parts better than they can. You can pantomime the old sage on the mountain better than they can. And there's no doubt that you should be the king's daughter."

"Then you want to book me all by myself? I won't know what to tell my loyal dancers."

"No," Mr. Jerome continued. "You won't be ready for a long time. By the time you have it rehearsed and ready, I will be long gone. You have a unique thing here. You're a Ruth Draper of the dance. Work on this idea: a one-woman show, a dance company of one. You have the ability to create the illusion of an entire company by yourself. Very few can do this. Now I must go. I am tired, but I am very glad that I came up to see what you can do. Goodbye now, and break a leg." He smiled, shook my hand, and left.

I sat alone for a while. I remembered seeing the one woman shows of Ruth Draper, Agna Enters, Cornelia Otis Skinner. I saw them as a very small child. Now I had been encouraged to go and do likewise.

I felt a warmth inside me, not from the hot night, but from the kind, fatherly encouragement I had needed and looked for all of my life. Now there was no one to hold me back except me, but somehow the idea of going solo gave me confidence. There was no one to let me down.

For the next year, I floated about looking for any kind of work I could get. Television dancing work faded but before it was through, I worked on the *U.S. Royal Showcase*, *The Kate Smith Show* and then the *Manhattan Towers* special. Everything comes to an end, so there I was, faced with unemployment. During periods like these, it is easy to become involved in situations which later in life, you wished you hadn't.

I joined a small group called the Monica Lind Dancers because I was told I would understudy the lead, Monica Lind herself, and I could design the costumes. The salary was only twenty-five dollars a week during rehearsals, and a flat twenty-five dollars for designing all the costumes.

Monica Lind was a very strong dancer. She could do "millions of this" and "millions of that" like a machine. She would step into an arabesque like a steam shovel would attack a pile of rocks. Our styles were completely different.

The company was to tour the big nightclub and theater restaurant circuit. Backers would come in and out during rehearsals to watch. Because I was the understudy, I sat on the sideline most of the time, with occasional stabs at a bit part here and there.

I ached to dance. However, I did not look forward to the time when Monica would get sick, because I was not the strong dancer she was once out there on the floor. I would probably improvise something I could do so that I wouldn't fall flat on my face.

Our first booking was to be in Buffalo at the Town Casino, Thanksgiving 1952.

Monica had come down with a bad case of flu, and there was no way that at the last minute I could get out there on that floor and dance the way she did and be partnered exactly the way she was, without rehearsals. I was becoming petrified.

I did have a small dance with a partner, which I fairly enjoyed, and I performed in a lyric style which Monica tried over and over to change.

Opening night went fairly well, but did not receive a big ovation. I don't think the dancers were any big hit. Our pay was soon fifty dollars a week, with room and board thrown in. Our hotel rooms were horrible, and the coffee shop downstairs was depressing. All the time in Buffalo, the lights flickered from Niagara Falls. The only place they didn't was in the casino.

I would get letters and postcards from Mother, telling me all about things going on back in New York. She sent me one card to say George Abbott was auditioning girl dancers for a musical called *Wonderful Town*, choreographed by Donald Saddler.

Immediately, I gave my two weeks notice. Monica Lind was furious. The dancers in her troupe gave me a party and seemed really sorry to see me go.

Marta dances in the Garden Party, *1968.*
Photo by Tom Williams.

Wonderful Town

I boarded the train to New York and made the audition at the Wintergarden Theatre the next afternoon.

Running in the stage door, I could see the auditions were already half over.

"Hurry up!" said Bobby Griffith, the stage manager, who had been with *A Tree Grows in Brooklyn*. "You're late!"

I rushed into my rehearsal clothes and, with the few remaining dancers, watched Donald Saddler demonstrate some steps.

Donald Saddler was a quiet, soft-spoken man. I liked him. He did not intimidate, as so many choreographers do. I enjoyed the audition. He liked me, and I got the job.

Wonderful Town was set in Greenwich Village of the thirties, my child-hood stamping ground. George Abbott came in across stage and greeted me as though time had never passed since *Tree*. Rehearsals were to start in a week and contracts were signed that afternoon.

I knew it would have a good run, as all George Abbott musicals did. Rosalind Russell was the star. Her leading man was George Gaines. Eileen was played by the young Edie Adams, who later on married Ernie Kovacs.

I was happy again, and looked forward to the start of rehearsals. I assumed that Mana would be pleased I had landed another Broadway show, simply because it would be steady employment for awhile. However, when he asked me who was writing the musical score (it was Leonard Bernstein) he was not overjoyed.

"Well, that's not Rodgers and Hammerstein," he remarked. "It won't be a great show without a great musical score."

I had learned by now that no endeavor I embarked upon would please him.

Now that my security looked stable for awhile, I began to plan my future. I was twenty-eight going on twenty-nine. I made up my mind that this would be my last Broadway show. From now on, I would concentrate all of my efforts on creating my own one-woman show. I would design and choreograph vignettes and dances in which I would play and dance out several characters. It would be my own evening of theater. I knew I could do this. Whether I could make a living from it or not didn't deter me. I wouldn't be given a second chance. This was it!

I foreknew I would need money for costumes, music, and a rehearsal hall. I would be making good money now. I always did when I worked in a show. Up to this point, I had never been able to save anything. Mother would scoop large amounts for her big buys in the market. I knew I would have to put a stop to this use of my earnings.

I rehearsed and delivered a speech to Mother, "This money is going to support a dream that I have had. My own theater of dance pantomime, and I must start now. Later will be too late. I'll never be twenty-nine again. This is my life, my money, and my dream. I will not have you taking any more out of the bank. The money will be invested in me from now on, not in stocks."

"Well if that is to be the way it's to be," she said softly. "That's the way it's to be. I was only doing it for our old age, dear. I'm always thinking of you."

After my speech, I left the flat and went out. I needed air. I took a long walk, alone. I felt strong. I looked at all my familiar haunts; Fifth Avenue, Rockefeller Center, the stage door at the Music Hall. I will never go back there again, I promised myself. My best friend, my imagination, cried for joy.

Dance rehearsals for *Wonderful Town* were held at Orest Sergievsky's studio. Dody Goodman and Babs Heath had been on most of the television specials I had done, but outside of that, *Wonderful Town* was an entirely new family. I made close friends with a modern dancer named Margaret Cuddy, and we roomed together when the show went on the pre-Broadway tour to New Haven, Boston, and Philadelphia.

I again enjoyed life away from Mother, Mana, and home. I would practice daily up in the balcony, while rehearsals were being held on the stage.

In Boston, Margaret and I stayed in a boarding house across the Boston Common.

The walk back to our lodgings after the Friday night performance, through the snow and sleet, with our weekly wages in our purse, was a thrilling experience. Each time we made it safely to the rooming house was a triumph. Our rent was half what the others were paying at the big hotels surrounding the theater, but the Boston Common was known for muggings, which is why no one else dared stay in a place where they would have to cross it.

There were several dance productions in the show which I liked very much. One was a jail scene in which characters, mixed up in a midnight brawl, were thrown into a row of cells which stretched from one side of the stage to the other. The character I played was a society lady, bedecked with diamonds. The jail house ballet was cut in Boston, so the assistant costume designer let me keep the fake diamonds. I use them to this day.

There was a scene that took place at an outdoor art show. A painting got ruined when it was bopped over one of the character's heads. I was asked to supply this work of art, each day, back stage. I spent ten minutes on a poster-painted cartoon of modern dancers, which was torn and replaced eight times a week.

In this scene, I wore the costume of a gypsy fortune teller, and as I crossed over from one side of the stage to the other, I wore a sandwich board advertising The Gypsy Tea Room.

We were all different characters, which made the show interesting. Dody Goodman, who later became famous from her appearances on the Jack Paar show, played Violet, the village prostitute, who goes about handing out business cards.

The dance sequence in the Village Vortex Nightclub was fun. I was carried upstairs, upside down by Billy Weslow, doing a kind of scissor motion with my legs. Everybody else was dancing closely, up on a raised dance floor. These few bars of being carried up the stairs with a spotlight on me, I cherished. It was my solo. Even when I had a bad cold, I wouldn't think of letting anyone else replace me.

During the run, I ran into an assistant photographer who had worked for Louise Dahl-Wolfe, the fashion photographer for *Harper's Bazaar*, back in 1948. He was now working at Doubleday and said they were looking for an illustrator to do the drawings for George Balanchine's new book, *Complete Stories of the Great Ballets*. He suggested I see the art editor. I did, and in a few weeks was given the assignment to illustrate the glossary for Balanchine's book. I suppose the fact that I was a dancer, as well as an artist, sold Doubleday on the idea.

Between scenes in *Wonderful Town*, I would work on drawings.

It was tedious, tailoring my style of sketching to Mr. Balanchine's forced turn out positions. Whenever I drew dancers, they were either soaring, poised en pointe, or in transition. The drawings for this book were more like diagrams. I made $400 dollars and stashed it away for my plans.

From this job, I got the assignment to illustrate Walter Terry's book, *Star Performance*, a children's book about the lives of the great ballerinas from the age of Catherine de Medici. The work for this was intricate line drawings which looked like etchings, very delicate on the original rendering. However, in the published book, the ink appeared heavy and thicker than I had wished. Several critiques of the work were none too kind. There were a few good ones, but the fact that two were not good, crushed me to the core. Doubleday was pleased with my artistic efforts, and I was paid $700 for the book. I put this away as well.

When I wasn't on stage or working on sketches, I was practicing for my one-woman show. I worked with the carpet for *The Mirror, the Carpet and the Lemon*. With three masks I bought at Woolworth's, I practiced changing from the prince to the king's daughter, with the quick removal of a crowned veil and circular skirt, to a turbaned mask, my transformation was complete.

I remember Dody Goodman, with her high pitched voice, saying, "My God, there's Marta again, always pretending to be some goddamn princess."

Her digs would hurt, but I would go on practicing anyway. After awhile she stopped.

A choreographer and teacher named, Paul Szilard, asked me if I would design a stage set for his ballet *Night Fright*, to be performed in Tokyo with the Komaki Ballet Company. The star was to be Nora Kaye. He told me that if I would design the set for him, he would get me into the Stage Designers Union.

I agreed to do it. I made a sketch from scale, and gave it to Paul, who took it to Tokyo. There, someone made it to scale, and it was used as the backdrop for the ballet. A month or so later, one of the singers in *Wonderful Town*, came running to me with a copy of *Variety* in his hand.

"You've received a rave review for your stage set in Tokyo. The ballet was panned, but your set received critical acclaim," the singer said.

I bought a copy of *Variety* and showed my review to Mana.

"A review in Japan doesn't mean much," he said. "Don't let it go to your head."

Paul, returned from Japan, had forgot his promise to get me into the set designer's union. Instead, he handed me a box.

"For you my dear. A gift for the wonderful set you designed for me."

Inside was a pair of Japanese tights. To me they looked no different than American tights.

"The best tights in the world, my dear, guaranteed never to wear out."

I remember a forced smile. "Thank you," I said, as I turned and left.

There was a replacement for one of the girl dancers in the show, and Doris Wright joined the cast. We became close friends and attended class together daily at Caird Leslie's. We were both very fond of ice cream, and could eat a whole pint each after class on a hot day.

A one-hundred performance anniversary was held for *Wonderful Town* on stage after the show. Rosalind Russell bought an enormous ice cream cake which nearly filled the stage. Her image in sugar was at the center.

After the curtain rang down, Doris and I changed and went down to the stage to join the party. To our shock, everyone had gone. There was the cake, sitting in the middle of the stage, with only the ghost light on. "Where is everybody?" we asked a stage hand who was sitting by the light board.

"All gone to the bar," was the answer. "Everyone prefers to drink. Cake is for kids."

Doris and I approached the cake timidly. It had begun to melt. "Go ahead, have all you want," the stage hand said. "It's just going to melt anyway. By two o'clock in the morning all that's gonna be there will be a puddle of cream."

Doris and I both felt sorry for the ice cream cake, a masterpiece constructed in a medium that was meant to be admired and then consumed. We began eating piece after piece as if we were trying to make up for all those who had ignored it. No matter how much we ate, the cake didn't seem to grow any smaller. We just felt more uncomfortable as we downed one plateful after another, until we finally had to call it quits.

By the next day's matinee, the cake was gone. No one even mentioned it. Doris and I kept our gluttony a secret, but from then on we had a bond.

I was close to completion in planning for my solo program of dance pantomimes. My program would start with a curtain raiser, which I called *The Eternal Triangle*. In it I portrayed Columbine as the wife, Harlequin as the husband, and Pierrot as the hidden lover. It was a light frothy piece, set to the overture to *The Merry Wives of Windsor*.

Columbine offers Harlequin her heart just as he is about to leave for work. He is too busy and too interested in his *Wall Street Journal* to be interested and he leaves. Enter Pierott, playing his mandolin. Columbine offers Pierrot another heart which she pulls from her bodice. Just as Pierott is about to accept Columbine's second heart, Harlequin returns home sooner than expected. Seeing Pierrot cringing in the closet in his cape, Harlequin picks up the cape and flings his competition out the window with slapstick anger. Harlequin's actions have once again proven to Columbine that he loves her after all. At the end, Columbine pulls from her bodice another heart for Harlequin.

Another piece, called *Gossip,* I created one afternoon in our cold-water flat. I was excited to discover a short musical selection on the back of a record which I bought primarily for the other side. It was one of five pieces for string quartet, called *Valse Ridicule.* From it, I arranged another three character work involving two prissy Victorian ladies who gossip about a cabaret dancer.

There was only one work in my entire repertoire in which I did not write the story for myself. It was from a story called *Her Lover,* by Maxim Gorky. It was one of those Russian short stories I had to make into a dance pantomime because I understood the lonely peasant girl so well. The music for this was by Alfredo Casella, the same composer who wrote the piece for *Gossip.*

The final piece on my program was *The Mirror, the Carpet and the Lemon.* I decided to keep the cast of characters pared down to four: the king's daughter and her three suitors.

The girls in the dressing room sometimes ribbed me about my preoccupation with designing or drawing between the acts. I was becoming obsessed with time. I resented wasted moments, and as I look back, I believe my constant concentration on what I was working on irritated them. Once we took a poll backstage. If any one of us had only three dollars left to spend, and a choice between taking class, or an empty practice studio as our last wish, which would it be? Everyone present chose the ballet class.

I chose the empty studio. In that precious hour, who knows what I could conjure up?

Of course, I realized at that time, nobody cared about what I might fathom.

My bank account was pretty good. Mother had done as I asked and had not withdrawn any of my savings. She agreed to make some of my costumes for me and attend some of my rehearsals.

The producers of *Wonderful Town* were planning a new show called *Pajama Game,* and they were looking for backers. They had a notice on the call board asking for one hundred dollar investments from the cast of *Wonderful Town.* Mother and I had an argument over the fact that I did not want to invest in it.

"Just think dear, when *Pajama Game* is a hit, you will receive royalties from the road shows, the film, and perhaps later on, television."

"I don't particularly like the show." I replied. "I'm going to invest in myself now. No more diversions. All my energy, money, and time are going to make my dream a reality, and that's it."

George Abbott took a liking to Doris and me. He would often show up at the stage door just before the curtain came down and invite me for an ice cream soda at Howard Johnson's. Sometimes he would invite Doris and me out to his country place in Port Washington. He would meet us at the train station and drive us to his rambling house which was surrounded by trees, with a large swimming pool in front.

Some thought Mr. Abbott had a part for me in a new show. Doris and I could never understand why Mr. Abbott invited us so often. He didn't converse much. He would doze beside his pool, while we swam and played with his dog Butch, who looked a little like a pig. Mr. Abbott said all Chinese bull dogs looked like pigs. In the winter, Mr. Abbott would ship Butch down to Florida for a vacation of his own.

A few times Mr. Abbott invited me out by myself. On one of these occasions I was a little apprehensive. Mr. Abbott enjoyed my company at breakfast, lunch, and dinner. He gave me free reign of his place all day, and then would enjoy a piano concert played by me after dinner. Upon my return to the Wintergarden, upstairs in the dressing room, I was greeted with curious glances, half smiles, and pummeled with questions.

"Well, what's the new show?" some asked. "Do you have the starring role? Were you alone? Was somebody else there?"

I was uncomfortable, but grinned and bore it. Bobby Griffith, our stage manager, helped out by saying that Mr. Abbott was tired of girls who immediately started questioning him about future musicals and that I was probably a welcome relief.

One night, Mr. Abbott invited me to dinner at the Hampshire House where he lived when staying in the city.

When I met him in the elegant public dining room, he had an amused smile on his face.

"Let them talk," he said. "There goes George Abbott, sixty-seven years old, out with another young thing."

I was twenty-nine, not so young anymore. But I looked much younger, and I sat there, feeling quite privileged to be dining with a great theatrical director. All I ever knew about his personal past was that he had been married for some time to an actress named, Mary Sinclair, but they were divorced.

"Let's go upstairs to my apartment and have some cheese and wine," he said.

"Alright," I said timidly. We went upstairs. Mr. Abbott went to his refrigerator and got out the cheese, crackers, and wine. He set it in front of the television and arranged two chairs before the screen.

"An amazing new medium," Mr. Abbott exclaimed, as he sat down in the chair opposite me. "I am fascinated by it. There is no end to its possibilities. Have some cheese and crackers and, here, have some wine."

I was surprised to see Mr. Abbott indulge in wine, for the story was that he was a teetotaler, and didn't smoke either.

The evening was quiet, punctuated by the crunching of cheese and crackers, and the dialogue from the television, and the explosions of blue and white light flickering from the set upon our faces. It was getting quite late, eleven o'clock or so. I mentioned I should think about getting home.

Mr. Abbott rose from his chair, put his arms on my shoulders and kissed me right on the mouth. I was paralyzed! The blood rushed to my face and I couldn't see for a moment.

"There, he said grinning, "Go tell that to your mother."

"How do you know about my mother?" I asked, with a quivery voice.

"Oh, you'd be surprised the things I know," he answered. "Come, let's get you home."

We went downstairs, where he hailed a taxi, gave me some money to pay the fare, and bid me goodnight. I never told Mother about this kiss. She never questioned me about my visits with Mr. Abbott.

Wonderful Town ran for a little over a year. Rosalind Russell had left the cast about three-quarters of the way through, and Carol Channing was her replacement. She was so good, the show ran a little longer than expected. However, our crowds were thinning and a road company was formed. Only one member in the chorus went on the road. A few of the bit parts had the same actors playing them, but on the whole, the road company was a brand new troupe.

We were invited to see the road company preview. There is nothing more difficult for the cast of a road company than performing for the original cast. And there is nothing sadder for the cast of a closing show, than to see the preview of the road company, all new people wearing the familiar wardrobe, the familiar sets, and music.

None of us out front watching wanted to go on the road. Still, it seemed unthinkable that our costumes were being worn by someone else, and our dances were being brought to life by others.

You can't hold time back by staying with a production to the bitter end.

But it's too bad that a great show can't die a dignified death, with the original cast.

I remember seeing a watered-down version of *A Tree Grows in Brooklyn* at a theater in Coney Island. To me it was like witnessing the dying gasps of someone I loved. The actors were mediocre, there were no dancers, the scenery had been cut in half, and the orchestra consisted of a saxophone, a trumpet, drums, and a piano.

There were many from the cast of *Wonderful Town* who went into *Pajama Game*. Margaret Cuddy went into *My Fair Lady*. Dody got on the Jack Paar Show, and the rest scattered to the four winds of Broadway.

Marta plays a composite of the characters in The Mirror, the Carpet, and the Lemon, *1955.*

ACT THREE:

A Fulfillment of Promise

Scene One

A Program of Dance Pantomimes

I was rehearsing in Michael Kidd's old studio in Hell's Kitchen, over what was once a stable, but now was a plumber's shop.

My costumes were about done, a combined effort between Mother and me. I was ready to show what I had to anyone who would come up and see it. Margaret Cuddy came a few times, and so did Doris. Two *Wonderful Town* stage hands were a great audience, the best I had yet. They applauded after each piece, and gave me a ten dollar bill and a mechanical counter.

"Take this," the younger of the two said. "You'll need it. Have your mother stand at the door and count the number of people coming into your show. Tally it up with the box office to make sure nobody's cheating."

A concert manager obtained a few bookings for me in the Catskills. My performance fees were painfully small, but chicken dinners and plenty of chopped liver sandwiches were provided. I would perform two or three numbers.

The same concert manager who booked these small dates introduced me to a manager in her building who booked college tours; a Sherman Pitluck. I would joke with Mother and call him Sherman "Potluck."

He finally came up with a concert date for me at the State Teacher's College in Edinboro, Pennsylvania. It was to be a one hour program of my dance-pantomimes. The only problem was that this date was booked for September 29, 1954, one whole year away!

My concert fee was to be $105 from which Mr. Pitluck was to take one-third. I signed the contract and when I left his office, I stopped in to see the lady manager who had introduced me to Mr. Pitluck.

"I won't take my cut out this time," she said. "Your fee is so small."

"However," she continued, "let's hope Mr. Pitluck can deliver some more dates for you, with bigger fees. Then we'll all make some money," she smiled.

For a moment, I felt like a ripe peach out of which a fruit fly has taken a sizable bite, and another was approaching and perhaps more in the distance were threatening.

The concert at the State Teacher's College was one whole year away. I would have to find some sort of income in the meantime. I scanned the want ad pages for free-lance art jobs which would leave me free to rehearse and seek future bookings.

Among all the ads in the *New York Times* classified section, there was one that caught my eye: "Ripp Studio, artists wanted, bring your own brushes and portfolio."

I gathered all my sketches, tempera painting, and cartoons, and prepared to apply for the job. I stepped out into a room filled with Santa Clauses, huge Easter bunnies, a smiling clown, huge flowers with faces, and swags of sparkle tulle with tiny electric lights that twinkled constantly. There was a table where a dark-haired man and an artist were pouring over a portfolio. An office behind a glass wall was beyond that. I was told to wait.

As I waited, I turned and saw a large room in the back which had huge windows looking out on Twenty-third Street. The room was filled with display scenery. Long tables stretched from the windows to the doorway which led into the front display room. Boys were seated at the tables, constructing artificial flowers with colored paper and green wire. One of them waved frantically, and finally attempted to call my name softly. The voice was familiar. I put on my glasses to see who it was. It was Charles, one of my dancers. I felt suddenly elated at finding someone who knew me; and a dancer besides.

The dark-haired man who was interviewing the artist before me said, "I don't see anything of potential interest we can use here, but thank you for coming."

He beckoned for me. I walked over to the dark-haired man, set my portfolio on the table and spread out my work before him. He began to leaf over it.

"Very interesting," he said. "My name is Boris and I am the art director here. You will sit here at this table and create designs for window display. We work at least one whole season ahead. When you have completed enough designs, you can go in the back and help the boys make flowers, or whatever. Your pay will be a one dollar and twenty-five cents an hour. You come in in the morning, punch the time clock, and begin work. You are paid only for the hours you are here working. Would you like to start now?"

I said I would like to start the next morning.

"That will be fine," Boris said. "We open at eight thirty a.m., and close at 4:30 p.m."

The elevator door opened, and a large man who looked like a prizefighter stepped out.

"This is Bill Price, owner of Ripp Studio. Mr. Price, I want you to meet our new designer."

"Vell, vell," the big man said. "I hope you volk out better than the odders dit. Dis has been getting to be a vaste of time." He shook my hand so hard it ached the rest of the day.

"I will try and do my best," I said timidly.

Charles came to see me out. "You're the first artist they've taken in three weeks," he said." Even when they do hire an artist, he's fired after two days. Oh Marta, I hope they won't fire you. It will be great to have you here. At least we can have lunch together."

When I arrived at home, I spent the afternoon devising my schedule. I would rise early and go to the Ripp Studio by eight thirty a.m., and be home at five p.m. I would then have a quick supper, and proceed to the dance studio to rehearse.

At least the time-clock allowed me to take days off for auditions, to go out of town on concert engagements, or to work extra hours during the day if I needed.

The next morning I began to work at the Ripp Display Studio. All through the winter and into the summer, I joined the rush-hour crowds and punched the time clock.

Every afternoon, Bill Price would come to my desk and feel the thickness of the pile of sketches I had made. Quality did not seem to matter to him. Although I had not been fired, there was no mention, from either Boris or Bill Price, about being pleased with my work. However, I saw construction of many of my designs going on in the back room.

I confess it was rather thrilling to see my ideas come to life; three dimensional forms, built by the dozens, then crated and shipped to many parts of the country. I had heard that they were sold for at least $200 apiece. I was paid the same as the boys who made flowers in the back.

Once, I was asked to actually paint one of my own designs. It was one of six knights in medieval armor standing in a gothic archway, for a men's clothing store.

I began the work enthusiastically, believing that because I was asked to paint my design myself, I would have full control over all six. It was working out beautifully, but the day ended at four-thirty p.m. and I had to stop. I had an audition the next day, so I didn't return to work until the following day. I was dismayed to see that someone else had finished my armored knight, and had begun to work on the other five.

"But that was my project," I exclaimed. "I thought I was going to finish it."

"You weren't here yesterday," Boris said. "Everybody works together on these units. Nothing belongs to anyone."

"You'd vetter get vack to da drawing table and make some more designs," called Mr. Price from his glass covered office.

I returned to my small desk with a lump in my throat. My mind went blank. Mr. Price was staring at me through the glass.

I put my pencil to the paper and, moving it about, formed a Pegasus, a mythical horse with wings, flying through the air. My Pegasus became a unit for a perfume display.

Whenever I wasn't turning out designs, I was in the back room constructing artificial flowers, or miniature Santa Clauses, or tiny felt Easter rabbits. I usually ate my lunch sandwich with Charles and the boys.

Sometimes I would go to Reed's Cafeteria. There I met a lady who was a personal friend of Pauline Koner, the modern dancer. We talked about dance, and I told her about my forthcoming engagement in September. She was curious as to why I was wasting my time working in a display studio. She said Pauline never had to be concerned about money. Her father was one hundred percent behind her, and besides, she got government grants.

Whatever she or anyone thought, I had to do what I had to do. I worked faithfully at the studio until the end of August. I made arrangements to return, right after the engagement in Edinboro. Whenever I wasn't dancing, my little desk in the corner was always waiting for me. The security was reassuring to me.

Finally the date for the teacher's college engagement arrived. I bought my bus ticket ahead of time, so I would be ready to board the bus without delay. I was so excited. I was going to take my very own show out on the road. As the bus sped through the Holland Tunnel and out into the spoils of New Jersey, the whole venture felt more right than anything I had ever done before.

In Edinboro, the hotel was the only form of hospitality visible. Down the other road was a small wooden structure, a grocery store with a gas pump.

Feeling abandoned, lonely, and confused, I carried each piece of luggage, one by one, over to the hotel. When everything was sitting on the front porch, I knocked. I asked if a reservation had been made for Marta Becket?

"Not really," an elderly lady said. "But we have rooms, come in."

The college was supposed to have a reservation for me, and their negligence made me feel they didn't even expect me.

I called the program chairman who transferred me to the theater lighting department, who informed me that they planned to have a lighting rehearsal with me, that night at seven thirty p.m.

I was relieved that someone had expected me, and although I was tired after twenty-four hours on the bus with no sleep, I agreed to have someone pick me up at 7 p.m. and take me to the college for the lighting rehearsal.

I had an early supper at the hotel, went upstairs to my room, unpacked a few of my costumes, and decided to do a small practice barre. My body wanted sleep. However, I knew that I was expected to dance for this rehearsal. With numbness in every muscle, stiffness from sitting, and burning eyes from lack of sleep, I forced myself to go through an entire barre.

By the time I finished practice, I could see there was no time for a short nap. It was already six thirty p.m. I gathered my costumes and makeup, went downstairs, and waited in the hotel parlor for a Miss Riley to pick me up.

Friendly, but businesslike, she drove swiftly for what seemed like at least ten miles to the college. Although it was dark, I could see that the college had many buildings, possibly dormitories, surrounding the main building. Upon arrival at the stage door of the auditorium, she briskly led me inside while students fetched my belongings.

Once dressed, I set my stage, quickly warmed up my already tired muscles, and then told the lighting crew and the director that I was ready. I cued someone to operate the record player with the records in their proper sequence, then stood ready, as Columbine in my first selection. My feet were swollen from traveling so long. I wondered if my body would obey my commands. And tomorrow at nine a.m., would it reach peak performance?

I pushed my body from one vignette to the next, changing costumes in rapid order. All the while, the lighting director's voice could be heard over an intercom, and at times, the changing lights almost blinded me. However, I pushed on. By the time I had reached the Turkish fairy tale and squatted in my starting pose, my body felt transparent. I was weak, and as I rose and began to dance, I felt as though at any moment I would keel over from exhaustion. At the final pose, there was a smattering of applause from the few drama students seated out front.

All I wanted was to go back to the hotel, take a cool bath, and go to bed. But the lighting director said, "Let's go over to the cafeteria and talk theater."

Whatever spirit I had left sank to rock bottom. It was eleven thirty p.m., and all too soon I would have to rise early for my big performance the next day. However, I thought I'd better comply with their wishes.

Since it was a warm evening, I had a bowl of canned fruit, while everyone else had pie, or hamburgers. I was exhausted and the conversation about theater was becoming meaningless to me as my tired mind slowly sank into a state of wishful sleep. I was afraid to glance at my watch. I was afraid to see how late it was. Finally I dared look. It was one thirty a.m. Although the conversation was in the throes of heated debate, I ventured to interrupt.

"Please, could somebody drive me back to the hotel?" I pleaded. "I have to get up at almost five in order to eat something and practice before the performance at nine."

The students looked at one another with puzzled expressions. How could anyone think of sleep when discussing theater?

"It's almost two o'clock," the lighting director said. "We'd better call it a night."

Miss Riley drove me back to the hotel. I bid her goodnight, made it upstairs, took a warm bath, and fell into bed. I fell asleep immediately. The alarm clock on the night stand was set for five thirty a.m.

It seemed I hadn't been in bed for five minutes when the alarm went off. I assumed I must have gotten into bed about four a.m. I felt as if I had one hour's sleep after I had been looking forward to this for one whole year.

I had forgotten to ask if someone would be picking me up in the morning. I decided I had better go downstairs and see if there was someplace where I could get something to eat, such as breakfast or a cup of coffee. The dining room was closed. No one was around.

I began to worry about finding something to eat. I was still hungry from the night before. I walked over to the grocery store, with the gas pump out front, and fortunately, it was just opening.

"Have you any donuts for sale, some hot coffee or juice?" I asked the proprietor.

"Nope," was the answer. "We've got Tastykake, cookies, and canned pop."

I spotted a box of saltines and I settled for those. Hoping to find some coffee once I got to the college, I decided that would be my next move.

"How far is State Teacher's College?" I asked.

"Straight down the road, two miles," was the answer.

I turned and made my way down the dirt road, makeup bag and tights in one hand, saltines in the other. I munched my meager breakfast en route.

I was feeling very weak by now. When I finally reached the college, at about seven fifteen a.m., I found the cafeteria so crowded I knew I would never have enough time for a good warm up, or to set my stage.

I turned and found my way to the auditorium. The faint daylight from the rafters above the stage filtered down on my waiting costumes and props. In only one and one-half hours, this room would be filled with students, assembled for the purpose of sharing my world.

As I warmed up, I was starting to become shaky, and I silently scolded myself for falling apart. How could I fail to meet the standards I had set for myself? I began to work harder, and soon I was beginning to feel an extreme nausea.

The saltines were gone. I began scooping up the salt in the bottom of the saltine box, when Miss Riley suddenly appeared.

"Is there anything you need for the performance?" she asked.

"Please, a cup of coffee, a donut, anything." I was desperate.

"It's already eight forty-five," Miss Riley exclaimed. "I haven't time to go to the cafeteria, but I can get you some instant coffee from the green room."

In a moment, Miss Riley returned with a paper cup of real, lukewarm coffee. I gulped it down and felt worse than before.

Whatever happened between the time when the auditorium began to fill up, and I stood as Columbine was a complete blank. When the music swelled for my first leap from fourth position into the dance itself, my mind was not inside me. It was somewhere, above me, hovering like a puppeteer over his marionette.

Finally, the last piece, *The Mirror, the Carpet and the Lemon* was hypnotic. I was feeling slightly drugged at this point and at the final pose, which was the Oriental squat, I nearly keeled over. The applause went on for some time, and although I was grateful for their appreciation, I wanted the curtain to come down so that I could collapse. I not only lost all the saltines and the coffee, but was taken to the infirmary. When I came to, I was in a hospital bed with a thermometer in my mouth, and a temperature of 103 degrees.

"Look at the drawings the students from the art department made of your performance," someone said. As my eyes opened, I saw about five students leaning over me, arms extended, thrusting drawings in my face of Columbine, Gossip, the peasant girl from *Her Lover*, and the king's daughter.

"It was a great performance. We hope to have you back again," said one of the heads leaning over my bed.

"What happened?" I asked.

"You just collapsed, fainted after your performance. You have a very high temperature, and must stay in bed until it goes down to normal."

Around two p.m. that afternoon, my temperature was low enough for me to leave the hospital, and someone agreed to get me back to the hotel. At the hotel, I asked when the bus for Pittsburgh would come through.

"About five forty-five this evening," the proprietor said. "But ya gotta stand out there an' wait for him. He's not likely to stop if there ain't nobody there."

I had time for a chicken dinner. I was hungry and desperately in need of food. The dining room opened at five p.m., and advertised a chicken dinner for two dollars and ninety-five cents. I remember sitting by the dining room window, behind white organdy ruffled curtains, devouring a delicious chicken dinner, complete with homemade biscuits. Now that my hunger was appeased and my brief sojourn in the college dormitory had rested my weary body, I no longer chided myself for getting sick. Instead, I celebrated the fact that I had now given my first solo dance concert.

On my way home, in Pittsburgh, I discovered *My Fair Lady* was playing at one of the local theaters. I knew that Pat Drylie was dance captain of the road company, so I decided to spend my hour and forty-five minutes between buses going to see Pat, and see if perhaps there was anyone else I knew in the show.

When I arrived, the show was under way. I went to the stage door and asked to see Pat. When she arrived, she was in her costume, and was happy to see me. Inviting me in, she got me a spot backstage where I could watch the show for as long as my time allowed. Our visit was short because she had duties backstage, and I would have to leave before the final curtain.

The dancers stood in the wings, waiting to go on in a mob scene. I was so close to them, I felt I was going out on stage with them. I knew several of them.

I boarded the bus back to New York at ten thirty p.m. It was quite a journey for just one concert.

Marta as the Marquis in
An Entertainment.

SCENE TWO

My First Big Tour

One cold afternoon I was making the rounds of concert managers when I met Roy Raymond, a member of the glee club at the Music Hall. When I told him I was trying to crack the concert circuit he was interested. His wife, opera singer Vera Brynner, had just cut an album of Russian gypsy songs. Vera was Yul Brynner's sister.

"Vera knows Richard Pleasant and Isadora Bennett who are the publicity people for the Ballet Theatre. I'll have her mention your project to them and give them a ring next week. Perhaps they can be helpful," Roy said.

I didn't bank on this prospect too much, but I did follow through. I took the day off from the Ripp Studio and prepared to meet Isadora Bennett.

She was very attractive, older, with white hair. Her enthusiasm and warmth filled the room. She invited me to describe my program while she leafed through my glossies.

When I was finished with my descriptions, without a word, she lifted the phone and dialed.

"Hello, is this Anna Molyneaux? Anna, I have a young dancer here in my office who is trying to break into concertizing. She has a wonderful program; a one woman show in which she acts and dances all the characters in her own original scenarios. She is a company of one. I want you to see her. Whether you can do anything with her or not, I know that you can help her. Give her some words of wisdom. By the way, isn't this the time you're holding auditions for the University of Minnesota?"

She hung up, faced me, and said, "My dear. The National Music League is holding auditions at Carnegie Recital Hall. The Music League only handles musicians, but Mrs. Molyneaux said that at the end of the session, time permitting, you are to be there and ready to audition. You know, my dear, you never know what might happen."

I canceled the rest of the week at Ripp Studio and Mother and I prepared for the first important audition of my new career.

When we arrived in the concert hall, an audition was already in progress. Several musicians were seated on a bench outside the hall entrance.

A young man told me I would have to wait until the others had performed.

Mother and I went to the top gallery of the big hall. I got into my tights to warm up and put on my Columbine costume and went out on the top gallery and looked down onto the great stage where the symphony was rehearsing.

At about five thirty, the young man guarding the door invited me in. He introduced himself as Al Rossin. Then he introduced me to Anna Molyneaux, who was out front in the small auditorium. As I walked onto the stage, she welcomed me.

"Let us know when you are ready. I've invited the two directors of the bureau of concerts and lectures, from the University of Minnesota, to stay and watch," she said.

I set my stage and began to dance. The slippery floor was obviously not designed for dancing. But I continued on, sometimes taking a small ride on a chair, ending up near the wings and hardly making it to center stage again to become someone else. This evoked laughter from my small audience. I was not sure whether they were laughing at me or the pantomime. I chose to believe the latter.

At the end of the *Curtain Raiser*, I was encouraged to go on. I skipped the *Solo-Divertissement* because of the slippery stage and went on to *Her Lover* and then *Gossip*. Then I performed my Turkish fairytale. I slid from one end of the stage to the other on my knee at the finish. There was applause after each piece, but this one affected them the most. I stood center stage waiting for a response.

"Do you have any more? Another dance or pantomime to show us?" a voice from the darkness called.

"Well yes," I answered.

Fortunately, I had brought the costume and props for a new piece, *The*

Marta at age 1 is held by her mother, Helen Beckett, 1924.

Marta at age 2 is held by her father, Henry Beckett, 1926.

Marta's last New York home was an old brownstone at 400 W. 40th Street. Marta's loft was on the extreme right over the sign that says ABC. Photo by Aina Balgalvis.

Marta appears as the Virgin Mary in a Radio City Music Hall Christmas pageant in 1943

Marta poses on the roof of the Radio City Music Hall, 1943.

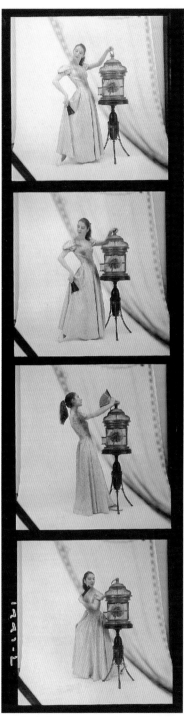

Fashion shots from Marta's modeling days.

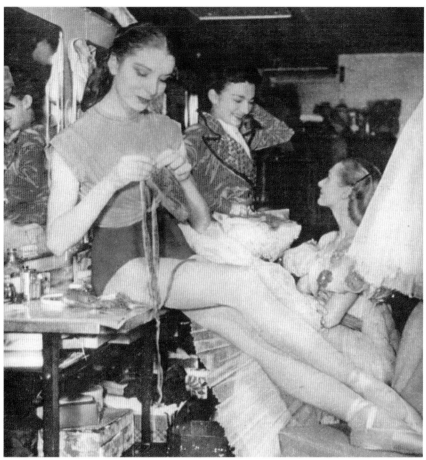

Marta prepares for a July 4 number in the dressing room at Radio City Music Hall, 1949.

Marta dances in a gypsy costume next to Ed Balin in Wonderful Town, *1954.*

OPERA HOUSE

Marta poses in front of the opera house, 1974.

Marta chats with agent legend William Morris, who became a guild member, 1975.

Marta dances on the road in front of the opera house, 1974.

A full house, in the 1980s.

Marta and Tom Willett dance in the Good Time Cabaret, *1995. Photos by Tony Scodwell.*

All opera house photos by by Aina Balgalvis. The revelers returning from a ball. A guest pours wine into a lady's slipper in the balcony below. Bottom: Noble women.

The gypsy fortune teller reads a girl's palm.
Below: Mother Superior sits in the center of a group of nuns with a certain look.

Marta's original pencil sketches for the opera house murals.

Ceiling was completed in 1974. Photo by Aina Balgalvis.

Completed murals. Finished in 1972. Photo by Aina Balgalvis.

Marta works on costumes for The Dollmaker, *2003. Photo by Aina Balgalvis.*

Marta and Tom Willett celebrate the closing night party for the Second Mortgage, *1988.*

Above: Marta and Tom Willet do scene from The Farewell Letter *to music by Mozart. Right: Tom Willett plays Cupid opposite Marta's Esmerelda in* Cupid's Mistake. *Photos Tony Scodwell. 1985*

Marta dances to Scott Joplin in Maxi's Burlesk, *1975. Photo by Tom Williams.*

A commissioned piece. The Life of an Elephant, *1964.*

Whistle Stop, *1984.*

Back Yard at the Circus, *1987*.

The Marionette Shop. *1988*

Bryant Park *in New York, 1989.*

The Cardboard Lovers, *1988.*

Two Gossips and an Eavesdropper, *2004.*

Fruit Market on 9th Avenue, *2000.*

Time Marches On, *2004.*

Corps de Ballet, *1990.*

Marta dances as a dust devil in On With the Show. *1993. Photo by
Aina Balgalvis*

Urchin's Dream. The music was *Blues in the Night* played on a harmonica. When it ends, the stage is covered in play money, huge playing cards, and diamond rings, and I am lying down asleep on two chairs just as I began.

At the finish of *The Urchin's Dream*, there was more applause and the two men from the University of Minnesota came up on stage to help me pick up my props. Then they deluged me with questions.

"Do you need much time to set up for a performance?" one asked.

"How much time do you need to pack up after a performance?" the other quizzed.

"How many miles between concerts can you manage?" asked the first.

"Do you drive, and do you have your own car?" both men wanted to know.

All my answers seemed to please them except that I didn't drive or have a car. They conferred for a moment and then turned to me.

The oldest said, "I'm Harold Alford, head of the concert and lecture division of the University of Minnesota. This is George Michaelson, my associate director. We would like to have you tour for us in the summer of 1955, appearing in colleges throughout Minnesota, Wisconsin, Iowa, and perhaps the Dakotas. It will be a very concentrated tour with a concert every day. The highest fee we can offer you is $300 per week, with your transportation assumed by the university. Mr. Michaelson will act as your stage manager and chauffeur. We both hope that you will find our offer to be satisfactory." Mr. Alford extended his hand and we shook in agreement.

"How long will the tour be?" I asked.

"A maximum of three weeks, with a concert every day," Mr. Michaelson said. "Mr. Rossin here will keep you informed on how many concerts there will be. The tour will be three weeks, regardless, but we hope to sell your program to fifteen colleges between now and then."

Sometime later, I learned that my attraction was the only one bought by the university that day. All those other musicians had not even been considered.

I returned to Ripp Studio the next day and informed Mr. Price that since my tour was not far off, I would have to quit soon. All he could say with a smirk was, "You'll be back. Then you'll go off again, but you'll always be back."

After I signed my contract, I called Isadora Bennett to tell her the happy news. "Just think," I said. "If it hadn't been for your enthusiasm describing my program over the phone that day, I would never have had the opportunity to audition."

I half expected Mrs. Bennett to say something about a commission. Instead she said, "If you hadn't been good, you wouldn't have gotten the tour, no matter what I might have said, my dear. It was really up to you. I simply opened the door. That's all."

I couldn't believe it. After all she had done for me, she didn't even demand a commission.

I continued to work at Ripp Studio through 1955. In the spring I received a phone call from Mother with a message that I had a one-shot job waiting for me as a chorus dancer on the *Milton Berle Show*, choreographed by Herb Ross. I was to leave immediately. Arriving at the Center Theater, I was told to get dressed and on stage. The stage was full of actors, dancers, and a few specialty artists. I signed a one-show contract for $300, plus additional rehearsal pay. It seemed too good to be true.

Many of my old friends were there, and for a week I again felt like a Broadway Gypsy. My friend Pat Drylie had a spot on the show doing a pas de deux with a short fellow dressed as a clown. She was very tall, so it added to the humor of the skit. She was so good, I told her she should pursue a career as a comedienne, doing parody on classical ballet. She laughed and thanked me, but did not show any interest in devoting herself to a solo career.

Because I made as much money on this show as I would have made in two months at the Ripp Studio, I decided to invest the rest of my time to preparing for my upcoming tour. I phoned the Ripp Studio and asked to speak to Borris. Before I could say "good-bye," he switched me over to Mr. Price.

"Alright, you go. Go!" Mr. Price shouted. "You'll be back. You show business people are all alike. You come, unt you go vich ever vay de vind blows. Und ders alvays the Ripp Studio mit good old Villiam Price. You'll be back." He hung up and I never went back there again.

Through my friend Margeret Cuddy who had been in *Wonderful Town*, I secured a free rehearsal studio in the Des Artists Building on Sixty-seventh Street owned by a dance teacher named Anita Peters Wright. The studio was almost three stories high. A gallery ran around the upstairs section where there were several small rooms. Margeret rented one of these rooms while she lived in New York.

Mrs. Wright was a lovely lady, about eighty-three, who taught ballroom dancing. Saturday evening she would give senior soirees, complete with tea, cookies, and ice cream.

If I would perform at her soirees, she told me then I could use her studio anytime I wished, as long as I called first. Also my rehearsals must not interfere with those of Pearl Lang, a former Martha Graham soloist who had struck out on her own. She rented the studio eight hours a day, several times a week.

Mrs. Wright and I became close friends. I would go to her studio three or four times a week at ten o'clock. I often mopped the floor for her and then worked on my dances for several hours.

The Des Artists Building had many studios in it. Each studio had an elaborate organ. I used to wonder what it would sound like if all the tenants played their organs at the same time.

Mrs. Wright introduced me to an artist upstairs who needed models for his oil painting classes.

I posed for his classes on quite a few occasions in my different costumes. The students would arrive in evening clothes, straight from attending parties. Others came in fine business suits. Students wore blue smocks to protect their clothing. Up on the podium where I posed, I had a good view of the progress. The teacher had a strong painting style and his work hung around the studio in various conspicuous places. I liked his style and noticed that all his students emulated him, except one.

This poor soul, who did not paint at all like the instructor, had a distinct style of his own, but was constantly called down for it. "Why does the teacher want you all to paint like him?" I asked.

"Who else would we paint like?" The student said as he turned to face me.

"Yourself," I replied.

"Oh, I'm afraid he would never approve of that," he said.

Meanwhile, the teacher strutted around his studio, criticizing each student's work. When he came to the lone man in the rear, his face got madder than ever.

"You're not even trying to do what I say!" he exclaimed. "You might as well not even come here as long as you insist on doing what you want." He threw some brushes down on the floor and walked away.

The lone artist quietly packed his things, cleaned his brushes, wrapped up his smock, and closed his paint box. He just left. I never saw him again.

The year of 1954 passed quickly. My performances for Mrs. Wright's soirees were perfect for me to try out my dance mimes before a real, live audience.

I would often bump into Margeret as she was leaving for the theater to do *My Fair Lady.* When she would mention going to cleanup rehearsal or the big house they had the night before, I would have a silent case of wistfulness. Had it not been for my upcoming tour, it would have been worse.

I hoped that if my tour was successful, the National Music League would sign me up as one of their permanent artists.

Travel arrangements were made and paid for by the university. I would be taking The *Silver Streak* train from Pennsylvania Station, travel by coach to Chicago, then change trains to one of the dome top models that would take me directly to the Twin Cities.

While I was packing, I could see Mother bent over some last minute sewing and a sudden feeling of love for her came over me. All these years she had shared my dreams and now she was going to be left behind. It didn't seem right. She should share in this first triumph and go on the tour with me, but it hadn't been arranged that way.

"Mother," I said, "I want you to come with me on the next tour. I didn't have anything to say about it this time, but if I'm a success on this one, perhaps I can have something to say about it next time."

"Oh, I was hoping I could go with you, but I see it's not possible this time. Perhaps next time," she said as she began to cry.

I went over to her and hugged her. I knew I shouldn't have said what I said to her. It was a commitment for the future that I had no right to make.

The day for my departure arrived. Mother and I went down to the lower depths of Pennsylvania Station where the long distance trains sat waiting for passengers. The hissing of steam, clouds of mist around the platform, occasional bells and whistles, and voices calling trains added to the excitement. I promised Mother I would write and send money each week.

The conductor came through the car calling for all visitors to leave. Mother slowly rose from her seat, but as she left, her eyes clung to me like a lover who is saying his last farewell.

She blew me a kiss. It seemed as if everyone in the car was watching. Finally she was out of sight and I was on my own for three whole weeks.

I was to stay with Harold Alford's family while in Minneapolis. He and George Michaelson were waiting at the station when my train pulled in. They both greeted me warmly.

A dress rehearsal was arranged for the next day in Northrop Auditorium, where Mr. Michaelson would practice his announcements before each of my selections and set the stage for my pantomime vignettes.

Harold Alford's house was a huge rambling place on a summit of grass. His wife, Winifred, made me feel quite at home, and their two small children were delightful.

The next morning, George and I packed my things into a rented Chevrolet. The university provided a tape recorder, and I brought along all my newly recorded selections. Leaving the city of Minneapolis to find myself on rural two-lane country roads was like having a vacation in the country.

Flyers had been sent out announcing my performance. Posters were about, hanging on university hallway walls. I was welcomed everywhere I went.

Skimming along the back roads was inspiration for a series of paintings. Our first stop was Ellendale, South Dakota. Moorhead, Mankato, and Winona, Minnesota were next with Eau Claire, La Crosse, Superior, and River Falls, Wisconsin, followed by Dubuque, Iowa, then back to Worthington and Bemidji, Minnesota.

My show was applauded with an enthusiasm I had never dared hope for. I performed in little theaters, gymnasiums, high school auditoriums, town halls and, once, in a college cafeteria. I learned to adapt my show to all conditions.

George and I got along perfectly, with a short break at his parent's place in Luverne, Minnesota, for a wonderful home cooked supper. I got to meet his wife, Joanne, and go on a picnic the next evening.

In every town, on every campus, I received excellent reviews. Seeing the titles of my ballets in print, with my name in headlines in some small town paper was a thrill for me.

I could hardly wait to show Mana. Certainly printed proof of my excellence would convince him my talents were worth something. The newspaper was Mana's "Bible." When he came to take us to dinner, I had the reviews ready to show him.

As he scanned each one spread out on the table before him, my heart thumped with hopeful anticipation.

"Well, these reviews are alright," he finally said. "You must remember that they appear in small town papers, which doesn't mean very much. Besides, it says here that *Her Lover* and *The Mirror, The Carpet and The Lemon* were the highlights of the performance, not mentioning the other pieces. I assume they didn't think much of them. You mustn't let these reviews go to your head. Reviews out of New York don't mean anything, anyway. It's New York that counts."

In spite of my father's lack of support, the success of my first big tour changed me. When friends met me on the street, they noticed an air of confidence about me they never thought possible.

Mrs. Wright was overjoyed and happy to have me back. But when I went to pose in the evening, the art instructor demanded, "Well, how was your tour?"

"Just great," I answered. "Every town and college loved my show and I got rave reviews from all fifteen concerts."

There was a painful pause. The instructor glared at me and dropped some of his brushes. His face flushed and his blue eyes were piercing.

"Do you know what that means?" he cried. "When an artist gets rave reviews he is appealing to the lowest common denominator. He is on the way out. He will never amount to anything."

He glared at me with disdain. I stood paralyzed under his gaze.

"You've hardly begun your career and you're already overjoyed at the reception from your loving audiences, the reception which will inevitably be your downfall before you have even gone up high enough to fall. You will never, never be great. You, who yearn to be loved by your public, you sicken me."

His wife came in to try to quiet him. The students stared in disbelief.

When I told Mrs. Wright of the incident she said, "Oh, dear, dear, that poor artist has been a serious painter all his life, studied in Europe, taught for years at the Art Student's League, and had never had one good notice. In fact, no one has ever noticed him at all, and he is almost seventy. All he has ever done is teach, and I believe he has always hated it."

I never knew what happened to the art teacher. I was often concerned I might bump into him, but I never did. I found other art schools to pose in.

I received a letter from George, who said they wanted me in their 1956 winter concert series. I started planning a new program immediately.

Not long after, I received a letter from Al Rossin informing me the board of directors had decided that it would be unwise for the National Music League to represent me. He told me to look for new management.

My heart sank. I thought they would be pleased with the success of my tour. I worked hard, paid my commissions, got good reviews and my show proved to be a success everywhere I went.

I was so desperate to find out what went wrong that I got up the courage to phone Mr. Rossin and tell him I wanted to see him.

When I arrived at his office, he greeted me with a defiant smile.

"If the National Music League won't negotiate for me, where am I supposed to go? How many times must I audition? I want to work," I demanded.

"First of all, you're a dancer," he said. "We specialize in musicians. Second, you're thirty-two. The National Music League specializes in helping young musicians under thirty, just out of the conservatory. I suggest you find a manager who handles special attractions, or better yet, why don't you just get yourself into another show?"

"How did you find out how old I was?" I asked.

"Oh, one of the ballet girls you worked with at the music hall told me. She lives in my apartment house. Her name is Pat Drylie. It's a small world," He said, grinning.

I had suspected Mr. Rossin didn't like me, but now it was obvious.

When I arrived back at the flat, I lunged through the yellow pages looking for concert managers. I checked off 137, wrote a form letter for each, invested in Photostatted copies off all of my reviews reduced to fit on one page, and walked to the corner mailbox and stuffed them in, one-by-one; a sort of ritual.

It was almost Christmas. Two weeks had passed since I had dropped the 137 hand-typed letters in the mailbox. I knew that Harold Alford and George Michaelson were going to be in New York soon after the New Year to sign my contract. I was hoping desperately that I would find someone to handle my bookings for me before they arrived.

Finally, a letter came from a Willard Matthews. I immediately wrote back and made a date the last week of December to audition. I rented a studio on Eighth Avenue and Willard Matthews arrived on time.

I danced everything in my repertoire. Mr. Matthews seemed pleased. He told me he could definitely book my program and he expressed a desire to sign a three-year contract. However, there was one thing that seemed to concern him.

"The second dance you did was very technical and difficult," he said. "In ten years you probably won't be able to do it. It's going to take you ten years to get established. What do you plan on doing then?"

"But I'm ready now," I said, puzzled.

"Yes, you are ready, but the public isn't. Right now, they haven't even heard of you. They must hear about you over and over again. This takes time; my time, your time, ten years."

I didn't believe him. Would I be required to tailor my choreography to what I might be able to do in ten years?

"I am not a nonprofit concert manager like the National Music League," he said. "Organizations like the League make it very difficult for managements like ours. This is why I must explain to you that, not only do we take a commission, but we require a retainer fee as well."

"What is that," I asked.

"When you and I sign our three-year agreement, you pay me a sum of money which will cover promotion, brochures, travel expenses, and the time I will devote to getting the public to know about you. Are you prepared for this?"

I nodded weakly and swallowed.

"Well, then," he continued, "For you, my retainer will be $750. From most artists, I ask at least $2,000. However, your attraction will be easy to sell. I have great hopes that you and I will have a very rewarding three years. If all goes well, we have an option to sign for another three."

I felt numb.

"What's more, I'll only take fifteen percent of your concert fees," he added.

The $700 I had from the two books I had illustrated was still in the bank. I must have been saving for this. I agreed to sign the deal. I was surprised when Mr. Matthews asked if I could get him the money that same afternoon.

During the second week in January, George Michaelson and Harold Alford were due to arrive in New York. One morning, Al Rossin phoned to find out if I had a manager, since he would have to inform Mr. Alford and Mr. Michaelson. I told him my new manager was Willard Matthews.

"Why didn't you ask me about him before you signed?" Al Rossin screamed over the phone.

"Well," I answered meekly, "I didn't really think you were interested."

"How much money did you give him," he demanded.

"A $750 retainer," I answered.

"Willard Matthews is a thief! He takes money from artists and doesn't do a damn thing for them. You fool, why didn't you ask me?"

"With only one door open to me, I certainly didn't need you to tell me not to go through it."

"All that money. It's highway robbery," Mr. Rossin said.

"Well, Willard Matthews is now my manger. He was the only one out of 137 managers listed in the phone book who answered. I had no choice."

The following week, Mr. Michaelson called to talk about the upcoming tour. We had a most cordial talk and he explained that Al Rossin despised Mr. Matthews probably more than any other manager and that the irony of it all was that they lived across the hall from one another. He assured me that it was strictly personal between the two of them and that he thought Mr. Matthews would do very well by me as he concentrated on booking special attractions and theater groups rather than musicians.

I felt relieved. He asked me if I would agree to the same fee I had the summer of 1955 and he said the University would print my program for me if I designed the cover.

"Of course," I answered enthusiastically.

As I spoke to George, I could sense Mother sending me a silent message. I knew what it was and I dreaded bringing it up.

"George," I asked timidly, "do you think it would be alright if my mother came along on this tour?"

"Well, I suppose so," he answered. "Just let me know for sure if that is what you decide to do just before you come out. That will make a difference in hotel reservations we make for you."

Suddenly I realized that my hotel expenses would be double. Also, food bills would be twice as much, but I was saddled with this situation. I had promised Mother.

Marta appears as the king's daughter in The Mirror, the Carpet, and the Lemon, *1955.*

New York Bookings

I decided to use 1956 to work on a new program for the Minnesota tour and develop the *Turkish Fairytale* into a full length program.

I designed four different backdrops, each ten yards in length, to stretch across the stage. They were hung on a wire set behind the action. The first scene was the interior of the king's palace with eight oriental musicians playing exotic instruments appliquéd in a row on ten yards of green silk. The King's daughter was introduced here dancing with her hand maidens which were actually two palm fans with painted faces and veils. The second scene was a Bedouin marketplace painted in earth tones on brown silk. The third scene was a skyline of alabaster domes and spires appliquéd in silver lamé with the royal palace to the right. A silver crescent moon served as a cradle for the princes to rest on during their journey.

The wedding scene I designed was the most opulent of all. I appliquéd a courtly crowd including servants carrying great trays of delicacies. Great plates of golden curry were carried high by saried ladies in paisley garb and silver and gold scarves. Jeweled turbans worn by servants bearing plates of candies and fruits accented the scene. I wore masks for all the characters, except the king's daughter.

I bought a Masco portable reel to reel tape recorder. It had a mellow sound that no other tape recorder I owned ever had. I had all the music for my fairytale taped professionally. The show's narration was done by an actor friend of mine who did a superb job in a rather British accent; perfect for the Middle Eastern fable.

While working on the sets, I went shopping for silks, satins, paisley prints, and gold and silver lamé. The lamé scraps became the appliquéd eyelids of the royal court women.

My scenery remained at Mrs. Wright's place since it was too heavy to carry home on the bus.

After one of my rehearsals, Pearl Lang came in to dance after me, saw my appliquéd chorus and exclaimed, "That's what I'd like, everybody exactly where I want them to be, in place."

Staying up until all hours, sewing my little people on silk, worked me to a physical frazzle. I got a bad case of the flu. Mother sewed my costumes again and made the masks and props. Nothing mattered to me, except finishing this masterpiece. My scenery was beautiful and the production moved smoothly from the prologue through the grand wedding scene.

It was February of 1956, and I began thinking of giving a debut of the whole ballet before an audience. I went around to ballrooms and social halls where I might present the fairytale as a children's entertainment, selling tickets for seventy-five cents, with fifty percent for the house and fifty percent for me. I even went to grade schools in and around Brooklyn, the Bronx, and Queens to investigate presenting the show at assembly.

But no one knew who I was. And because no one had offered such an idea before, to disrupt the school schedule and take a chance would have been too much of a gamble.

I finally ended up with a date for April 8 at Sonia Hall in Brooklyn. Two older men owned the hall. They agreed to the fifty percent split and they offered to pay for an ad in a local newspaper. They seemed sure the show would draw an audience. They informed me that much of the audience would be black, and that was fine with me.

That same week, I offered my program to the Children's Series at Henry Street Playhouse. They offered me twenty-five dollars for an afternoon program. While discussing the show with series organizer Betty Young, I found out I could rent the playhouse for the evening for $125, with 350 seats in the house. I pinned down a date to present a program.

Mana was very upset when he heard I had rented the playhouse. He thought since I had rented the place rather than be booked by an agent, I was going into business for myself.

"You'll need a license for this one," he insisted. "I will contact the license bureau. I know the chief from interviews with him at the *Post* and I will inform him of what you are up to."

My heart sank. I begged Mana not to do this. If I had needed a license, wouldn't Betty Young have said so?

"I think I had better get in touch with the fire marshal, too," Mana said. "I know him well, and this will save you from going down to city hall yourself. I'm doing you a big favor taking care that you do these things now before it's too late."

"But why the fire marshal?" I asked.

"Your scenery and costumes should be fireproofed," Mana said. "You must play it safe. You're going into business yourself in this project."

Mana left with the address of my practice studio scrawled on the news pad he habitually carried.

I turned to Mother and said, "Mother, now I know what you meant when you told me how Mana meddled and spoiled everything you ever tried to do."

"Yes," Mother said. "Now you know."

The fire marshal was due to come to Mrs. Wright's studio to test my scenery. I looked at all my people; their dark black eyes looked back at me from beneath their golden eyelids. Spangles on turbines sparkled and I wondered how fireproofing would affect them.

The fire marshal didn't waste any time. He brought up my need for a license and handed me some forms to fill out and deliver to city hall when I went to get fingerprinted.

He took out a book of matches and, not even bothering to inspect my work, struck a match and held the flame up to the green silk of my scenery. Immediately it caught fire. I was horrified! I felt helpless as I stood there and watched this city employee burn my "child."

"Yep," he said as he blew the flame out. "You'll have to take this scenery to the New York Fireproofing Company. They'll fix you up. You should have made the whole thing out of fireproof cloth in the first place."

He handed me a card with the fireproofing company's address and then asked me when the event was to take place.

"April 15," I said.

"I doubt if you will get your license in time for that," he said. "It takes six to eight weeks.

As I fell asleep that night, the sounds of my exotic musical accompaniment played in my mind as visions of the king's daughter dancing with her two handmaidens restored my determination to see this nightmare through.

I must make sure that this creation of mine lived, even if I had to present my *Turkish Fairytale* in the street.

I took my scenery to the New York Fireproofing Company. In a few days, they called to say the job was done and was hanging up to dry. I hung up the phone and rushed over to see the results.

The cloth had shrunk, some had stretched and some had puckered. The hemline was uneven. The lamé was tarnished and the golden eyelids gone. The sequins were cracked and speckled with rust. My little people stared back at me from underneath a gray film. It was as if they had died.

All this damage, for just one performance, I thought. I probably would not have done this for the tours or the out-of-town performances, but it was too late now. I had made the commitments for the playhouse and Sonia Hall and the children's matinee. I had to plow through these commitments the best I could.

Mana offered to pay for the $300 for the fireproofing. After all, it was his idea.

In a few days I took the scenery home, and then to Mrs. Wrights where she let me hang it up to let the wrinkles out. It was much heavier now, and as I opened the suitcases, the heavy fumes filled the air.

Mr. Bolu didn't sound too encouraged about gathering an audience at Sonia Hall. However, I had enough problems sprucing up my scenery with new sequins and rhinestones.

I had taken care of the license problem by going to city hall for the demeaning experience of being fingerprinted. Then I prayed I would get the license in time for my debut.

Mana insisted on helping me take my show to Brooklyn. I was not happy about this. He was promptly there at ten in the morning; hooded in some sort of ridiculous rain cape. He was covered in snow and ice. Almost looking like Saint Nicholas, if it had not have been for his stern expression.

The three of us trudged down the narrow stairs, bumping the luggage into the banister. I was carefully guarding the tape recorder while Mother carried the handmaidens in the shopping bag so their fragile bamboo faces could safely peek out.

The subway ride was an ordeal. When we arrived at Sonia Hall, little handbills, which I had block printed in bright red with the princes riding on a magic carpet and the synopsis of the scenes on the reverse side, were already placed on each empty chair.

The Bolu brothers had tried to make this matinee a success. They showed me the advertisement they had placed in the newspaper.

"The blizzard will keep a lot of people away," one of them said.

"Have you sold any tickets?" Mana asked.

"Well, no we haven't, but that doesn't mean anything," the other replied.

"I didn't think you would sell any," Mana said. "This was a ridiculous idea in the first place."

"No it wasn't," said one of the Bolu brothers. "There was a time out here in Brooklyn when we would have filled this hall for an event like this. We were hoping this event might start the ball rolling again. This was for us as well as for Marta."

I opened the suitcases and unraveled the scenery. Mother began stringing it up on the clothesline and the Bolu brothers helped by rigging the line from one side of my performance space to the other.

"I'll go out and bring something back to eat," Mana said.

"Does your father do this sort of thing to you often?" Mr. Bolu asked.

"Yes, a lot," I answered.

"He's no friend of yours," said the other Mr. Bolu. "He may be your father, but he sure is no friend."

Mana returned at 1:15 p.m. with sandwiches and hot tea. While putting on my makeup, I downed half a sandwich and a paper cup of tea. At exactly 1:30 p.m., the door opened and Marc and Karl from the Ripp Studio came in. I watched them from my prologue curtain. They walked down the center aisle as if it were a full house and took their seats in the front row.

Mana was seated in the back row on the aisle, while Mother sat in the very end of the front row. The Bolu brothers stood at the door ready to greet the people who never came.

At the stroke of two, dressed as the king's daughter, I came from behind the curtain. I pressed the button on the tape recorder and suddenly the exotic sounds of the Middle Eastern overture filled Sonia Hall. When the narration began, I was transported to another time.

The empty room, for me, was filled with people. The music transported me so vividly that even if the Hells Angels had come in, I couldn't have stopped now.

Once the narration proclaimed that "everyone lived happily ever after," Marc and Karl rushed up to hug me. When I apologized for the small audience, they looked around in amazement as if they hadn't noticed.

"It doesn't matter," Marc said. "You did it, you did it, and it is positively beautiful. It will be a big success. I know."

He squeezed my hand.

"Things like this always take time," Karl said. "It will take years, but believe me, you are on your way."

"We're coming to see you at the Playhouse next week," Mark assured me. "We wouldn't miss an opportunity to see this again."

The Bolu brothers complimented me as well. Mana said nothing about my performance. Mother squeezed my hand and I could see that her eyes were moist.

"Well," said one of the brothers. "We made exactly one dollar and fifty cents. Seventy-five cents for you and seventy-five cents for the house."

"Who knows?" the other brother said. "Maybe we can talk about trying this again sometime."

As I prepared for the Henry Street Playhouse performance, I sold about fifty tickets and hoped that the playhouse box office would be selling tickets as well.

My license had not yet arrived and this made me nervous. My anxiety prompted Betty Young to suggest I cancel the whole thing. I was hurt by this and felt it strange she didn't share my philosophy that the show must go on.

All of the boys at Ripp Studio bought tickets, so did a few of my dancer friends who were not working at the time, and there was Fernand Fonssagrives, a photographer introduced to me by Margeret Cuddy, and a few board room friends of Mother's. Mana bought a whole block of tickets for his friends at the *Post*.

By curtain time, no one from the license bureau had arrived, and I wasn't sure I would get through the first number without being pulled off the stage. When the overture began, I took my pose anyway, determined to get through the evening alive.

The curtain opened, the lights hit me, and I was off and running. I made it to intermission without mishap, and I knew once I started the *Turkish Fairytale*, nothing could stop the show.

The audience was small. I could feel the warmth from the few friends out front. I was even able to erase the coldness coming from Mana's friends.

After it was over, I received some curtain calls. Then Betty Young came back to congratulate me and tell me she was looking forward to my performance in the Children's Series. I believe she was surprised at how delightful *The Mirror, the Carpet and the Lemon* was. I had been such a neurotic about the license and the fireproofing, but my show made up for all that fuss.

Marc and Karl came to the dressing room to tell me what a charming ballet I had created. Fernand Fonssagrives took many photographs of the entire performance, which I used for years afterward. Alwin Nickolai, resident dance director for the Henry Street Playhouse, and his associate Murray Lewis came to tell me how unique my show was. However, I knew my performance was just adequate.

Mana said nothing about my show until we arrived at home.

"Well," he said. "I just want you to know the truth. I have to be honest because I love you, as a father loves a daughter. Everyone else will tell you what you want to hear, but it's my duty, as your father, to tell you the truth. It wasn't every good, you know. My friend Fern didn't think much of it either. She thinks you should give up dancing and concentrate on your art. Your scenery shows some talent in that direction, but that's all. Don't take it too hard. You will have to find out sooner or later. It is better to know the truth now than when it is too late."

I sobbed until my eyes were so swollen and red I could hardly open them. Finally, there were no more tears left.

The matinee for the Children's Series at the Henry Street Playhouse was sold out. Someone even mentioned that there was a line of children and parents waiting to get in.

Marc and Karl were there and so was Fernand. The audience was warm and responsive. I knew I was giving them the best performance of the *Turkish Fairytale* yet.

When the curtain closed at the end of the performance, the house filled with applause. When I was alone for that moment with the curtain closed between calls, my masks, my props, and my scenery seemed full of life along with me. We were a company of one.

Two weeks after the matinee, I received a letter from the license bureau telling me there was no need for a license due to the fact that the performance was given in a theater owned by a nonprofit group dedicated to educational and cultural events. All that anxiety and fuss for nothing. If only I could remove the fireproofing from my scenery.

From the matinee, I was introduced to Francis Schram of Briggs Management. That summer, they secured many dates for my *Turkish Fairytale* in and around the New York area. These children's concerts kept me in performance gear while I waited for my tours to start. Also, Mr. Matthews allowed me to take these dates without any commission to him, which was unusual for a concert manager to agree to.

I would usually receive fees of $125 for one performance. Of that, twenty-three percent went to Francis Schram. My transportation expenses came out of that as well. Occasionally, I had to stay overnight in a motel somewhere out on Long Island. But I enjoyed being on my own.

Marta dances with Andre Van Damme
in the Charleston Ballet, 1957.

SCENE FOUR

The Charleston Ballet

Mr. Matthews did get me one exciting date for the fall of 1956. The booking was to appear as a guest artist with the Charleston Ballet.

As the Charleston performance got closer, I concentrated all of my efforts in that direction. I was to be in Charleston an entire week before the show; the first half rehearsing a piece I choreographed for myself and Andre Van Damme, and the rest coordinating my half of the program along with the rest of his company.

Mother saw me off at Penn Station on my first journey to the South. After the long night traveling by coach to Charleston, I was pretty tired. Andre Van Damme and his wife Maggy came to the station to meet me. I was charmed by their strong French accents.

While packing my luggage in the rear of their station wagon, I noticed that Mr. Van Damme was no taller than I. I began to worry about our pairing. As we sped to their house in the hills, the conversation was vibrant. I felt as if I were taking part in one of those passionate French movies. Regardless of the topic, rehearsal time, picture taking, interviews, publicity luncheons, Andre was dramatic with graceful hand gestures and an expressive face.

After a brief lunch, I was told there would be a publicity photo taken in our Brahms costumes. I was tired from my trip and concerned it would show. However, the photo turned out to be a very pleasant prelude to our working relationship. I could see that the costume I had designed for Andre turned out very well indeed. The design I had sent for his tailor to make came out just as I had hoped. Together, along with my romantic length tutu, we looked well.

That afternoon, we rehearsed the Brahms *Variations*. Even with Andre's lack of height, we managed to retain the lifts and finger turns I had choreographed for it. We each had a solo and then finished together.

At the end of the first rehearsal, we really dug into it and by the night of the grand performance, we had gotten to know each other's weaknesses and strengths and were able to use them to our advantage.

For the next few days, I lived and dined with the Van Dammes. Every morning, strewn on the table, were newspaper announcements for the show. I had never had such a drum-beating to announce my performances in advance. The local newspapers made me out to be a celebrated ballerina from New York, appearing for the first time as a guest artist with the Charleston Ballet and founder Andre Van Damme.

At dress rehearsal, Andre asked if his students could sit out front in the auditorium and watch me go through my dance mimes, which would be included in the second half of the show. Naturally I agreed. At the end of my rehearsal, there was a big round of applause from the front and the wings. I knew that I would live up to their expectations.

The Charleston Ballet experience was my first taste of celebrity. These four days were a whirlwind of interviews, rehearsals, money-raising luncheons, and picture taking. One thing annoyed me. I was constantly referred to as this "ballerina" from New York. Yes, I danced en pointe and wore a tutu, but I was not a ballerina.

The term "ballerina" traditionally describes the leading female dancer in a classical ballet company. I write my own shows and I dance alone. A ballerina is an exquisite diamond, placed in a proper setting of lesser stones. I was certainly not this.

The ballet performance was held in the municipal auditorium. The program was divided into two parts. Andre's company was to dance his famous ballet *Mateo* and then we were to dance our Brahms followed by my half of the program, including *Curtain Raiser, Cacion Triste* and *Gossip*; then *The Mirror, the Carpet and the Lemon*.

As the first strains of Brahms rose from the piano, we broke our frozen tableau pose and the ballet began.

This ballet gave me a taste of what it was like to perform a classical pas de deux with a partner in that romantic way only seen in the world of ballet.

The applause rolled on for several curtain calls. We did a great show. After *The Mirror, the Carpet, and the Lemon,* we all took curtain calls again.

There was a reception in the lobby filled with people in formal attire. Andre's wife, Maggy, had made a beautiful orange-lime sherbet punch in a huge crystal bowl. Canapés and cakes, hors d'oeurves, olives, and tasty sandwiches decked the huge table out front. There also was a bar for those with stronger taste.

I wore a lavender taffeta dress with a huge skirt that flared out from the waist. It was marked down at Gimbel's because it had been used in a fashion show, but it looked expensive and I felt elegant.

My cheeks were aching from the frozen smile I held for the reception line. I was introduced to Bayard Ennis, music critic for the *Charleston Gazette.* He was pleasant but restrained. The audience had loved me, but would the critic?

The audience began to disband. The bowl of punch was only three-fourths gone. Most had preferred something stronger. Andre's daughter, Marie Claude, took two more cups of punch and so did I. Together we must have consumed gallons of the satisfying drink.

Andre talked about another possible performance in the future and we all hugged.

When the train pulled into Penn Station, I could see Mother and Mana.

"How was it," she called as Mana fetched my luggage.

I wanted to pour out the happy events to Mother, but Mana's presence subdued me.

"I bought a copy of the *Charleston Gazette,*" he said.

"Have you read the reviews?" I asked.

"Well, not yet. We'll have to wait until we get home," he said.

The trip home was grueling and I knew the reading of my "report card" from the *Gazette* would follow.

We finally made it home and waited for Mana to open the *Gazette.*

The headline read, "Marta Becket is Impressive in Ballet Performance Here."

Bayard Ennis' column continued, "A dynamic and agile young dancer from New York was introduced to Charleston."

The review went on growing more complimentary with each line. It was fabulous.

After Mana finished, he set the paper down on the living room table and said, "Well, it's a pretty good review, as reviews go. Don't let it go to your head. It's still not New York."

Somehow, having a favorable review along with all the reviews I had received for my Minnesota tour, and approval, all written in black and white, opened a door on a new world for me. I had created my own niche, and the challenge of improving what I put into that slot was exciting.

Scene Five

My Second Tour and the Buffalo Philharmonic

The date to audition my *Turkish Fairytale* for the University of Wisconsin tour arrived. As I waited in Mrs. Wright's studio for Marvin Foster to arrive, it seemed the characters I was preparing to portray were there in the studio around me.

I expected Mr. Foster to be a more imposing man. He was pleasant, but his mind seemed elsewhere. He sat in a chair I placed out front for him and I began the show.

Halfway through the marketplace scene, he called out, "Stop!" I thought I was hearing things, so I kept on. Then he called out again.

I was stunned.

"Mr. Matthews said you don't drive. Is that right?" he asked.

"Yes, that's right," I said.

"Well, we'll get you a college boy," he continued. "He can drive you from place to place and act as your stage manager."

"But, I haven't finished auditioning," I said. "Don't you want to see the rest, find out what happens at the end?"

"No, that's fine. It's good. I don't have to see anymore. It will be just fine for our schools."

I was to receive $200 per week for a tour of twenty-one weeks. My travel expenses were to be paid by the university. They would also provide a stage manager/driver. Of course out of the $200 a week, I had to pay Mr. Matthews and I had to pay for my food and hotel expenses. A maximum of three short programs a day with travel in between each was planned. I didn't see how I could afford to take Mother along. I wouldn't be making that much and the tour was the longest I had encountered. So, it would be grueling and many of the towns were so small there would be no board rooms for Mother to watch her stocks.

Mr. Foster expressed a need to make a lot of money fast. His wife had contracted polio. Mr. Matthews said his wife had cancer. I realized my problems were miniscule by comparison. I was confident Mother would understand, I just couldn't afford to take her along.

For the spring tour for the University of Minnesota, I changed the program quite a bit. This time it began with a piece based on the old nursery rhyme, *The Queen of Hearts.*

I designed costumes from authentic playing card characters with a clothes tree and dressing table from which I could change right in front of the audience in time to the music as part of the choreography.

I painted a narrow back drop to resemble a medieval kitchen with an old stove and I used the music of Boccherini's *Schula De Ballo,* which in English means *School of Ballet.* Every count and note of music was used. Not a beat was wasted.

My second piece was *The Three Graces,* in which I portrayed a dancer from the past, a dancer from the neurotic present, and a dancer from the hectic future. For the last character, I wore a helicopter headdress with a constantly moving propeller on top of my head. I composed the future music myself.

Next came a dance called *The Mermaid and Her Soul,* which was based on *The Little Mermaid.*

This was followed by *Gossip, The Urchin's Dream, Her Lover* and then my opus *The Mirror, the Carpet and the Lemon.*

My programs for the evening audiences were long, about two and one-half hours with a fifteen minute intermission.

It would be wonderful if I could have taken backdrops for every number. I would have had no trouble painting them, but to carry along such a burden would not only be impractical, but impossible in a small car with only a college boy and Mother to assist. There would be no room to carry a larger show.

The prospect of going out on all these tours was challenging. Merely changing the repertoire was not enough. I longed to use the other talents I had as well, such as my painting in the form of scenery and perhaps, one day, my composing.

The big day for departing on my second tour finally came. I was happy to leave New York to go where I was wanted. Mother was excited and arranging all of her stock market affairs so that they could be taken with her. She said board rooms could be found in almost any town in the country.

Mother's constant chatter on the train helped me realize, I'm lonelier when I'm with someone. When I'm alone, my mind is free for plans for projects. I'm not like other dancers. I don't need the parties, the boyfriends, nor the social life. I like people out front, on the other side of the footlights. When the show is over, they go home, leaving me alone with my best friend, myself. I may be a dancer, but I have the temperament of a painter who must work alone for hours. Solitude is my fuel.

By the time we reached Chicago's Union Station, I was very tired. Keeping Mother entertained all that way was exhausting.

Once on the Vista Dome to Minneapolis, I perked up a bit. This train took us through territory Mother was unacquainted with, so she was occupied looking out the window.

We had a nice hotel reserved for us in Minneapolis, downtown. Someone met us at the station and took us there. Rehearsal at Northrop Auditorium was to be the next day, with my new stage manger. After that, we would head out to our first evening concert engagement in Worthington, Minnesota.

The rehearsal with my new stage manager, Allen Lotsberg, went well. I liked him. He even hit it off with Mother.

Traveling along on the two-lane rural roads was peaceful. Allen would give us a travelogue lecture as we rode into the hinterlands, for this was his world. He was born in Minnesota and grew up there.

My show was welcomed wherever we went. Posters and place cards had been put up beforehand. Announcements in local papers were clipped and given to me by each program chairman.

Mother would be very sociable whenever people from the press showed up. She told them all about her column in the *Cincinnati Post*. When I would comb the paper for reviews, there was no mention of the program I had given. The story was always about Mother. Here's a sample: "Mama Beckett traipsed around Europe with a typewriter before Marta was born. But when Marta showed talent in dancing, Mama Beckett gave up her career and devoted herself to Marta's career. Through the years, the two of them sacrificed the comforts of life so that Marta might dance."

The tour itself was a happy one and the applause I got after each performance was all mine, not Mother's.

At the tour's end, we bid farewell to Allen and had a goodbye supper at Harold Alford's house.

Toward the end of the tour, Mr. Matthews sent a telegram asking me to phone him immediately upon my return. When I called, he asked me to come to his office for a talk; a confidential talk.

As I made my way to Mr. Matthews' office, I had a premonition of something unpleasant ahead. When I was ushered into his purple office, the room was hushed.

"Marta," Mr. Matthews said, with measured reserve. "You are not to take your mother on any more of your tours. Do you understand?"

"Yes," I answered.

"There are excellent reports of your work now, throughout the Midwest. A great future awaits you and your program, but without your mother. I have an important audition for you, regarding a school tour on the East Coast for the Red Path Bureau. This tour could be up to thirty weeks for the spring of 1959. These university men want you and your program, but not with your mother. Do you fully understand?"

"I will tell my mother that she cannot go on any more tours," I said. "This past tour was the last and only tour she will ever go on."

"Fine," he said with a smile. "I'll arrange to have you meet Howard Higgins of the Red Path Bureau and make a date for you to audition for him. He really wants you on this tour and now, since our talk, I believe we can make great strides, but without your mother."

Following my initial meeting with Mr. Higgins, an audition was arranged. I booked Karl Schook's studio on Eighth Avenue.

In the meantime, I had a talk with Mother about the impracticality of taking her along on these school tours. Financially and physically, they would be too draining. She took the news stoically.

The following Tuesday morning, Mr. Higgins and his wife arrived at ten a.m.

"We have heard wonderful reports about your work," he said, looking more like a minister than someone involved in the performance circuit. He wore silver rimmed glasses that reminded me a little of my father. I danced my three short pieces, one in which I wore a tutu, and Mr. Higgins spoke again.

"Perhaps you could do that selection in a longer skirt. And the photo of you in the short costume could be eliminated from the brochure. I'm afraid our school men might be concerned about that."

"Well, you are good," he said, when I finished. "Just a few changes in costume and I think our school men would heartily approve of your attraction. I would suggest you present your *Turkish Fairytale* in Chicago, for the final auditions there. It's just the right length and the costume covers you completely."

Mr. Matthews hadn't told me the final rehearsal was in Chicago. Several hundred school representatives from all over the country would be there to see auditions. The possible tour could be as long as forty weeks with three assemblies a day. I would have to pay my own expenses to get to Chicago, but as Mr. Higgins said, "If you get the tour, it's a small investment to a career."

"I'll do it," I said. "You can count on me going to Chicago."

Mr. Higgins suggested I save money by sharing a hotel room with the "Umbrella Lady," a nice older woman who lectured on the history of umbrellas and parasols going back to 1800.

When I got home, Mother informed me Mana was coming to take us to dinner; the last dinner for a while because he was leaving for a European vacation. I was relieved. Now I wouldn't have to tell him about my audition in Chicago.

All through dinner, a silent satisfaction dwelt in me, knowing I was going to Chicago to audition for a big school tour.

As the train pulled out of the station toward Chicago, Mother saw me off at Penn Station. She stood waving and blowing kisses. I was alone at last with the company of my best friend. I wanted to embrace the world.

When I arrived in Chicago, I was excited. The cab driver sped me to my hotel as if the streets were his. I slid so hard right and left on the plastic seats, I thought I would get black and blue.

I paid for my room in advance, and the desk clerk gave me a big old fashioned key with a large brown tag attached. It was a small hotel by big city standards, but it was comfortable. As I entered the room I was to share with the Umbrella Lady, I could see that the door to the adjoining room was open.

"Hello," a voice called out. I looked in the direction of the voice and could see that the room was filled with suitcases, valises, and a "garden" of umbrellas. We introduced ourselves, but I never did remember her name.

A note from Howard Higgins informed us auditions were to be held the next morning at ten and eleven, respectively.

The Umbrella Lady and I had a very pleasant dinner. After a quick breakfast, we took a taxi to the high school. The Umbrella Lady was to present first while, behind her backdrop, I could set up my scenery and be ready to go on next.

I was impressed with her presentation and her array of umbrellas and parasols. I could see that she loved them and took great pains to handle them carefully.

Two stage hands helped rig up my scenery while I got into costume for the king's daughter. When the Umbrella Lady had finished and her applause had died down, I heard my name over the load speaker.

I took my position for the opening scene. The music began and the warm stage lights bathed me in that make-believe glow of illusion. The stage was enormous and the distance between me and the audience was covered in darkness. I finally arrived at the wedding scene, the grand finale. The applause from out front gave me assurance that all had gone well.

Howard Higgins came up on the stage with several school men and shook my hand. "We'll send you a letter in about a week. I think your presentation went very well and we look forward to contacting you soon," he said.

It was two weeks before I received the anticipated letter. I unfolded it so I could read the verdict in Mr. Higgins' own words. He told me I had a twenty-week tour of the East Coast covering Pennsylvania, Maryland, Delaware, and New Jersey. Then it would be up to Maine, Massachusetts, New Hampshire, and Vermont. My eyes welled up with tears of joy. The tour would be in the spring of 1958. I would have three programs to do each school day with enough time in between to get from one town to another. I would receive a fee of fifty dollars per forty-five minute program. This was the highest fee paid on the Red Path Circuit. I would have to supply my own stage manger, transportation, hotel, and meals. I figured it out. I would be making $750 a week with this schedule. Of that, one hundred dollars would go to my stage manager. I thought of trying to hire Allan Lotsberg. Out of the remaining $650, I would have to rent a car, pay for gas, hotel, meals, and give a fifteen percent commission to Mr. Matthews.

Then, of course, I would have to send money to Mother. Any extra, she could put in our joint account at the bank. If I were lucky, I would end up with $200 a week for myself, but that was what I ended up with on other tours, so it all came out the same in the long run. The important thing was, I had a tour.

Mr. Matthews came up with another interesting engagement; guest artist with the Buffalo Philharmonic Pop Series. This confirmed my confidence in him. My fee for this guest artist appearance was $300 for the evening. A rehearsal with the orchestra was scheduled and I would be required to supply my own orchestrations.

This was first time since my nightclub days that I would be accompanied by live musicians. A full symphony orchestra was a far cry from the tiny three-piece bands I so often had to contend with. I chose to perform *Curtain Raiser* and *Gossip*. Because *Gossip* was performed to one of the five pieces for string quartet, there was no piano conductor sheet. With the small amount of music instruction I had combined with a fairly good ear, I was able to write the piano score myself. All of the orchestrations, plus the parts for the string quartet, I purchased at Shrimer's Music Store. It wasn't until I had rehearsed with the orchestra that my apprehension about my ability to write a piano score was quelled.

The Buffalo Philharmonic date was the highlight of that summer. I danced on top of the orchestra pit, which was covered with a temporary stage, while the orchestra played behind me.

Willis Page, the conductor that season, was most cooperative working with me to obtain the tempos of the musical selections to my liking. I was so used to recordings, never having to adjust to different styles or tempos of conductors, that I was spoiled in this respect. The evening went well, and I received a huge ovation along with an excellent review in the *Buffalo Courier Express*.

Although I had quite a bit of work that summer of 1957, I was still worried about money. I was definitely not going back to the Ripp Studio, but I was looking for something like that to tide me over until the fall tour. Fortunately, I got a call from an artist named Sebastian who used to work for the Ripp Studio. He was opening his own studio and wondered if I would do some designs in ceramics for tiles, pottery, lamp bases, and plaques. I gave it a try and was introduced to Sybil Cooper, a woman who had a pottery business in Greenwich Village and also fired other artist's work.

I got to know Sybil quite well as I took bisque lamp bases and tiles down to her nearly every week. Sebastian paid me by the piece, which was great because I could work and then stop anytime I needed to pick up the life I was meant to live on tour.

The flat I lived in with Mother was filled with bisque lamp bases all over the place. My costumes hung in their doorless closets, unfinished music sheets sat on the piano, and a few of my paintings hung on the wall. Mother sat by the open window, amidst the art, working on her stock sheets. These were warm summer evenings with the curtain blowing out the window, the night sky dotted with lighted office building windows. Everything seemed right with the world.

Marta performs dressed as a maid in
The Garden Party, 1968. Photo by
Tom Williams.

Scene Six

Touring on My Own

M r. Foster wanted to have the musical accompaniment for *The Mirror, the Carpet and the Lemon* taped by itself without the narration. He planned to have my stage manager, a drama student named David Starkweather, do the narration live. I was apprehensive about this, but went along with it.

I bought a three-tiered parasol made of silk to be set stage right. David would be seated cross-legged, attired in a robe and turban, reading from a large prop book.

From the Rockford Women's Club, to the Women's State Prison in Taycheedah, Wisconsin, I danced my way through Illinois, Michigan, and Iowa. From the Art Museum in Milwaukee, Wisconsin, through the back roads of rural communities and Indian reservations, I performed in schools so small, that all grades from kindergarten through eighth, attended. Often, a make-shift stage would be put up especially for me, behind which windows looked out on a field of cows.

David and I got along pretty well on the road. He was hard at work writing a play during the evenings. He would lock himself up in his room after our dinner together, and write. Sometimes I could hear him through the wall talking to himself.

I, on the other hand, was pretty tired, and whatever time I had after supper was used to wash tights. I usually had to rise pretty early the next morning to stretch.

I received a check for $200 each week, which I cashed at a local bank. I would send one hundred dollars home to Mother for her expenses, the remainder to be deposited in the bank. I kept that money for hotel and meal expenses. David was paid by the university.

I had weekends to myself, because David had to return to Madison where his family lived. I cherished the weekends in rural towns. I would take long walks and window shop down Main Street.

I would write down my thoughts on cards and local hotel stationery and send them back almost daily to Mother. I needed to share these experiences with someone, and Mother was the only one I had.

There was only one review from this school tour. That was the one from the Rockford Woman's Club appearance. The review went on and on, glowingly, making up for the other sixty-three performances which had no reviews. School tours generally reap no ovations, no flowers, and no fancy receptions after the performance. However, a school tour offers an opportunity no other performing experience does; the exposure of an art form to first-time audiences.

I returned home to New York, happy about my tour. Mr. Foster was now talking about another tour, possibly for the fall of 1958. Again, he said he would supply my stage manager and driver. But, for this next tour, he wanted a program of varied short dances and pantomimes. This was agreeable to me. For the grand finale however, I could give the wedding scene from *The Mirror, the Carpet, and the Lemon*.

There wasn't much time between the fall tour for the University of Wisconsin and the winter tour for the Red Path Bureau which was coming up in just a few weeks after New Year's, 1958.

Mother clung to me constantly, knowing I was to be gone again for a long time. We did enjoy shopping and preparing for the next tour together.

Earlier, I had contacted Allen Lotsberg about stage managing and driving my show in the Northeast for the Red Path Bureau. I told him I wouldn't be able to pay much, one hundred dollars a week, but he seemed to like the idea, saying that it would be a sort of paid vacation.

Arrangements were made for him to head east, from Minneapolis to New York, in a rented car which would be the one we would tour in and the one he would return to Minneapolis when the tour was over.

My first check was waiting at Penn Argyle Post Office in Pennsylvania. This was following a week's performances, fifteen in all. I had to lay out a great deal of money just to get started on this tour. But once I had that check of $750 in my hand, I felt triumphant. Howard Higgins wrote a beautiful letter to accompany the check, welcoming me to my new adventure.

Traveling through Pennsylvania was truly a trip back through time. There were tiny rural towns with brick sidewalks, rolling hills and farmland, as well as old fashioned schools with upstairs auditoriums. The morning performance was usually at seven o'clock. The second program would be about eleven thirty, and approximately 150 miles away. After lunch at a main street café, there was a drive of some 200 miles to the third performance of the day, which might be at four o'clock. Sometimes our schedule was so tight we had to eat in the car en route.

After a final school performance, we would drive part way to the next town on the itinerary. That way, we would be practically there for the morning program at seven o'clock.

We would usually eat supper, then go to the hotel. I would spend the evening washing tights. Then exhausted, I would fall into bed. I knew I had to rise at five o'clock to do my stretches and be ready to perform the next morning at seven.

My deep sleep was often interrupted by the lock on Allen's door clicking open, followed by footsteps down the hall that made the hotel's old floorboards squeak. I would pull myself out of bed and run to the window, where I would see Allen crossing the street to the local bar. Allen was always up bright and early, regardless of how late he turned in.

After Pennsylvania, the tour took us to New England. The golden fall quickly turned to cold winter. The rural roads of New England were tunnels of white lace, with huge snowflakes constantly drifting down.

The schedule continued at a backbreaking pace. The schools in the Northeast had large old fashioned auditoriums, almost like theaters. The backstage areas were so large; they had to put a screen on the stage for me to dress behind. In one school, it was very difficult to make my quick changes.

Once I was changing from *Slavonic Dance* to *The Urchin's Dream* and feeling fairly secure that everyone was out front in the auditorium. Allen was announcing my next number and filling up time for me to change. I was standing in just my tights. I looked up and there in the corner stood the school principal, leering. So much for the prim and proper censorship of my tutu for Mr. Higgins' school men. Hypocrites, all of them, I thought.

Following a performance in a small town near Boston, I was signing autographs and packing to go, when a young girl came up to me with tears in her eyes. "Where can I go to learn to dance? To do what you do. To live the life that you do?" she asked. "There's no dancing teacher here. You are the first live ballet dancer I have ever seen. Sometimes, I see one on TV, but not much. Where can I go to learn to dance?"

"Can you get to Boston?" I asked. "There are several fine teachers in Boston," I said, my heart aching for her.

"I can't go to Boston myself, and my parents won't take me. My father's a farmer and my mother has problems. Where can I go? What can I do?" she asked almost crying.

I would have enjoyed talking to her, if only we hadn't had to hurry onto the next school. She remained alone on that empty stage. I remembered the dull ache I had felt inside when I watched Dania Krupska dance in Philadelphia.

In New England, every town had at least one white church with a steeple. Railroad tracks crossed and crisscrossed, sometimes running right down the street which backed up into Main Street. It snowed constantly. One time, we stopped late for supper at the only establishment we could find on the edge of a forest. It was a hunting lodge. I remember feeling uncomfortable dining while surrounding us on all the walls were the magnificent heads of a buffalo, elk, deer, and wild cat. I never approved of hunting for sport. The fixed glass eyes of those once proud creatures didn't do much for our appetites, so we left, still feeling hungry.

After New England, we went down to Delaware and Maryland. We had quite a few engagements in all black schools. At one very tough school, in Annapolis, Maryland, my stage was the gymnasium. The students sat in bleachers, while I performed under a basketball hoop.

Another school had an obstacle right in the middle of the stage, the principal's prize rubber plant. She seemed very hurt when I refused to dance around it. She assumed it was so beautiful I would have been delighted to use it as a stage set for my program. I guess I was the first performer in years to insist on its removal.

The last leg of the tour took us to New Jersey. We were now getting closer to New York and home. For me, the tour could have gone on forever. There was one date where we had to spend the night in Teaneck. I felt guilty that I did not take the short ride over the George Washington Bridge to Manhattan and Mother. Finally, my guilt left me. I was glad that I had saved this time for me.

I returned to New York soon enough and picked up where I left off. The dates for Francis Schram got more interesting as time went by. I had a booking from her management at a private Catholic school, which was connected to a convent in Tuxedo Park.

The convent's custodian picked me up at the train depot. At the convent, a nun greeted me.

"I'm Sister Claire. Welcome to our school," she said, extending her frail hand. "It is almost time for vespers, so I will show you to your room now. I will give you the room where our young novices stay when they first come here. Breakfast will be served to you in your room at six o'clock. In the meantime, we will be looking forward to your performance tomorrow afternoon. We have a dance department of our own so our students are very anxious to see you perform. Follow me," she said.

Sister Claire unlocked the heavy door which had a small window at the top. I entered the small room with a tiny high window. A narrow, high iron bed stood in the corner. Turning my head, I saw a huge crucifix on the wall opposite, facing the bed.

I felt as if I were entering the convent myself, and was about to renounce my life and past, the very next day.

"Our dance instructor is Ingaborg Tarrup. Have you heard of her?" Sister Claire asked.

"Yes indeed," I answered. "Miss Tarrup was my very first teacher. Do you think she will attend my performance tomorrow?"

"No," Sister Claire answered. "She never attends these events. She's very strict with the girls and stays pretty much to herself. Have a good night's sleep my dear, and we'll see you tomorrow morning at six."

Sister Clare locked the door of my room with the same large key with which she had opened it. It had a final iron clad clank to it. I couldn't get out if I wanted to.

The bells announced morning Vespers. There was a loud knock at my door. A grate opened at the small door window and a nun's face appeared. Soon the heavy door was unlocked with a great clanging and a Sister Theresa entered and put my breakfast tray down on a night table near the bed. A white cup, a small pot of tea, one hardboiled egg, and a piece of dried toast stared back at me. A surge of panic went through me as I thought about how much I had to do from this moment until my performance was over, and I could get home to civilization to eat what I needed to sustain myself.

"We will be back for you at twelve," Sister Theresa said. "We'll take you to the auditorium and help you set up for your performance." Then she left and locked me in again.

At noon, the nuns came and helped me hang my scenery. My performance went well, considering how weak I felt. I was hoping Miss Tarrup might drop by for at least part of my program. But I heard she was angry when she learned her props and stairway had been removed to make way for an outside performance, so she disappeared for the rest of the afternoon and evening. She wouldn't have known who I was if someone had mentioned my name.

After my performance, I got to meet some of the students. I was disappointed none of the novices came. I was told that they no longer attended such events.

I continued rehearsing at Mrs. Wright's studio. Mornings I would arrive about ten, clean the floor, and then rehearse. One morning, after going over *Curtain Raiser* and *Divertissement*, I started to go through *Age of Gold Polka*. I got up to the fouette turns and my supporting leg began to give way. I tried again and again, but it got worse. There was no pain, but the leg just wouldn't obey. I became frightened and paced the floor like a mad woman.

"What happened to me?" I wondered. I used to perform those turns on command. Now I was terrified to try. I remembered Mr. Matthews remark, "That second dance you did is difficult, what are you going to do ten years from now when you can no longer do that dance?"

I realized the polka was that dance. It had only been three years. Was his prediction coming true?

I tried convincing myself it was all mental. I began pushing myself. There was no longer any joy performing the polka. I punished myself. I was angry at this failing, just when I was reaching a plateau in my career. Also, there was the fear that this weakness, taking over my left leg, might be the start of a breakdown in other parts of my body, my instrument. Finally, I had to give up the polka. I cut it completely out of my program. I couldn't help but wonder which dance was next. I loved them all.

I thought by becoming a dancer, I could become like Peter Pan, always in flight, forever dancing, forever striving for beauty. I didn't realize how short-lived a dancer's life is. Unfortunately, being a dancer does not make us immortal.

In the summer, Francis Schram came up with a most interesting booking, the Baltimore Museum of Art, for their summer children's concert series. I was to present three short pieces followed by the *Turkish Fairytale*. It seemed that I was getting more engagement from Francis Schram than from Mr. Matthews.

Nina Collier, founder of Young Audiences, Inc, and head of the museum's children's concert series, was there to greet me when I arrived by train. I was a guest in her home that night and the night of the performance. She had a huge house, attached to a dairy farm that she and her husband owned and operated. The Collier's had several daughters. When we all sat down to dinner, I was taken back to a time when family farm life was once a common reality.

The performance the next afternoon resulted in an excellent review from George Kent Bellows of the *Baltimore Evening Sun*.

When Mana read the review, I knew what he would say and he said it.

"It's still not New York. A review doesn't mean a thing unless it's New York."

My next tour was to start in only two weeks and preparations were frantic. I was excited but apprehensive. Mr. Foster had assured me there would be a stage manager driver to accompany me, yet he still had not told me who it would be.

Mother clung to me, and Mana asked for a list of the towns I would perform in. "Wonderful, he's taking an interest," I thought. All I got back was the list returned along with population, elevation, as well as the agricultural and industrial importance of each town.

The goodbyes at Penn Station, with Mother there to see me off, were the same as usual. She stood blowing kisses as the train was swallowed up into the black tunnel.

Out in the sunlight again, we sped westward to the life I loved. I love New York, and always will, but New York was the backdrop to my life, not part of my life.

When I finally reached Madison, the platform was jammed with college students. There in the midst of the milling crowd stood Marvin Foster. His head had been shaved to the skin. He could be Yul Brynner's understudy in *The King and I*.

A porter got my luggage and set it on the platform, while Mr. Foster grinned and looked down at me as if I were a tasty morsel.

"Well, how was the trip?" he asked, still grinning. Then he informed me he would be my stage manager for the trip.

We got into the station wagon and sped toward the student union where I was going to stay prior to the tour. My mind was swimming with problems. I knew Mr. Foster had a wife. I knew too, that she had polio. However, that was not my problem. I had come to Wisconsin to perform.

I tried to convince myself I was imagining Mr. Foster's innuendos. After all, he *was* a married man. Married men don't do things like that. But then I thought of Mana, who was once married to Mother, and here I was.

Scene Seven

Girl Meets Boy

I was not imagining Marvin's advances. He was angry when I rebuffed him, but kept his distance. With three weeks left in the tour, he dropped me off in Elgin for the weekend. I decided to take a walk. It was a balmy evening and I thought perhaps I would find somewhere downtown to eat.

Lost in my thoughts, I found myself in front of a movie theater. The entrance was crowded with children. Over the marquee it read, *The Life of St. Ignatius.* Buses thundered up along the sidewalk and more children piled out. It was so crowded, I could hardly get through. The box office read "fifty cents."

"I can afford that," I said to myself. I thought the film might have interesting costumes and even old music. I went to the window and bought my ticket.

I glanced over my shoulder and saw an interested man of medium height, gazing at me intently. As he took tickets from the children entering the theater, he never took his eyes off me. He smiled. I could feel my face flush. He took my ticket and looked into my eyes and smiled the kindest smile I had seen in weeks.

"Have you had dinner?" he asked.

"No, I haven't yet," I replied.

"Well, how about meeting me right after the movie, after all the children are gone? I have to close everything up and then we'll have dinner. How does that sound?"

"That will be fine," I said.

His name was George Hahn. He was touring his father's films around the country for parochial schools. His father was Catholic; George was not devout. He was a writer, but like many writers had to rely on other things to earn a living.

He was from Greenwich Village. He said he hung out with his cronies at the White Horse Tavern where they would play chess.

When he left me at my hotel that night, he stood for a long time, just looking up at my window. He planned to come to every town where I danced and when he couldn't make it, he promised to write.

During the following week, George was to attend one of my performances. I had mentioned him just briefly to Marvin, so that he wouldn't be surprised when a strange man showed up.

The Wednesday afternoon performance went fine, and after it was over, I looked everywhere for George. "Well, where's your George," Marvin quipped.

Then I spotted George slowly walking up the center aisle. As he came closer, his expression seemed sad.

"What's wrong," I asked. "Didn't you like my show?"

"Oh sure," George said with a forced smile. "It was great, just great. I just didn't expect you to be that good."

"I think you would be disappointed in me if I had not been good," I said.

"You don't understand," George said. "You're great! That's the problem."

Marvin came in and hardly acknowledged George standing there. He informed me he would be unable to accompany me to Muskegon, Michigan

"We'll have to cancel that date. I'll call and tell them it's off," he said.

"You will not. George here will be my emcee."

I looked over at George and he smiled back. "Sure I will," he said. "We'll drive there together. Do the show and then I'll take you wherever you need to go next."

Marvin wasn't pleased, but George and I made arrangements to meet at the Elgin Hotel and do the show together that afternoon in Muskegon.

Wednesday morning came, and as I did my stretches and warmed up my muscles, I wondered what kind of emcee George would make. Would he speak with eloquence? Would he move props about the stage with ease or would he be uncomfortable before an audience?

We picked up the luggage and the tape recorder and loaded them into George's car. Much smaller than Marvin's station wagon, the car was stuffed to capacity. It hardly left any room for us. Sitting so close to George sent my head spinning. At the same time, I tried to squeeze myself into as tight a ball as possible. As I looked down at my protruding knees, I wished I could become invisible.

"We'll have a nice dinner at O'Hare Airport," George said. "The show should be over in plenty of time for us to get there before dark. There's a great restaurant there."

I thought how nice that would be, but worried about it afterward.

"You're awfully quiet," George said. "Are you okay? We're almost there."

I brought myself back to the present. I had a show to do, and George and I would have to at least talk over the mechanics of the production.

There wasn't much time to set things up for my performance. It was a small stage and I had to warm up behind a curtain on the side so no one could see me. After all the children were seated, and my program had been announced by the chairwoman, George ambled out on to the stage. For a moment I wondered what it might be like to share this life of mine with him forever.

He stood there, center stage for a moment, looking a bit uneasy. Instead of immediately announcing my first number as I had told him, he began telling the audience about a lovely lady who had come all the way from New York City to dance for them. He went on and on, in a monotone voice which was more suitable for intimate conversation between two people, not for a full performance hall.

The children were becoming restless. In desperation, I flipped on the tape recorder, hoping the music would signal to George that it was time for me to come out and dance. The music started for my *Divertissement*. I ran onto the small stage and went into my dance. George smiled, confused, and went into the wings. At the dance's conclusion, the children applauded and some small boys whistled. I left the small stage to change into my next costume, leaving George to face the youngsters.

I was frantic, trying to change as fast as possible so I could rush out and relieve George. This routine continued until it was time for my *Turkish Fairytale*. At last, I was able to hold the stage for fifteen minutes because I changed costume and character right in front of the audience. There was a sense of relief now, for the worst was over. George was not the great emcee I had hoped for. He was too subdued. However, my feelings for him were still romantic. Perhaps with a little more practice, he would improve.

It was very late afternoon now. As we got into George's small car, steam drifted from our nostrils with every exhale. Then George's hand on the stick shift brushed against my knee and we were off to O'Hare Airport for dinner.

It was a large restaurant overlooking the runways. Planes slowly taxied on the ground while others, like giant birds, swooped down to land. Hardly anything but taillights and the tips of wings could be seen, but the movement in the dark was constant.

Little candles in votive glasses were centered on each of the restaurant's tables. George was overly attentive to the pretty hostess. For moment, I felt as if I had ceased to exist.

Alone at our table, we made small talk, as George scanned the room, watching all the pretty waitresses. It was the first time I had seen him act this way, and it made me anxious. When one of the girls came to our table to take our order, George exchanged a few jokes with her.

After our table had been served with all the food and wine we wanted, George began telling me the history of his life. He had been married once, had two daughters, eight and ten years old. His wife had come from a wealthy family and until they separated, he lived in style. Now that was over, and since the divorce all that was left were visitation rights.

George never asked a single question about me. It was just as well. Everything there was to know about me was reflected in my performance. My life with Mother was hardly anything to discuss with George.

As we left the restaurant, I began to worry about the next episode in this adventure. I don't think that I loved George yet. But I was charmed by him.

After dinner we went to a small motel nearby. George had stayed there before. We checked into adjoining rooms. I looked at the door that led to his room and a streak of fear passed through me.

George took it all so casually, as if he had experienced it a thousand times before. When he entered my room later that evening on the pretext of watching television together, his manner was soft. When he climbed into the bed with me and called me "honey," put his arm around me and started unbuttoning my night gown, my head was pounding. I knew this was not a scene in a movie. This was the real thing. I wanted George to hold me but I was terrified of being a disappointment. I longed to be as expert in lovemaking as I was in dancing.

He reached through the opening of my gown and touched my breast. I flushed. The caress intoxicated me. I wanted more, yet I knew I wasn't ready for more. I had to tell George to stop. And yet, something told me not to.

Finally, I had to call out, tell him that this was my first time, before he discovered it on his own. I was afraid he would laugh at me, be angry, or just leave.

I was interrupted by a smothering kiss. I didn't know until later that it was called a French kiss. As he smothered me with his entire body, visions of me dancing passed before my eyes. I pictured the flat were I lived, my easel, my piano and yes, even Mother managed to work her way into my mind, too.

I wondered if this experience would affect my art and my dancing.

"George, please, not yet. I have something to tell you first."

"Honey, what's wrong with you?" he asked gently. "Tonight I thought we would make love. We only have one more night together. Then we must go back to New York, to the separate lives we left there. What's wrong?"

"I just need more time, you see. You don't really know me," I said avoiding the real issue.

"All right," he said softly. "I'll meet you at Union Station next week at the end of your tour and we'll spend one night together before we take the train back to New York. Meanwhile, just allow me to gaze at your body. I won't do anything. I just want to look at you. C'mon honey, I'll help you take your gown off."

George undressed me. I lay there, naked, while he, naked also gazed down on me. I wished he would look at my eyes or my face. But he didn't; just my body.

After awhile, George lay beside me, put his arm around me and went to sleep. I couldn't sleep. Our nakedness, lying next to each other aroused thoughts and feelings that invaded my very soul.

Next morning, I made us some instant coffee with the electric coil I always carried. George dressed hurriedly. I felt numb, strange.

During the drive back to Elgin, George made all kinds of plans for us in New York.

"I want you to be with me at the White Horse Tavern where I play chess every night. I want you beside me all the time. I want my cronies to know you," he said.

"But I can't be with you every night," I said.

"For God's sake, why not?" he asked, looking at me aghast.

"I paint at night," I answered.

"You paint, too?" he said with amusement.

There was so much George didn't know about me. I didn't know where to begin to try to tell him. The fact was he didn't give me a chance to talk about myself.

"Listen, honey," he said, in earnest. "If we're going to have a relationship, you're going to have to be with me all the time. No getting away from that. I want to be with you when you practice, when you paint, and I want you to be with me when I write or when I'm with my friends playing chess. Isn't that the way it is when two people are in love?"

Is this what love is all about? I had fallen in love with his attitude toward life. I loved his personality, his "good-time-Charlie" charm. I was intrigued by the way he wore his hat, the twinkle in his eye and the ne'er-do-well commitment he seemed to show to his writing. The return to New York, for him, was like coming home to a big party.

To me, returning to New York was like returning to childhood. Living again with Mother meant giving up freedom. In Mother's eyes, I would be tarnished, because I had fallen in love.

The final week of the tour was uneventful. Marvin was brusquer, angry at my interim with George. I was not looking forward to my return to New York. The romance with George sparkled like a diamond compared to the singular life with Mother.

The rendezvous with George in Chicago was going to be my final test. Could I measure up to a love affair? I was as nervous as I would be approaching my first performance before a live audience.

The train pulled into Union Station. My baggage was put down alongside me. As the shrill whistle blew, steam emanated from below the train in great puffs, enveloping me completely. I couldn't see a thing. Finally, the steam parted like a curtain of thick fog and there before me stood George, like an apparition, in a swirl of lingering steam.

He smiled, head cocked to one side. I knew then, that nothing mattered but our being together. This was my night with George. Now was the time.

We had dinner at a small restaurant and talked a blue streak. I asked him about his writing, but his response was one of indifference. Trying to find out if he wrote short stories, novels, or poetry, all he mentioned were periodic articles in the *Village Voice*. He never asked about my life.

We checked into a small hotel under the El. My feelings for him overwhelmed my disappointment over the fact that this very special night was to be spent in a cheap hotel.

As I watched George brush his teeth in the narrow bathroom off the bedroom, I wondered what it would be like to live with him. As he undressed and climbed into bed, his slight but strong build attracted me. The tilt of his head through the smoke from his cigarette as he snubbed it out in the ashtray on the nightstand could have been from a painting by Edward Hopper.

"Come on, honey," he said. "Climb in and I'll keep you warm. And take off that Victorian nightgown."

"In a little bit," I answered meekly, climbing in beside him. Outside, the El went past and the room shook. George put his arms around me. Impulsively, I hugged him. This was the first time I had ever held a man in my arms. As I did so, he unbuttoned my nightgown, rolled it up over my head and flung it off, leaving us in a naked embrace. Our bodies, held flatly against each other, couldn't have been closer. As George fondled me intimately, terror went through me. The consequences of making love could change up my life. George continued probing, soon learning that I had never made love before.

"My God, honey, I'm your first!" he exclaimed.

"Are you angry with me?" I asked, frightened almost to tears.

"No, no, honey," he said softly. "Just surprised. I thought all this time you were very experienced. And here you are, I'm your first lover."

George rocked me in his arms while I cried. Perhaps cried for joy because he hadn't laughed at me or become angry.

"I'll tell you what, honey, when we get back to New York, we'll get you fixed up so you won't have to worry about anything. And if for some reason you get pregnant anyway, I'll marry you. How's that?"

"But I'm not ready to get married now," I said. "I just want to love you and have you love me and then in time, we'll know whether we want to make it for life."

We just held each other and soon drifted off to sleep. I was exhausted. Although this first attempt at making love didn't end in disaster, neither had I passed the test.

Next morning, George was up brushing his teeth with my toothbrush. He had lost his.

I made our morning coffee with my coil, feeling unsettled, different somehow; knowing something between us was unfinished. It would be weeks before we could pick up where we left off.

George was hurrying to dress, to take off for parts south, to tour his father's film. I was in less of a hurry. My train wasn't due to leave until later afternoon. We gathered all our belongings and George drove me to Union Station where I could wait for my train to New York.

George kissed me and promised to call me when he got back to town, just before the New Year.

"We'll spend New Year's Eve together. We'll paint the town red," he said. "We'll go party-hopping and I'll show you off to all my friends."

He hugged me and he was off. I felt stranded, with too much time on my hands.

I wandered aimlessly about the station waiting for the hours to pass. I didn't want to go back. What I really wanted was to get on a westward bound train which would take me further away from my problems, away from Mother, where I could get on yet another tour and perform forever.

The return to life with Mother was a strain. She followed me everywhere. Instead of sleeping on the Italian sofa, as she used to, she put her mattress down on a board, on the floor, about two feet from my bed in the alcove. She claimed that sleeping on a board was good for her back.

"You could still sleep on the board, Mother," I said, "without being almost on top of me."

I could see that my being away for so many weeks had not cured her hold on me. In fact, it had become worse. Fifteen years before, she had friends of her own, and even went out on occasion with a male companion. Now, she had no one but me.

I set my easel near the piano in the front room so I could be as far away from Mother as possible. I began painting on shirt cardboards a neighbor downstairs saved for me. I didn't have the money to buy canvases. Each evening after supper, I rushed to get back to my painting while Mother was in the kitchen.

"I'll be with you as soon as possible, dear," she would call out, "Don't worry, I won't be long."

The tears would stream silently down my cheeks. Sometimes I could hardly see what I was painting. The few moments alone were soon over, and Mother would be back in the front room. She would settle down into a chair beside my easel to study her marketing charts. She sat in my painting light, intruding on my creativity. I had nowhere to go.

On some evenings, when I wanted to work at the piano, Mother would lounge full-length on a Victorian chaise she had bought at Tobias Auction House.

"Mother's ready for the concert, dear," she would say.

"But I want to work on some ideas this evening," I would say, trying desperately to make her understand that I hadn't planned on giving a concert.

"I have been alone so much, dear," she would say pathetically. "I haven't heard your music for several months now. I'm lonely for your music. Please play your *Spanish Rhapsody* for me, please!"

Dutifully, I would play, hating myself every minute.

With Mother sleeping so close to me, I could hear her breathe, sigh, toss and turn during the night. I lay awake for hours, wondering if I could ever bring this to an end.

When it got close to time to tell Mother about George, it was almost like planning a cruel blow. The day finally came and it must have been good timing, because Mother's thoughts were far away as I told her I was going out New Year's Eve with a man she had never met; a man I met on tour.

The thought of losing George because of my strange environment or eccentric Mother haunted me. I was hardly in the mood to paint the town red, as George had said. I simply wanted someone to love, someone to pour my heart out to.

As New Year's Eve neared, apprehension about George's reaction to Mother, and the way we lived mounted. Finally, I realized that if I could just completely forget Mother, for the time I was with George, New Year's Eve would be a respite from her.

The morning of New Year's Eve was bitter cold. The ruthless knife of time would soon slice off another year, crowded with past evenings. There was no time for regrets.

I wondered what 1959 would hold for me. Was George going to be a part of it? I hoped so and yet, what was really more important was my life's work.

George arrived at six thirty p.m., right on time. How was he going to react to this moldy stage set and what of Mother, with that look of fear on her face? Was this new acquaintance of mine going to threaten her security?

I was afraid George would hug me or, worse, kiss me. This was fine out on tour, but not in front of Mother.

"Hi, honey. Happy New Year's," George said as he breezed into the room. He gave me a long discourse on his near accident on the Pennsylvania Turnpike. His car had slid down the ice and completely turned around.

"Like a pirouette," I chimed in nervously.

"Yes, like a pirouette," George said. He laughed. Mother stood with a forced smile, taking it all in. As far as George was concerned, Mother could have been anybody; a friend, a roommate, a neighbor, or an aunt. Even after I introduced them, his regard was casual.

He seemed in a hurry to get underway. I hugged Mother and assured her I would not be too late, even though it was New Year's Eve. I was thirty-four years old and this was the first New Year's I had spent away from her.

As we left, I glanced back. Mother stood in the doorway blowing kisses. I was glad that George had not looked back. He took the stairs two at a time.

We wended our way down to the subway, briskly scooting around the corner by the newsstand where Eggplant, the cat, held down a pile of *Herald Tribunes* and *World Telegrams* like a tremendous paperweight.

"We're going to Chinatown," George said.

Another couple was to meet us on Mott Street, where George knew a good Chinese restaurant. When we arrived, the other couple was waiting for us. I liked them and the young lady and I struck up a conversation immediately.

After dinner, George took us party-hopping, a whirlwind series of events. We made several stops in Greenwich Village, one in Little Italy and then one in an old fashioned basement bar on Allen Street where the jukebox was playing polkas. George put his arms around my waist and we danced polkas all over the place. I was wearing a big purple taffeta skirt which ballooned out as we turned. People were standing around clapping. I was deliriously happy. I believed now that I was truly in love.

George was intent on introducing me to his friends at the White Horse Tavern. Although I had seen it many times from the outside, I had never been inside. There, George's cronies sat, playing intense games of chess. Many of the players looked unshaved and unkempt. George said some were writers and artists who gathered for camaraderie. I was unimpressed.

We made one more stop, an apartment where his friends had already been drinking heavily. There was an upright piano and someone was playing the cancan. By this time, I had downed a few glasses of champagne myself, and I guess the combination of the drinks and the music combined to prompt me to jump on a table and perform the cancan kicking my legs up high.

Suddenly, I was the life of the party and George was looking up at me with admiration.

Someone said, "Midnight!" and everyone yelled, "Happy New Year!"

George grabbed me, hugged me, and kissed me passionately. I hugged back. I wanted to make this moment last. Suddenly, I realized how late it was.

"I've got to get home," I said. "My mother will be worried if I'm not home by one thirty."

"Mother?" said a heavy young man. "What the hell does Mother have to do with New Year's Eve?"

"My mother and I live together," I answered. "We're kind of like roommates, sisters, you know. It's cheaper that way." I laughed a nervous laugh.

"Wow, she lives with her mother. That must be interesting, a real trip," the young man said, loud enough for everyone to hear. Laughter filled the room. The admiration I had from this small group was suddenly gone...

"C'mon, honey," George said. "Let's go by my apartment and have a night-cap. Then we can be alone together for awhile before I take you home."

"I've got to get home soon," I said softly. This was the latest I'd been out. How was I ever going to explain to Mother? It was one forty-five a.m. before we left and I could tell George was not too happy. I longed to be home.

In George's small, slightly unkempt apartment, we approached another session of lovemaking. I had no enthusiasm for it. Worried about being home before the sun came up and confronting Mother distracted me. Whether I passed the test and made love to George was inconsequential now. It had been so much easier in Chicago, but in New York, Mother dominated the scene. George did not go any further than the first time. I was too frightened. I just wanted to go home.

He took me home in a cab and made arrangements to have lunch after my rehearsal the following week. The goodbye kiss at the door did not linger.

"Is that you, dear?" Mother called out.

"Yes, it's me," I answered.

I undressed in the cold room, put on my nightgown and stepped over Mother's body to get to my bed. I hoped she would ask no questions, at least not now. It was late and I wanted to black out.

It was not easy for me to get back to normal, if normal was before George. The moment I sat still, Mother would start with questions. She knew I was different since my return to New York, but didn't broach the subject. Perhaps, she was as afraid to know the truth, as I was to tell it. Her behavior was not unlike that of a husband who knows his wife will eventually leave him, but puts off thinking about it for as long as he can.

The day finally arrived for my lunch date with George. As I turned the corner at Sixty-seventh Street and Columbus Avenue, I could see the beanery where I was to meet him. My heart was pounding hard. Maybe I *was* in love with him.

It was exactly one thirty. I was right on time. As I opened the door to go in, the man on duty asked if he could help. I told him I was meeting some-one.

I looked around for George, but he was not there. I sat down on the rear booth feeling dejected. I decided to have a cup of coffee. I nursed it slowly, waiting another fifteen minutes. At the top of the wall was a little electric train that kept running on a track around the restaurant. I must have watched it roll around the track over a dozen times. It was after two o'clock when I finally got up and left.

I had a painful lump in my throat that swallowing did not relieve. I decided to walk home. The traffic helped divert me from the realization that George had stood me up.

I didn't tell Mother about the lunch date that never happened. In a few days, George called.

"Honey," he said. "I'm sorry I didn't make it the other day. Shall we try again?"

"Okay," I said, hoping he had a good excuse, but afraid to ask.

We agreed to meet at a little restaurant on the Upper East Side. I hung up, relieved to have heard from him again, but annoyed with myself for agreeing to see him so soon after he stood me up.

It was bitter cold the night George and I were to meet. Mother was going to visit her friend Helen Laird in an apartment on East Seventy-fourth Street, not far from where I was to meet George. I did not feel guilty about leaving Mother this time. I set off, in good spirits. Again, George was not there. I sat for half an hour waiting. Out on the street, my hot tears turned cold on my cheeks.

I made my way to Helen Laird's apartment. Her place was always warm, and I needed warmth. I was trembling all over. When I reached the building, my feet went right on by. I instinctively knew that Mother should know nothing about this episode. Running against the wind, sobbing, I made my way over to Fifth Avenue. The sobbing never stopped.

When I finally reached home, I threw myself down on my tiny bed and wept, hugging an old curtain which had been flung across my pillow. It was the only thing I had to love now, and I hung onto it for dear life. I decided to get on with my life.

It was winter turning into spring of 1959. I did not have a single tour ahead of me, but I was continuing to do dates for Francis Schram. I also continued painting ceramic pieces for Sebastian. I was even doing some to sell to friends; mugs with faces wearing peasant costumes, the handle being the hand on the hip. I painted quite a few large oval plates with rows of cancan dancers.

A letter arrived one day from Notre Dame University inviting me to appear at the National Catholic Theater Conference the following summer. I was to present my *Turkish Fairytale* with a few short numbers, first to an audience of priests, nuns, cardinals, and bishops from all over the world. I also was to prepare a lecture to be given the next day, about my medium of dance and mime. This appearance would give me the seal of approval from the church hierarchy for appearances in any Catholic schools or universities in the country.

Between ceramic work and the children's programs for Brigg's Management and the small paintings I was doing on shirt cardboards, I decided to tackle a new dance, for which I would write the music. *The Betrothed* depicted the final five minutes of a young girl's thoughts before her marriage to someone she doesn't love. It was for soprano, viola, and two cellos. I wrote out the parts myself, transposing for the strings from a book on orchestration. The music was reminiscent of Menotti, whose opera *The Medium and the Consul*, I idolized. My friend Helen Rice sang the solo part. I had met Helen in *Wonderful Town*.

The rehearsal sessions, and finally the recording of the work were very expensive. The very last section suffered from lack of recording time. The final chords ended with the soprano, viola, and one cello playing in one key, while the second cello was a quarter note lower. For this reason, I never did perform the work. It was an experience that I am glad I had, but at the time, I was frustrated. I needed another hundred dollars so the last section could be re-recorded, but by that time, I had run out of money.

Scene Eight

Elephant Love

In spring, the circus came to Madison Square Garden. One of the things that Mother, Mana, and I did each year was go and watch the elephants come out of the stage door on their departure from New York. They would go over Ninth Avenue and then up to Fifty-seventh Street where they would head over to Second Avenue, then go north to the railroad yards. Mana was in Europe, so Mother and I decided to go alone.

As we approached Madison Square Garden, the stage door was crowded with men, women, and children all waiting for the parade of elephants. Mother and I stood by the chain link fence. Next to me was a young man, hanging his hand through the links of the fence. He turned and looked at me.

"You've come to see the elephants, too?" he asked.

"Oh yes, I come every spring. It's a ritual," I answered.

"Well," he said. "I live around the corner on Fifty-first Street. I heard all the commotion and the neighbor told me the circus was leaving town, so I decided to come out and watch. My name is Tom Williams," he continued as he handed me his business card. It read, "Tom Williams, Transfilm" I was impressed. "What's your name, if I may ask?"

"My name is Marta, just Marta," I answered, afraid of how forward it would be to give my whole name. Mother seemed oblivious to my conversation, so for a moment I felt free to talk to Tom.

"What do you do?" he asked.

"I'm a dancer," I answered.

"That must be an exciting life," he said.

"The theater is always exciting," I responded.

"Where do you dance?" he asked.

"I'm between engagements now," I replied, wishing I had an impressive tour to tell him about.

Suddenly, I remembered and began talking about my upcoming Notre Dame University appearance. Then I began describing what it is I do, and I became more animated. Tom appeared to be genuinely interested. No man had ever been interested in what I did before.

"A one-woman show," he said. "Like Hal Holbrook does in *Mark Twain Tonight*?"

"Well, yes," I answered. "Except that I don't impersonate anyone. I create my own characters and then portray them in scenarios I write myself, through dance and pantomime."

"I hope I can see it one day," he exclaimed.

Suddenly there were shouts from inside the cavern that served as a stage door for animals. A few roustabouts with sticks appeared, along with some New York City cops. They moved us all to one side to make way for the elephants. Then a small man with a German accent came out, calling to his charges in elephant language, a thick, guttural vocabulary that preceded the sudden appearance of the elephants.

By now, it had grown dark. The parade of elephants with followers running along either side stopped traffic. The elephants barged onward through blowing impatient whistles and horns. It was all we could do to keep up.

Noticing Mother, Tom stayed back and helped her along. I ran ahead a little. Then I would slow down so they could catch up. Then I would skip ahead, like a child.

Walking across Fifty-seventh Street to Second Avenue was exhilarating. The pedestrians were delighted. Drunken laughter erupted from bars we passed. "Why aren't the elephants pink?" yelled a man stumbling out of a cocktail lounge.

The elephant parade passed Carnegie Hall just as the concert goers poured out of the doorways. It continued on shuffling along Fifty-seventh Street.

The parade continued toward Fifth Avenue, crossed Madison and Lexington until it reached Second Avenue where it turned north to journey up to the railroad yards in the Bronx. By the time we reached Second Avenue, Mother was beginning to show signs of fatigue. We all agreed to head for home. Tom walked with us until we reached Fifth Avenue at Forty-sixth Street.

"Chance will have us meet again," he said. "What is your last name?" he added. "We mustn't leave it to chance."

"Our name is Beckett," Mother said before I could answer. I wonder to this day if she ever regretted revealing my last name. Would I have dared to say it in front of her? She saved me from the decision.

"Good night," Tom said.

"Good night," I answered. He went off into the night, and Mother and I wended our way home.

Two weeks went by, filled with rehearsals and ceramics work. I was beginning to sell quite a few ceramic mugs. I also was painting more on cardboards; imaginative and childlike figures dressed in flimsy white gowns, holding a sunflower set in a background of Queen Ann's Lace, or dried grass in front of a backdrop of a depressing coal town.

One day, I got a call from Tom Williams. He invited me to see Hal Holbrook in *Mark Twain Tonight*. I jumped at the idea.

We agreed he would pick me up Thursday for dinner around six o'clock. I hung up looking forward to the evening. Suddenly, I noticed Mother gazing at me with a puzzled expression.

I swallowed, "You know the young man we met at the circus? He invited me to see Hal Holbrook." I rose from my seat and went to my easel to hide behind a painting I was working on.

"You never did say what happened to that other gentleman you met on tour. The one you went out with on New Year's Eve," Mother said.

"Oh, he had to go out on the road again with one of his father's films," I answered, swallowing my white lie.

"You never mentioned him again," Mother persisted.

"I think not, Mother, he's out on a long tour," I answered hoping she wouldn't ask any more questions.

Tom showed up Thursday at exactly six. I could feel Mother's clawing gaze as we descended the stairs. Once we were out on the street, I felt free. Tom looked at me with the setting sun on his face and asked where I would like to have dinner.

"Doesn't matter," I answered. "I like all kinds of food."

"I know a charming French restaurant on the West Side; small, intimate, and real French home-cooking," he said.

The restaurant accommodated only about seven tables. The food was delicious, and I can still remember the cream of broccoli soup. The food was cooked by a French couple who also waited on us.

After dinner, we meandered over to the Forty-first Theater, where Hal Holbrook was performing. He was so believable. It was an inspiring evening. The fact that it was a one-man show made it even more so to me. When Tom took me home, we made a date for him to visit Mother and me the following Tuesday.

We said good night. Even though it had been a lovely evening, I did not have that romantic feeling I felt with George. Perhaps it was too soon. Whatever I was missing was replaced by Tom's genuine interest in me and my work.

Tom arrived promptly at eight the following Tuesday night. He brought along a pint of vanilla ice cream. Later, I asked him why he had chosen such an ordinary flavor.

"I wanted to play it safe," he answered. "Everybody likes vanilla."

That visit was the first of many. Tom would bring exotic flavors of ice cream and Mother would buy day old layer cake. While we enjoyed these treats, the conversation was always strained.

The unrelenting schedule of the visits at the flat and the Thursday evenings out on the town with Tom, Saturdays at the zoo or the Metropolitan Museum of Art, or a ferry boat ride, made my life a sort of stage play. Tuesday evening was "scene one," Thursday evening "scene two," and Saturday, "scene three."

Between my work and Tom, I had very little time for Mother. She felt abandoned and I felt guilty but I was caught up in the whirlwind in spite of myself.

After awhile, Tom told me he was recovering from a divorce and now lived alone in a walk up in what he called Hell's Kitchen. He had three children whom he supported and visited regularly. He was seeing a psychiatrist to help him through the trauma.

I told Tom about Mother, Mana, and the Nice Lady. I stressed the fact that I was devoted to Mother to make up for what my father and her former best friend had done to her.

"Still," he said. "You should hear your father's side. Two sides to every story you know."

"Yes, I guess so," I replied.

I began preparing for the big performance in August at Notre Dame. I was working on the lecture I was required to give along with the performance. I was a bit apprehensive about this because I had never spoken before an audience out of character.

My paintings on shirt cardboards were developing a style of their own. I was devoting more time to them than the ceramic work. I wanted to find a gallery or perhaps a store where I could sell them on consignment. I thought of Milo, whose gallery used to sell my pastels.

I collected about eighteen tempera paintings and went to see Milo. He said he remembered me well, as a little girl in pigtails on roller skates. He and his wife, Florence, remembered Mother as well.

"Yes, leave them here. I can definitely sell them," he said. I'll make frames for them as well and make an extra profit for myself." We shook hands on the deal. We agreed that I would get sixty percent. I left the gallery elated. When I returned home, the flat seemed empty without my sunflower children.

In a few days, Milo called to say he had sold everything and wondered if I had worked on anything else. I quickly got to work painting more.

Tom and I continued spending Saturdays together, usually starting with a trip to deliver bisque lamp bases to be fired for Sebastian. Then we would go over to the gallery to pick up my profit from the paintings sold the previous week, and drop off new paintings. I was full of ideas. The rest of Saturday was often spent browsing around Fourteenth Street or, if it was a pleasant day, at the Bronx Zoo.

I was beginning to feel close to Tom. His interest in my work spurred me onto something more than just infatuation. There was stability in him. I sensed that he not only loved me, but wanted to help me fulfill my dreams. I called him my "big tree." I would put my arms around him and feel safe, cared for, and loved.

I had acquired some bookings up it the Catskill Mountain resort area. One show was booked at a place called Maude's Sun Ray, a summer haven for Jewish seniors.

"How would you like me to take you up there," Tom asked. "I'll be your stage manager. Let's try it and see how it goes."

I loved the idea. I wondered what Mother would think? We would have to stay overnight. Would we share the same room? I longed for the freedom I had out on the road.

One Saturday afternoon, Tom and I went to Coney Island. We rode all the rides at Steeplechase Park. We ate hot dogs, cotton candy, and ice cream, and walked endlessly up and down the boardwalk. As the sky began to darken, the Ferris wheel beckoned. At the very top we were stuck for almost thirty minutes. Tom and I were alone, swinging softly in the little car high above

Coney Island. The lights and sounds were far below. Tom put his arm around me and kissed me in a way I had never been kissed before. He fondled me in places which sent my head spinning. No one knew where I was or what I was doing at this moment, except for Tom. I was intoxicated. I put my arms around my "big tree" and held him close. Suddenly, the Ferris wheel began to turn again and swiftly our small car came back down to the ground.

"I think we'd better go home, to my place," Tom said.

By the time we reached his place it was eleven thirty p.m. Tom had love-making in mind.

"Tom," I said. "Please, can we make a time when I can tell you something about myself, something you should know about me, please, before we go any further."

"Well, alright. If that's the way it has to be. We can do that," Tom seemed impatient. I knew he was disappointed. He agreed to pick me up for dinner the following Thursday. It was then I planned to tell him my terrible secret.

Tom arrived promptly at six thirty p.m. on Thursday. We went to a romantic Italian restaurant called Vesuvio. The waiter took our order and as we sipped our wine. I broke the silence and began.

"I have been in love a few times before, but I have never made love," I said. I could feel my face flush. Tom looked at me with amusement and surprise. "I've never slept with a man in my life," I continued.

"But why not?" Tom asked. "If you were in love before, why not go all the way?"

"The two men I was in love with were engaged to marry other girls. The first one knew I was in love with him. The other...well, I kept my feelings to myself."

"Would you have made love with them if they had not been engaged?" Tom asked.

"I don't know. I worry about getting emotionally involved with someone because of Mother and my work. I always felt that a career in the theater mixed with a marriage would never work. I worry about spreading myself too thin."

Tom fiddled with his glass and I played with my napkin. "Perhaps if someone loved me and shared my dedication to my work. As for Mother, my loyalty to her just doesn't fit in with a love life. I don't really know what I would do if I fell so deeply in love that I had to choose. I could never give up my life's work, but Mother.... I just don't want to hurt her. She's been hurt enough."

Tom reached over and touched my hand. I thought he was going to cry. He hadn't laughed at all.

"How old are you, if I might ask?" Tom said gently.

"Thirty-four," I answered looking down.

"Heavens! I thought you were in your early twenties," Tom said with surprise. "Do you know you are older than I am?"

"I've always been taken for much younger than I really am," I said. "I've told you everything. I wanted you to know these things before our relationship went any further. If you want to break it off, it would be better for me if you do it now instead of after we make love."

Tom reached over and touched my hand again. I could see he didn't believe me. He looked a bit amused. How could a thirty-four year-old woman be a virgin?

I could hardly eat a thing and was too concerned about the rest of the evening to notice what Tom ate. He was gentle with me, trying to understand. After dinner, we walked down Broadway, held hands and enjoyed the warm summer evening. Tom was reserved.

"Well," he said with forced cheerfulness. "Shall I pick you up Saturday at noon again?"

"Oh, yes," I said with relief. "I will look forward to it."

When Mana and his wife returned from Europe, it was difficult for me to slip back into my role as his little girl. Mana would be overjoyed to learn that I was in love. He had remarked that nothing would make him happier than to see me marry and leave Mother. I was not about to provide him with this pleasure.

"I don't care who it might be who sweeps you off your feet." Mana once exclaimed. "It could be a truck driver or even a bum; anybody, before it is too late." At thirty-four, Mana viewed me as someone who was doomed to spinsterhood.

When I told Mother that Tom was going to stage manager my show up it the Catskills, I eased her concern by telling her that Tom and I would be staying in separate rooms. It was a lie, but I was beginning to feel more comfortable in lies like this.

On Tuesday evening, when Tom came over to the flat for the usual coffee and cake, we would rehearse for the show. Mother would sit in the back room, oblivious. It would annoy me when Tom would steal a kiss from time to time or caress me as we tried to work. I was determined that my show would run smoothly. Intimate intrusions didn't help.

The engagement finally arrived. We headed up the narrow winding roads to the Maude's Sun Ray. We received a hearty welcome and were shown to the room where the performance would take place. Dinner was part of the performance fee and what a dinner it was, chicken in a pot with dumplings, gefilte fish, herring, coleslaw, plenty of black bread, and a choice of pastry and ice cream.

It was hot and sticky, the air so humid it was hard to hang the scenery. I knew when I started to dance I would be dripping with sweat. Finally, show time came and the guests began filing into the room. When Tom went out in the front and began announcing my program, he did it with eloquence and confidence. He was made for the part.

The Middle Eastern music for my Turkish dance began. Narration started as I rose from my oriental squat as the King's daughter. As the story unfolded, my face was soaking wet under the masks. Mascara was running down into my eyes causing a painful stinging sensation. By the time the elaborate wedding scene ended I was drenched.

After the hearty applause, everyone left and Tom and I sat on the floor folding the scenery.

"I could do this for the rest of my life," he said.

We stopped to get a bite to eat and then went directly to the motel. I had bought a small jar of espresso to boil with my electric coil. I thought this would perk me up. But one cup just made me nervous.

The preliminaries to making love did not seem to do much either. I had little enthusiasm for what was to come. I was just too tired to cope with the unknown, but I knew I had no choice.

When this experience of lovemaking was over, I felt as if I had been invaded. I felt a sense of disappointment. If this was my first lovemaking experience, were they going to be like this ever after?

"Oh, it's true. We must get married now, we must! It's true. I am your first."

He hugged me again, grateful to have discovered my virginity for himself. To Tom, I was unique among women. Now he wanted me for himself. I didn't understand at all.

On the way back to New York, Tom seemed exuberant. All he could talk about was marriage.

When I returned, Mother was waiting. Tom's enthusiasm clashed with Mother's pained expression.

I headed into the flat. Tom followed with the trunks. Mother's eyes fixed on him like daggers. She was anxious for him to leave so she could start the inquisition. As Tom reached over to kiss me goodbye and make plans for our next visit together, Mother came out and stood there, watching us.

"Goodbye," Mother said, as sweetly as possible. "Don't forget, coffee and cake next Tuesday." Tom glanced back and then raced down the stairs.

Once I was alone with Mother, she searched my eyes for clues.

"He didn't say goodbye to me," Mother said in a wounded voice.

"You didn't give him a chance to say goodbye to *me*, Mother. You wouldn't leave us alone for a moment."

"You were alone with him for two whole days, how much do you want?" Mother retorted.

It was so hot I didn't want to argue. After I hung everything up, I ran a tub of cool water to soak in. Unfortunately, the tub was in the kitchen, right under Mother's nose as she prepared the dinner I didn't want.

"Was it awful dear? Was it terrible? Was it painful? You haven't said a thing since your return," she said. "Mother wants to know all." She looked down at me as I sat cramped in the small tub and studied me, her daughter, who to her was now soiled.

There were three pressures now; Mother, Mana, and Tom. And my concern was my work. I was very concerned about bookings. The only one I had was the Notre Dame University, in August. My paintings were selling well at Milo's. I continued to rehearse daily at Mrs. Wright's, and I lost myself in painting every afternoon. The demands for my work seemed to siphon off my troubles.

One day, the phone rang and at the other end was a familiar voice. It was George.

"Hi honey," he said. "I've been thinking about you a lot and I'm sorry I stood you up. I want to apologize." I really didn't know what to say.

"The responsibility of being your first lover made me afraid to go any further. But I can't get you out of my mind. I want to give it another chance. Will you let me try again, honey?"

"It's too late," I answered, "I'm involved with someone now. I believe this time, it's permanent. It wouldn't make sense to see each other now."

"Maybe we could just meet somewhere and say goodbye nicely then. It's not right to end it this way. Maybe we could have lunch somewhere," he said.

George and I agreed to meet at the fountain in the restaurant of the Metropolitan Museum of Art. This time, he was on time. It was good to see him again. It was comforting to know he had been thinking of me and I wasn't just another of his many encounters.

After we ordered, we just sat for awhile, staring at one another. He put his hand on top of mine, gazed intently at me and asked, "So who is this man who swept you off your feet?"

Tom had not swept me off my feet. It was George who had done that. It was Tom's stability, his growing love for me, and his great patience with Mother that had slowly made me fall for him.

I didn't know what to say. My heart was pounding. There was something about George's voice that seemed to go with that twinkle in his eye. I hadn't forgotten.

Tom's interest in my work made me know he was right for me. So why was my head spinning as George held my hand. I knew he didn't care about my career. I told George how Tom and I met at the circus.

"He loves me and I love him, and that is that. There's nothing more to say," I said.

"Well, perhaps I opened a door to some feelings you didn't know you had. I was the one who goofed up. It's my loss. But I can feel perhaps that I was, in a way, responsible for your new found happiness."

We wandered through the impressionist paintings of the French school. George would take my hand, and I would withdraw it, gently.

My dates with Tom were pleasant, but the subject of marriage always hung in the air. He was upset I hadn't told Mana about him. He also couldn't understand why I wasn't ready to be married. My three year contract with Mr. Matthews was about up. Although he offered me another, without a retainer fee, I declined, for I felt that I had gone as far as I could with him.

I was now getting some very nice articles written about me, in *Program Magazine*, which was mainly devoted to the lecture circuit. Occasionally, I would buy a small ad, and through this, had a running relationship with Agnes McTernan, the associate editor. She made a special effort to speak to Phil Tippin, who was head of the department of concerts and lectures for the National Concert & Artists Corporation, better known as NCAC.

An appointment was made for me to meet him in his Fifth Avenue office. Walking down the long hall to his office was like walking through a museum dedicated to the golden age of performers and the great impresarios who nurtured them. The walls were lined with photographs of past greats such as Toscanini, Kirstin Flagstadt, Fritz Kreisler, Lotte Lehman, and the great Spanish dancer Carmen Amaya.

I knew if I could be listed as one of the artists for NCAC, I would have arrived. My worries would be over and perhaps even Mana would approve.

Phil Tippin looked over my clippings and agreed to take me on. He mainly booked women's clubs and occasional colleges with a prospect for tours for organized audiences across the country. However, he could not promise a specific number of bookings within a given year, which disappointed me a little. The best thing about the contract was that no retainer fee was required.

I was to be under exclusive management after 1960, and I felt saddened that I would not be able to do any more of the children's dates for Frances Shramm after that.

My performance and touring days would be different now, but still, this was the best deal that had been offered to me to date. I left feeling elated. After spilling out the happy news to Mother, I called Tom. His reaction was not what I had expected.

"Well, goodbye," he said. "You'll go off on long tours and I won't see you any more."

"Oh no," I said. "NCAC is just booking me for a few dates at a time. We can do those together. Then after I get established, we can both go on long tours together. Doesn't that sound good to you?"

"Sure, sure, it all sounds fine. When do we start?" He responded.

August was suddenly upon us with the date for Notre Dame coming fast. Tom rented a car and the costumes, tape recorder, and scenery were all piled into the back. We could hardly see out the rear window. We left the flat with Mother standing at the top of the stairs blowing kisses.

Notre Dame University was an enormous campus with imposing buildings spread out on green lawns punctuated by shade trees. The spacious green lawn was bedecked with nuns, cardinals, bishops, and priests from all over the world. I had never seen French sisters before, with their medieval head pieces. As they stood in clusters talking, they looked like geese with wings spread, ready to take off. The cardinals also stood out, in their vermilion red coats that touched the ground.

We were welcomed and given a schedule for the week-long seminar. My performance was held in a special theater. Just before I went on, I peeked through the curtain and saw the audience. I believe even Tom was impressed. The audience consisted of nuns, priests and cardinals from all over the world.

The performance went well. The applause was enthusiastic, sounding like a rain storm during monsoon time. The lecture was the following day, and because I had already performanced and been well received, I felt confident during my speech. I told how I changed character on stage right before the audience. I talked about the difference between projecting a character while dancing compared to just doing a divertissement. I spoke about becoming someone else in a split second and then back to myself, instantaneously.

Tom enjoyed the Notre Dame experience very much, despite the fact he was an atheist. Whenever I mentioned the possibility of a life after this one, Tom would laugh.

That fall, Phil Tippin obtained a few women's club engagements, and Tom accompanied me on most of them. The rest of the time was spent rehearsing and staying prepared for whatever might materialize.

I remember one particular women's club in York, Pennsylvania. Tom and I were on the small stage, behind the skimpy curtain, which separated us from the ladies out front who were having cucumber sandwiches and tea. A precocious little girl of about seven came back and glowered at me. "You'd better be good," she said. "My mother paid $150 for your show. You'd better be better than good, that's all I can say."

The Rockford Women's' Club, in Illinois, was the best of all the women's clubs. It was there that I performed when touring for the University of Wisconsin. Having a real theater to dance in, and space behind the curtain to warm up, was a luxury compared to the other women's clubs Phil Tippin got for me.

Anzia, my old friend from high school, called to tell me she was now living in Tampa, Florida, teaching dance in her own school. She wondered if I might be interested in guesting with the Sun State Opera Company in a performance of *Aida* and also appearing with her dance company presenting my dance mimes. I jumped at the idea. The venture seemed to be alright with Phil Tippin who turned out to be more lenient concerning outside engagements than our contract indicated.

Tom agreed to fly down to Tampa the weekend of my performance with the ballet. Mr. Tippin even managed to get some pick-up dates while I was in Florida. One was a retirement community south of Tampa, the other a Catholic college in Cullman, Alabama, which was a detour on the way back to New York.

Anzia's husband offered to drive me and my show down to the retirement community for my performance there, as well as stage manage the show for me. Tom would then drive me and my show to Cullman for the performance on the way home. Everything was getting exciting.

"How can I be sure about you, alone with Ralph on that trip to the retirement community," Tom asked.

"How can a thing like that even occur to you?" I asked. "Anzia has been my friend since high school. Why would I betray her? And I love you. Why would I be untrue?"

When I arrived in Tampa, Ralph, Anzia and her entire ballet school were waiting for me with flowers. I stayed with Anzia and practiced in her studio behind the house. Afternoons, I rehearsed with the opera company.

It was cold in Tampa, thirty-two degrees, which is rare. Rehearsing with the ballet was a shivering experience there since the theater they were given was not heated. We had a beautiful baroque theater to perform in at no cost, so we had to forget the comforts of heat.

The opera performance was scheduled for January 22 in the armory with elaborate stage sets and an excellent singing cast. Anzia's Tampa Civic Ballet provided the dances while I did the solo parts.

The performance with the Tampa Civic Ballet, in the Centro Asturiano, followed a week later. I remember Anzia's little girls in their Degas costumes in the wings watching as I was performing my *Grand Performance*.

At the retirement community, Ralph and I set up in a large room usually used for meetings and occasional banquets. There was no theatrical lighting or curtain to separate my performing area from my audience. The chairs were arranged in rows facing my makeshift dancing area and there was a sign, set up on an easel in the lobby out front which read "Marta Becket, Dance Mime, 8 p.m., Tonight."

I had to walk out, after Ralph announced me, at each selection, take my pose and go into my dance, which detracted from any illusion I might have hoped for. After my performance, an old man with a cane walked up to me, shook my hand and remarked, "Your mother came to my office years ago, in New York, and asked me to see you audition, which I did. I regret now that I didn't sign you up. I certainly wish I had. If I had signed you up, I might still be in show business, who knows." He laughed, shook my hand again and left. I wish I had asked his name.

Tom arrived the day after my performance with the ballet. I remember seeing him come up the path to Anzia's house. I ran to meet him and he put his suitcases down to hug me. We went into the house and I introduced him to Anzia, her husband, and their seven year-old son, Keith. We all had coffee and then made our plans. Tom and I would be leaving the next day for Alabama, so this was the last chance I had to really visit with Anzia.

I was rather stunned when Anzia took me aside that afternoon and said, "I just hope Tom doesn't hurt you someday."

"Why," I asked. "You don't even know Tom. How can you pass judgment?"

"Just from what I've observed," she answered. "I can see things you can't. When you're in love, you don't see. Love is blind, remember?" She laughed nervously.

We arrived in Cullman, Alabama in late afternoon and stayed at a motel with paper-thin walls. A picture of Christ walking on water hung on the wall. This made me feel self-conscious when I realized what Tom had in mind after three weeks without me. I was tired and not in the mood, but Tom was, and he proceeded to make love to me as Christ watched from the water.

One evening when Tom picked me up for our mid-week date, he was in a particularly bad mood. He needed to get something off his chest, so before we went to dinner, we stopped by a coffee shop and had it out.

"What is all this about your mother and you not having enough to eat or enough money to live in a decent apartment?" he demanded.

"What are you talking about?" I asked.

"You know very well what I'm talking about!" he said angrily. "Yesterday, as I was walking through a building, I saw a brokerage house on the first floor and guess who I saw sitting in the first row. Your mother. There she was staring at the tape as if her very life depended on it. Did you know about this?"

"Tom," I said beseechingly, "When I was a little girl, Mother made me promise never to tell anyone about her stock market activities. My father was never to find out, because he had always stopped her from everything she had ever tried to do. In the market, Mother found her refuge. She hoped one day to make enough out of it that she wouldn't have to worry anymore. I felt I owed it to her, to keep her secret."

I pointed out to him how hard Mother had it after the affair between Mana and her best friend, after thirteen years of confinement as a house-wife.

"Although I love you, I love Mother, too, and I have known her a lot longer than I have known you."

Tom seemed to soften a little, but continued to barrage me with questions.

"Has your mother ever revealed what she has made in the market, if anything?" he asked.

"No," I answered meekly. "I have never seen any results from her investments. She tells me that she is making money for our old age."

"You mean she plans on the two of you growing old together and that's when the pie in the sky will come?"

"It makes her happy; the market. It's what she lives for. It's sad, but I can't stop it. Mother is addicted. When Mother is happy, there is peace. I have to live with her, you don't. All I know is that she doesn't take any of my money any more. Whatever she does, it's with money she has made herself."

"But where did she get the money to invest in the first place," he asked.

"Back in the Depression, my father gave her money for my support. She used that. Then when I worked in nightclubs, she began using my money. Finally I made her stop. She hasn't bothered me since."

There was a dead silence. Tom had discovered Mother's addiction himself. I hadn't broken my promise to her.

During the winter of 1960, Mother and I received an eviction notice from our landlord. The building we had lived in for seventeen years was about to be torn down to make way for an office building.

I began searching the neighborhood for loft space and found nothing. Uptown, I found an apartment, one huge room with an alcove where I could sleep and a bathroom with a frosted window overlooking a yard. The rent was sixty dollars; twenty more than our old place. I took Mother up to see the wonderful place, but she was reluctant to move out of our neighborhood.

I tried hard to impress upon her the benefits of the apartment. I felt she would like it once she saw it, but all she said was that big space and the dancing shadows of trees were luxury we could not afford.

"For only twenty dollars a month extra," I said. "We could live in a nicer place. I can afford it. It isn't that much more. Perhaps I would be inspired to do better work in this place." But my pleading fell on deaf ears. So my search continued.

Finally I saw a sign, "loft for rent," on the third floor of a walk-up on Eighth Avenue, between Forty-second and Forty-third streets. A Blarney Stone Bar & Grill was on the first floor, a Greek club on the second, and some kind of publishing company on the forth. I went to the fourth floor to inquire about the loft.

A rather seedy fellow with a mustache, who introduced himself as David Fish greeted me.

"We need the rent money for this loft up front," he said. "We want the first year paid in advance; one hundred dollars a month. That would come to a total of $1,200. Can ya handle that?"

"I'll have to think about it," I answered. I was wary, but when I brought Mother to see the place, she encouraged me to take it.

Mother insisted we move our things the cheapest way possible. She found an old man from Ninth Avenue with a large, open truck.

"What if it should rain?" I asked.

"That's the chance we have to take, dear. We don't have the luxury of choice."

When the man came to make the estimate, I was horrified at how small his truck was. Our piano would never fit.

"We'll just have to leave some things behind," Mother said.

"You mean even the piano?" I asked.

"You don't compose much any more, dear. I'm thinking of giving it away, perhaps to some piano student. Whoever will pay for the moving can have it. We can't afford the luxury of the upkeep of a grand piano now, and that's that."

"What about all these little things; our clothes, my paintings, drawings, and smaller furniture? It won't fit into that mover's truck." I was becoming more and more depressed.

"We can carry these things in a grocery cart. There will be a number of trips, but we will get it all over to Eighth Avenue eventually."

I was the one who made the countless trips back and forth with the grocery cart full of belongings and mementoes Mother insisted on keeping. Several times I almost had an accident, right on Times Square, trying to pull the cart over a curb.

There were three large rooms in the new loft, plus a huge bathroom which had a full-size tub, a luxury compared to the wash tub in our old kitchen. There also was a large space for a kitchen, so we bought a stove. This loft was well-heated and had big windows that brought in plenty of light. The middle room had no windows, so I selected that room to sleep in. Mother thought she would continue to sleep on her floor board, right beside me on my cot in the front room.

I told her I needed to be alone. I was an adult. Mother was wounded. The front room was our living room; the room to the rear, my studio.

When moving day arrived, it was raining hard. The open truck arrived and the old man and his son proceeded to carry our things down the stairs and into the rain. Mother's precious Italian sofa was drenched.

Finally, we were moved and things settled down to normal. There was one thing we didn't count on. The Greek men's club on the floor below us played wonderful music, but it continued all night long. And the men played dominos loudly under my newly acquired bedroom. Mother seemed pleased when this forced me to move into the front room with her.

David Fish would show up now and then. Groups of tough-looking girls would climb the stairs to his floor. Often we heard things at night which we would have rather missed.

Mother and I lived in the loft for a year when we received a visit from the manager of the first floor Blarney Stone Bar.

"You'll have to move, Miss," he said in his Irish Brogue. "You'll havta get out. The buildin's condemned and gonna be torn down. How soon can ya get out?"

This was a nightmare.

"But we've just paid David Fish another year's rent," I said. "We have nowhere to go right now."

"David Fish," the Irishman bellowed. "He's gotta get out, too. We need the whole building."

"What about all that rent money I paid to David Fish?" I asked pleadingly.

"How much did you pay 'im?" the man asked.

"I paid $1,200 for the whole year ahead. Did you inform David Fish about this?" I asked.

"Sure I did. A month ago, I did. Well, he's gotta get out right away, but due to the circumstance, you payin' him up front, and all that money gone, take the time ya need ta get out. Don't take too long, mind ya, 'cause we need the buildin' now. Is it just you and your mother," he asked?

"Yes, it will be hard to find a space like this for what we can afford. We've only lived here for a year. We were evicted from a place over on Forty-sixth Street that is being torn down. I need this kind of space to work. I'm a dancer."

"I don't know about that, young lady. I'm just telling you, time is up here. Meanwhile, we won't charge you nothin.' Just make it fast, okay?"

I knew I could not go through another moving day with Mother. If I decided to live in a place of my own, I would have two rents to pay and she would be crushed. If I was to go and live with Tom, or possibly marry him, at least that would be good reason to leave Mother; a normal reason.

Perhaps living with Tom would be easier on her than if I moved to a separate home of my own. I did not feel I was cut out to be a wife. However, I could not stagnate the way I was, in this role of the good daughter. I picked up the phone and called Tom at his office and told him the news of the eviction.

"Do you still want to live with me, marry me?" I asked.

"Well sure, what a surprise. You're proposing to me this time," Tom laughed.

"I have to know if you still feel that way. I know we're still going together, but I wanted to be sure. I can't move into another loft with Mother. I can't live this way anymore.

Something about Tom's voice, his reaction seemed strange. He wasn't the same Tom I had met at the circus. Ever since he had started that job as art director at the big advertising agency BBD&O, he had become more of a man about town. He was more confident, but along with it, rather cold. I longed for warmth and open arms to welcome me to this new life.

"Sure, let's get married," Tom said, as casually as if he were inviting me to dinner. "When should we tie the knot?"

It was winter of 1961. I didn't like making such a serious decision so fast, but I found myself saying, "How about June? June 30."

"Sounds great to me," Tom said. "I'll make the arrangements. We'll get married at the Elephant Hotel in Somers, New York. For a honeymoon, we'll go to the Catskill Game Farm. In the meantime, we'd better look for a place to live. See you tomorrow night, sweetie," he said. "I have another call on another phone." And then he hung up.

I was alone again. Mother would be home soon. First I would have to tell her we were being evicted. That would be hard enough. How could I also tell her Tom and I were to be married? It would kill her. I couldn't do that. Not now anyway.

As soon as I heard her footsteps on the stairs, I ran to help her with the groceries.

"How was your day?" I asked.

"Oh, things are the same. The market is down and there is a wonderful buy, but I don't have the money."

I decided to wait to tell her after dinner. When we sat down to eat, I couldn't wait. I plunged right in with what I had to say.

"Mother," I began. "Tom and I are going to …"

Mother let out a sort of scream and I couldn't finish.

"Oh!" she exclaimed, "I knew it would come some day. I just knew it. It had to come some day and this, I guess, is it."

She got up from her chair and began pacing the floor, wringing her hands. She went into the kitchen and prepared to do the dishes though neither of us had finished our dinner. I felt a sense of relief. She knew, without me even finishing the sentence.

Life was quiet for about a week. Then one afternoon I heard Mother racing up the stairs, crying. She burst into the living room and said. "I met Miss Glasheim on the street. She told me that Milo told her you and Tom are going to be married. She actually congratulated me on your engagement."

"Mother," I said. "I told you the other night, during dinner we were going to be married. Didn't you hear me?"

"Oh, I heard it alright. But I thought you and Tom were just going to live together. I can't believe you're really going to marry him. What does he want to marry for anyway? He's had three children. He's had his physical pleasures."

Tom's parents were delighted. Everyone was happy except Mother.

Tom and I did not want anyone at our wedding. His parents wanted to attend, but I knew Mother would not come. If she did, it would be too painful for her. We thought it better all around to be alone, together.

That spring, we looked for a place to live. After much searching, we settled on a loft at Fortieth Street and Ninth Avenue. We had an Italian landlord named Luigi Demaio. His Ninth Avenue office had a marble floor and a large roll top desk. There, we made our rental arrangements at $125 a month.

While we were doing all this, I was looking for a place for Mother. I finally found a theatrical hotel called the Park Savoy on Fifty-eighth Street, a hotel where actors and other struggling artists lived. Mother would have a room with a shared bath and cooking privileges and it would be well-heated. There was a switchboard downstairs and it was in a good neighborhood with access to the art galleries.

The move to the Park Savoy took much longer than I had expected. Mother clung to the loft for dear life. She would not budge until long after Tom and I had married and moved into our own loft.

Our wedding plans were kept secret from Mana. I didn't want him to know until he had to.

Neither Tom nor I seemed excited about the big day. I felt as though I was about to act a scene in a play, in a role I was unsuited for.

The big day arrived and Tom came to pick me up, just as he had done on other Saturdays for dates. I didn't buy a wedding dress. Instead, I chose a red calico I already owned.

Mother seemed tense and looked as if she was trying to hold back tears. I was not happy, and Tom was trying to be patient with both of us.

As I turned to say goodbye to Mother, it was not hard to weep. I was leaving a life I had shared with her for so many years, a lifetime of companionship with someone who, through all eons, had emotionally supported the artistic life I cherished.

"We'll call you as soon as we're back. Goodbye, Mother," I called as I was forced down the stairs.

The drive up to Somers was a pretty one. The sun was shining and it was a warm, balmy day. We were to be married the next morning, which gave us time for sightseeing after we arrived at our destination.

I remember that evening, sitting quietly on a park bench in Kingston, not saying a word. I loved Tom, but I really didn't feel that I knew him. He was a man of many moods, and I hoped that after a while these would go away. Then he would be the Tom I had met at the circus. Now I wasn't so sure of him, because he seemed unsure.

The next morning, I put on my red calico dress and Tom put on a fine suit, and we went to the justice of the peace where, under the statue of Old Bet at the Elephant Hotel, we were married.

Marta hands a painting to Rosalind Russell as a publicity stunt during Wonderful Town.

Scene Nine

The Life of a Wife

We went home to our new loft and the spaciousness reminded me that I would be practicing there tomorrow for the first time. The traffic going over the bridge at the Port Authority Bus Terminal was deafening. This loft had previously been inhabited by a band of Gypsies. As a result, remnants of their tenure were evident. One such remnant was a wall telephone from which you could call out anywhere in the world, without inserting a nickel.

Married life did not require too big an adjustment. At first, Tom went to work the next morning and after I phoned Mother to see if she was alright, then I proceeded to practice in my spacious new studio. As soon as I became involved in my barre, I was comfortable. This was my world, and for a short time I forgot about the tension between Mother and Tom.

After a week had gone by, Tom announced he was leaving the ad agency and going into business with Max Kerr, a friend who was starting his own advertising agency. Tom would be art director, but he would be making less money. But he would also have no boss hanging over him. I was concerned since more would depend on me, but I said nothing.

One day, I received a phone call from Florence, Milo's wife.

"Milo must go to St. Vincent's Hospital He has a brain tumor," she said. "Eddie and I will take care of the gallery and we are hiring someone to sit at the desk while we are at the hospital."

I told Florence I would be right down. I brought two paintings with me. Ordinarily I brought in three or four.

"You're not knocking them out as fast as you used to," Eddie said.

"But my paintings are getting better," I said.

"My rent here is $1,000 a month," he said. "If you can't turn out enough work, I'll be forced to look for another artist."

I never knew until then, I was Milo's only source of income. For two years, no other artist's paintings had hung in his gallery. With Eddie taking over all of Milo's legal affairs, I wanted out of my contract. I didn't trust him.

I was concerned about who would sell my paintings. I had no connections and I never knew who bought my work. Milo gave me a few names because some were famous people who were taken by my work: Kaye Ballard, Georgie Tapps, Perry Como, and Shelley Berman. I had no addresses and once my paintings were sold, they were gone.

Milo's new desk clerk, Ezra Stone, phoned to inform me Milo had been cheating me. He said Milo had been taking seventy-five percent of the profit from my paintings.

"How long has this been going on?" I asked.

"About a month after you began showing here," he answered.

"Can you prove this," I asked, hoping he was just being vindictive to get back at Milo for something.

"I have in front of me all of the books, a list of the sales of your paintings, who bought them, and what was paid."

"Could you send me a list of these names?" I asked.

He promised to have the list in the mail within the week. I decided to concentrate on painting for an exhibit I would hold in our loft. I would write to everyone on the list and invite them to an exhibit of my new paintings at 400 West Fortieth Street. As I continued to make plans, my hurt began to lesson. When Tom came home, I told him about Milo.

"If what Ezra tells you is true, we have a good cause to break that contract," he said.

When I had signed the contract with Milo, I was so happy to have someone to sell my paintings I hadn't noticed the small print said I was committed for ten years. For two years I had worked hard to please Milo. Once, when I returned home from a tour, I saw he had cut one of my paintings in two. The top half, clotheslines hung between tenements, was sold to Georgie Tapps. The bottom, old store fronts, remained.

"Georgie didn't want the bottom, he just wanted the top," Milo told me. "He's a good customer, and the customer is always right."

Now that my anger was surfacing, with Ezra prodding my memory like a surgeon probing a brain, I was recalling the times when Milo would tell me to paint more orphans flying blue balloons, circus acrobats, or six more ballet dancers waiting back stage. These were popular and I couldn't turn out enough of them.

Tom found a lawyer through his father, an executive with the American Smelting & Refining Company. The lawyer got me out of the contract and, though I wasn't happy about it, insisted on suing Milo for money I was due.

Now that I was free of Milo, I planned my solo show. Flyers were sent to the people from Ezra's list. When the big event arrived, I was surrounded by twenty-five paintings.

Tom and I sat on the couch and my work stared back at us. This was the first time I had been forced to sell my art. I was certainly no saleswoman. I knew my art had to sell itself.

Georgie Tapps was the first of my admirers to arrive. The art patrons arrived with cash and the loft was soon bustling. I was making money hand over fist. Amid all the activity, I noticed Tom had disappeared. Why would he leave at a triumphant time? By five thirty that afternoon, my walls were bare. I was sold out, but Tom was gone and I felt so alone. On the corner table was a cash bag filled with $3,000.

I sat in the loft as the sun set and darkness came. I wondered when Tom would return. I knew Mother would have loved sharing this triumphant afternoon and I felt a twinge of sadness. I wished she could have been there.

It was late when Tom finally returned. The next day, not a word was said.

In the evenings I would paint. To the accompaniment of Hindemith and Bartok, my imagination soared. Mother was no longer sitting in the corner of my eye sharing the light. I was free.

During these evenings of self discovery, I was unaware of Tom at the other end of the loft pounding out designs on a piece of leather from a Tandy carving kit. Sometimes he would read; other times he would lie in bed listening to Jean Shepherd. By the time I fell into bed, it was usually around three, and Tom was fast asleep.

Whenever I painted in the evening or rehearsed in the morning, I forgot I was married. I really didn't know what was expected of a wife and I didn't know what was expected of a husband either. I thought as long as we loved each other and shared certain hours of the day together, the rest of the day we could claim as our own.

Weekends were spent at the Metropolitan Museum or going out to Madison, New Jersey, to visit Tom's parents. The visit to Madison soon became a Sunday routine. Tom's brother Doug, an excellent musician, accompanied several well-known singers. When I met him, he was working with Judith Raskin.

Tom's Aunt Wyn, just a few years older than he was, had been in and out of several mental institutions and even had shock treatments. I enjoyed talking to her. She was absorbed in the study of religion. At that time she was into Emanuel Swedenborg. Wyn had two children and a devoted husband. When we all got together for Thanksgiving and Christmas, it made me feel I finally had a family.

During the week, Mother would come and watch rehearsals. I hadn't encouraged her to do so, but she had pleaded. She missed sharing my creative life.

On Sunday evenings, Tom and I visited her with a copy of the *New York Times*. She always had cake and coffee ready for us. It was a nice gesture except for the way she arranged the chairs; two at the coffee table and a third way over at the window looking out on the traffic on Eighth Avenue.

"That chair over there is for Tom," Mother would say. "He can sit there until we are finished with our visit, dear."

Tom lifted his chair and brought it to the coffee table. No one said a word. Mother had her stage set for an evening with just me, and Tom would religiously reset the stage to include him.

One Sunday, we arrived at Mother's loft and found it locked. The Greek club owner told us Mother had been taken by police to Bellevue Hospital.

"Bellevue?" I thought, "The mental hospital? oh my God!"

Tom and I rushed to the Sixteenth Precinct and asked about Mother. The officer on duty informed me Mother had fallen in the street and broken her arm.

"She told us she didn't have nobody. You say you're her daughter?"

"Yes," I said. "I'm her daughter."

"That does it," said Tom. "By saying she has no one, she hopes to get out of a hospital bill. I'm fed up with her. She can wait until morning."

I was surprised I did not feel a need to rush to Mother's side. She was safe in Bellevue. I was relieved that she wasn't there for some mental ailment.

The next morning, we went to see Mother. As soon as we entered her ward, we saw her way down at the end in the last bed in the row. As soon as we stepped in, Mother spotted us and started waving the cast on her left hand high it the air.

"Oh, Marta," Mother wailed. "Please call Joe and have him sell Preferred Data and buy Blessings right away. It's terrible being in here on a Monday."

"Mother," I said. "How can you think of buying and selling stocks when you are in the hospital?"

"I didn't mean to hurt myself this badly," she said. "All I wanted was to hurt myself enough so that perhaps you would stay with me for one night. Oh my dearest, I miss you so. You would have stayed wouldn't you?"

"No," I answered emphatically.

I couldn't believe Mother could be so desperate for my company, that she would deliberately injure herself! Living apart from Mother gave me the confidence to be more independent. But the more independent I got, the more she appeared to be a lost soul. Mornings were spent practicing and rehearsing. Although Mother came to watch these sessions, she left in the afternoon and I had time to myself. Tom didn't get home until about six.

We would then go over to Forty-second Street, to an Italian restaurant or to an Argentinean restaurant which served great steaks, yellow saffron rice, and huge salads, all for one dollar and ninety-five cents. I didn't cook yet. I really didn't know how. Besides, we were too busy exploring the city to eat at home.

Sometimes we would go to a triple feature foreign movie on Rotten Row for sixty five cents. We enjoyed New York together and although I would get twinges of guilt about Mother being alone, I knew my life had taken the right direction.

Phil Tippin did manage to book us into some woman's clubs in and around the New York area. He also consented to let us do some children's concerts, under Briggs Management. We did mostly schools, many out on Long Island and in Brooklyn.

At one that we did in Harlem, there were heavy plastic curtains that had to be padlocked after the performance. The principal had to come up on stage and hand me my fifty dollars in cash accompanied by a security guard. There were fluorescent lights on during the entire performance. Many of these auditoriums provided no illusion whatsoever, but we did our performances as well as we could.

Early in 1963, I made arrangements to have a one-woman show of my paintings at the Waverly Gallery, in Greenwich Village, right off of Washington Square. A woman named Mildred Milch managed the gallery.

My show was scheduled for November 23, 1963. The day before the opening night, President Kennedy was assassinated! I will never forget that dreadful night! No one was on the streets. Tom and I walked around Waverly Place and looked in at the lighted gallery, with my paintings locked up inside. There they were, waiting for the crowds that never came.

My paintings hung there for two weeks, but the grand opening for my art never materialized. I sold some of my work, but no one has matched Milo's salesmanship.

After my show at the Waverly, I just let my work gradually disappear, and I never took any more back. By the time December rolled around, I was busy getting my Turkish fairy tale ready for three children's concerts at Town Hall in New York. That helped soothe the disappointment.

During the time I was preparing for the three performances at Town Hall, I received a phone call from Mana.

"Why didn't you let me know about your marriage," he demanded.

I knew this moment would eventually come, but did not prepare myself for it. "Well," I answered, "The occasion never arrived for me to tell you, and besides, I knew how overjoyed you would be that I had finally left Mother, so I put it off for as long as I could."

"I phoned the other day, to invite you and your mother for dinner, and that's when she told me." Mana said, "I tried to find out from your mother who you had married, and all she said was, 'Oh, his name is William, or something.' She didn't seem to remember, or else she was pretending to not remember."

I was quite annoyed at Mother for not telling Mana who my husband was. She was just deliberately being uncooperative.

"His name is Tom Williams, and we had been going together for three years," I said.

This made Mana even more upset. "Why did you wait three years to tell me?" he asked desperately.

"I told you the reason. You always wanted me to find someone who would eventually take me away from Mother. I have simply saved Mother three years of extra pain by waiting. My getting married hurt her."

Tom was present during my conversation with Mana. He was edgy, and he made me nervous.

"May I come up to see you," asked Mana? "I'm right off Times Square now."

"Yes," I answered meekly. "If you come up now, you will meet Tom. He is here, right now."

"Good," answered Mana. "I'll be up in ten minutes."

I turned to face Tom.

"Well," he said, "I'm finally going to meet your father. It's about time."

It wasn't ten minutes before we could hear foot steps on the concrete stairwell leading up to our loft. My heart was pounding. I was dreading this moment. There stood Mana, in his overcoat, holding his hat with his left hand, reaching out with his right to shake Tom's.

"Come right on in," said Tom.

After the usual introductions, shaking of hands, and removal of Mana's overcoat, we all sat down.

"You know," Mana said, "I asked your mother if she thought it would be nice if we all went out to dinner soon, and I could give you both a wedding present of $500. I was so happy for you, and wanted to give you a good send-off financially, to show you my best wishes for a happy future. Your mother said, 'No, I wouldn't give them any money. That marriage won't last, and it would just be wasted.'"

I was shocked at mother's selfishness. Mana gave us the money anyway, even though I was reluctant to accept it.

Tom invited Mana to bring his wife to the loft for reconciliation with me. I was not happy about this. But Mana and Tom were winning now, and this reunion with the second Helen Beckett was now going to take place. The date was set, Mana and Tom shook hands over the deal, and I was in the middle, feeling wiped out!

My personal life was simply out of my control. Tom and Mana were arranging all kinds of family gatherings, without Mother, of course. Yes, there were a few times Mana took the four of us out to dinner which were tense occasions, but several visits up at our loft, both with and without the nice lady, were on the agenda.

It was at this time that the big Irishman from the Blarney Stone bar threatened Mother with eviction if she didn't get out in a month. As it was, she stayed there much longer than I had ever expected. She finally agreed to move to the Park Savoy. Now I would have to pay sixty-five dollars a month, and give her money for food.

The dreaded date for the reconciliation with the nice lady finally came. Mana brought her up to our home for coffee and cake. She had white hair, pulled back in a bun. Glasses were prominently fixed on her nose which kept her eyes hidden. All I could see where the reflections of Tom and myself in the panes. She was not tall; in fact, she was several inches shorter than I. Her coat which she had buttoned up against the cold was plain and shapeless. She certainly did not look like the glamorous professional woman Mother described. She looked like a nice homebody who bakes pies.

"Come right on in," said Tom with forced enthusiasm.

"This is my wife, Helen," Mana said. "Her nickname is Matie, because she is my mate you know." He laughed nervously.

Everyone went over to the couch, and I sat on a chair facing them. There was some small talk at first, and after I had gotten some cake and coffee served, the small talk turned into a heated conversation. Both Mana and Matie started talking at once. If one didn't start elaborating upon all the terrible things Mother did, then the other one would.

"Your mother wouldn't sleep with your father," Matie said. "Your father was hungry for love."

"It's true," Mana added. "The only time she would sleep with me was when you were conceived. I waited five years to have a family. You were supposed to have been born five years earlier."

"If I had been born five years earlier, I wouldn't be me," I retorted.

"Your mother wouldn't allow me to visit you when I went to Rose Valley to see you. I gave her money for your support and she still kept you away from me," Mana said.

"Mother told me that you gave her nothing for my support," I said, not knowing who to believe any more.

"I know where that money could have gone," Tom said.

"Where?" Mana asked.

"Helen was playing the stock market, dealing in cats and dogs from the time Marta was six years old. That's where the money went."

"Tom!" I screamed. "How could you betray me and my mother like this? I promised my mother when I was little I would never reveal what she was doing in the market. I regret that day you found out with all my heart."

"Why didn't you tell me about this?" Mana asked. "How could you keep a thing like this from me, your father? I could have had her stopped immediately, and I could have gotten custody of you from the beginning."

"Because I loved my mother," I answered. "I was closer to her than anyone else in the whole world. For the first five years of my life, I saw my mother every day, every night she would put me to bed. I never saw you except when you would take us to a concert, or Coney Island. After Mother and I left New York and went to Harrisburg, she had a hard time. The Depression was on, there were no jobs, and people stopped buying her furniture. Suddenly a door opened to her, she was accepted inside. It was the boardroom. There was hope. She kept it a secret because she didn't want you to take it away from her. It was all she had. I may have not turned out the way you wanted me to, but if I had been put in your custody, I wouldn't have been allowed to be what I am today."

I rose from my chair, disgusted with this reunion. I stood up and faced them all, sitting on the couch before me.

"Whatever you have to say about my mother that happened before I was born, is none of my business. Whatever happened afterward is only my business if it concerns me. What about the instances you had threatened to kidnap me? You hardly knew me. You still don't know me."

"Well," Matie finally spoke up. "Which boardroom does your mother go to?"

"She goes to the one in the Hotel Astor," said Tom bitterly.

"I think I'll just run up there tomorrow," the nice lady said. "I think we, too, should have a reunion."

"Please," I said. "Don't go in there; my mother won't be able to handle that."

Two days later, Mother came up to the loft to tell me about her encounter with Matie.

"I was sitting in the Astor boardroom, the front row, so I could watch the tape," she said. "Then this strange woman came down and sat beside me, as if she deliberately planned to say something to me. She turned to face me and said, 'The stock market has much excitement, doesn't it?' I knew that voice from the past. I looked at her, she didn't look like the other Helen, but I knew it was from her voice. How did she find me? Who informed her I was here?"

The pain I now felt for Mother was overwhelming. As she left to head back to the boardroom, I watched her walk toward Times Square. She walked like a zombie, as if her body was drawn to the boardroom, like a magnet.

A few days later, Mana came again to visit, and I told him it was too late to try and stop Mother now. He had calmed down. The visit was short, and soon Mana made ready to leave. I could hear Mana and Tom talking down on the sidewalk underneath the window.

"I don't know why in the hell I ever married Martha's mother," Mana said.

"Well, we all make mistakes in our youth," Tom said.

I was very hurt to hear Mana make this remark. He certainly must have loved my mother once. I wouldn't be here if he hadn't married my mother. Perhaps he was even sorry I was born.

Mana had had many affairs during the first five years of his marriage to Mother. The nice lady was the one who got him. Mana admitted to Tom that he didn't know how to say "no."

"I could have taught you how to say no," Tom said proudly. "I've had a lot of practice in that."

All I could do for the next few days was to practice, paint, and go about my chores as a routine. My heart was with my mother now and living with Tom was a great strain.

On the bright side, I found a new art gallery to show my work. It was the Park South Gallery in Carnegie Hall owned by Bert and Laura Gold. It was small, but had good exposure, as its two large windows faced right on Seventh Avenue. A few steps north was Fifty-seventh Street, the prestigious neighborhood of the classical music, art, and dance world. Other artists showed there as well, but even if one painting of mine hung, that would be good, because influential people passed by every day on their way to rehearsal, or dance class.

We often had dinner with the Golds. Laura was not too keen on our plans to go on another tour.

"How much longer can ya keep doing this?" she would ask. As far as I was concerned, I was going to keep doing it until I dropped.

"The older an artist is, the higher his prices," she would say.

"But I am a dancer, and I'm going to stay as young as I possibly can," I would retort.

Other than that, we got along well, and talk of a one-woman show of my work for the fall of 1965 was encouraging me to work at my painting with as much enthusiasm as I did my dancing.

One day, I received a phone call from the Social Security Office concerning an application from Mother to get Social Security for having been a professional costume seamstress. As far as I ever knew, Mother had only sewn costumes for my nightclub act, and years ago, for Hedgerow Theatre. For these, she never received wages of any sort; therefore, there would be no Social Security payments. I was asked to come up to the Social Security office to give some facts in person, and to bring my mother.

At my regular rehearsal time next day, when Mother came to watch as usual, I confronted her about her request.

"Well," she said, "I certainly should get something. After all, I worked as your mother for thirty some years, and besides, I am a human being. I need food and clothes just like anyone else."

When we went to the Social Security office, the woman in charge asked to speak to me alone.

"Oh," Mother almost cried. "Marta might need me to explain a few things."

"I still need to talk to your daughter alone, Mrs. Beckett." The woman behind the desk looked sternly at Mother.

The clerk asked me few questions pertaining to Mother's profession as a costume seamstress, and I told the truth.

"Are you aware that your mother is holding a $17,000 loss in the stock market the past year?" The clerk said this, looking up from her papers at me.

"What?" I said in alarm. "She what? Seventeen thousand dollars you say, and I have been struggling to pay her rent and buy her groceries all these years?"

"We have had many cases like this," the clerk continued. "Your mother is not the first, nor will she be the last. Needless to say, your mother does not qualify for benefits. I'm sure that you understand."

"Yes, I understand perfectly," I said.

Once we were in my loft, I started on a discourse I thought I would never be able to initiate.

"Mother," I said, "From now on, you will be on your own. I cannot afford to support your addiction any longer. You are going to have to sell some of your stocks to pay your rent, to buy your food. You have been taking me down the hole with your losses for too long. Do you understand?"

"What do you mean? I haven't taken you down any hole!" Mother was desperate now.

"Where did you get the money to invest in your precious cats and dogs? Where?" I asked.

"Why, some of it was your money, yes, but then the money I made out of it was mine, dear. I have been working all these years for our old age. I've been thinking about us," Mother answered.

"The $17,000 loss you had for the past two years was my money, all lost!" I said at the top of my voice. "Mother, you will have your cats and dogs pay for themselves at last. I have never seen you sell a thing from your investments to pay the rent."

"I can't sell stocks now, they're still working for us. They will, be going up again in no time now!"

"If you can't sell any of your stocks, then sell the two paintings I gave you, *Ghost Village*, and *The Children with the Blue Balloons*. Take them up to the gallery in Carnegie Hall and perhaps their sale will be able to pay your rent."

"What will I do after that?" Mother asked.

"That will be your problem," I answered.

The next day, I received a phone call from Laura Gold. She told me Mother had been in that morning with the two paintings under her arms, for sale.

Laura had put the painting of *The Children with the Blue Balloons* in the window right away. One half hour later Mary Tyler Moore passed by the window and bought the painting. I was hurt that Mother preferred to sell the painting I gave her instead of a stock.

All these years I thought that Mother had the highest regard for my art. But in a way, I was relieved to find that I was not my Mother's breath of life after all. Now I was free at last.

Phil Tippin booked a concert for us in a South Carolina. I considered it a warm-up to the tour ahead. The program was to consist of four short dances and mimes first, after which *The Mirror, The Carpet, and the Lemon* would follow intermission.

My performance was held in the high school at the edge of town. There was to be a reception afterwards held in a Southern mansion. The hostess and her husband were chairs for the Civic Music Association. They and the audience attending my performance were Southern aristocrats.

This whole evening was topped off by a remark made by our hostess as she looked up at Tom from her cup of coffee.

"Mr. Williams," she said. "I don't know why you don't get some nice colored man to pick up Ms. Becket's props and move the sets instead of yourself. Why, I declare, that does seem a bit degrading." Her husband nodded in agreement. Tom's face turned red, and he looked injured by the remark, but said nothing.

The next morning, while I was doing my stretches in the hotel room, Tom went out and purchased a gun. He told me it was to protect him from his first wife. He had the notion she was after him.

I didn't like guns. I never wanted one in my home. Now there was a gun under my husband's pillow, and I was frightened.

The morning after we had returned from South Carolina, Tom went to register his gun. As the sun set and the loft became cold, I became concerned. At about eight thirty p.m. the phone rang.

"I wanna speak ta Mrs. Tom Williams," a man's voice said in a gruff tone.

"This is Mrs. Williams," I answered.

"Your husband asked me ta call you and tell you he'll be home sometime tamorrow, an not ta worry," the gruff voice said.

"Where is Tom?" I asked desperately.

"Right now he's in jail. He was found having a gun without going through the proper procedure. Right now he's going through some litigation, and has a lawyer who hopefully will get him out by ta morrow."

"Who's his lawyer?" I asked.

"A John De Maio I believe," answered the gruff voice I later learned belonged to a cop.

"Please, please ask him to call me will you?" I asked pleadingly.

"Yea, yea sure, I'll tell him. Just don't worry." The officer hung up.

I couldn't paint; I certainly didn't feel like working on a dance number. I couldn't do anything. Suddenly, I had the desire to call Agnes McTernan, my loyal friend and editor of *Program Magazine*. She always worked late, and I knew I could get her ear any time of day or night.

"Agnes," I said almost crying, "Agnes, Tom is in jail."

"In jail?" Agnes echoed back.

"Yes, in jail. He bought a gun and was put in jail for being in possession of it before going through the proper paper work. I'm waiting to hear from his lawyer, and I'm so alone here. I just had to call you."

"Do you want me to come over and keep you company?" she asked.

I said yes. She came and waited with me. She was there when the lawyer called to assure me Tom would be out by morning.

"He'll probably never do anything like this again," Agnes said. "He's learned his lesson. I'm sure that once is enough."

As she made ready to leave, I thanked her for coming over, and she assured me that things would be alright now.

"Let me know more after Tom gets home tomorrow, will you?" she asked.

With the spring tour coming up soon, and Christmas and New Years holidays upon us, the gun incident soon became a thing of the past.

Christmas was especially difficult. I felt some guilt, thinking of Mother alone. As for myself, I not only had Tom, but a warm Christmas and Thanksgiving spent at his parent's home.

On the day before Christmas, while Mother was occupied in her boardroom, I decorated a small Christmas tree for her with all the ornaments we had had through the years.

Mother came home to her little room at the Park Savoy and I took her to Christmas Eve dinner, after which we exchanged gifts. She knew then, that I would leave, and have a second Christmas with Tom.

Just before I made preparations to leave, Mother presented me with a present for Tom. I was delighted and felt perhaps there might be a sign of hope in her attitude toward him.

Back at the loft, Tom had waited for me and was a little impatient. Our Christmas tree we decorated together was up. Millions of little pink lights scattered over it, with tinsel and a few ornaments.

After a bit of small talk, a cup of tea, and exchanging of presents, I handed Tom the box Mother had given me for him.

"I have no idea what it is," I said.

Tom opened the box and inside found a book titled *The Devil and All His Works*.

He threw the book down on the table and Christmas was over.

URLY URLY
SALON
ENTER
DUST DEVIL
GULCH-MINING CO
WHEN YOURE UND
ADDEUS THUNDER
INSHOP

SCENE TEN

Touring the West with Tom

For the spring tour of 1964, we bought an Econoline Van and equipped it for carrying everything. Mother did not come to see us off.

She became more and more engrossed in her boardroom activities, and I in my own life. Tom and I had friends to keep us company. We met Dorothy Lake and Mary Ruder through Columbia Artists Management. They helped with our mailing lists.

Dorothy and Mary would come to our loft for spaghetti dinner, after which I would give them a ballet class.

These ballet classes for misfits did not amount to anything more than just a lot of fun. After the class, we would indulge in dessert.

We finally embarked on our tour in the new van. Tom had printed on the side of the van, "Marta Becket, Dance Mime."

By nightfall, we reached Pittsburgh and spent the night in a Howard Johnson's in Ohio. At breakfast, in Howard Johnson's restaurant, I admired a stuffed purple hippo in the gift shop. After we were seated at our table, Tom got up and disappeared for a moment. Soon he returned with the purple hippo under his arm.

"Here," Tom said, "is your hippo. I think we should name him Howard, don't you?"

"Oh yes, he's great. Thank you, Tom."

I immediately loved Howard, and so did Tom. Howard became real to us; we would speak through him to each other as if Howard was doing the talking. I used a funny voice, and would say things that I would never say as myself.

Tom and I made many friends during this tour. In Livingston, Montana, we were house guests at the home of a ranching family who were members of the Community Concert Association. They had many head of cattle, and raised racing horses.

In Del Rio Texas, the chairman of the Civic Music Association was Reverend Wally Wallace, who took a great shine to our stuffed Hippo. I guess it was because Wally was very large himself, and felt a kinship to Howard. We also made friends with the concert chairman at Cañon City, Colorado. We returned to these towns for second appearances on later tours, and kept corresponding through the years, even after the concert associations had folded.

In Greeley, Colorado, I performed in a gymnasium which had a curtain stretched behind my performing area as a background. I felt, however, I could not do this wonderful space justice due to my difficulty in breathing from the altitude and the stench in the air from the stockyards.

To top it off, Mana's half brother Guy was at my performance and went around to everyone boasting he was my uncle. I was more annoyed when he told everyone what year I was born. To a dancer, this is like informing the world how many years you have left.

After Colorado, we crossed the Rockies. A new kind of sunshine seemed to prevail. Back East, the sun seemed old, used, tired. Out West, it was rejuvenated. Then heading farther westward to Globe, Arizona, we went through miles of Indian country. When we stopped in Gallup, New Mexico, we visited a Zuni village, and through some friends we made there, managed to witness Hopi tribal dances. When we reached Window Rock, Arizona, we were fascinated by the round meeting house. Bleachers surrounded the stage in a complete circle.

We didn't have to be in Globe until the following week, so Tom and I went to the chief in charge and offered a free performance of my *Turkish Fairytale* to the local Navajo children. The afternoon of the show, the children filled over half the building. Partway through the music, the children began to hum along as if they knew the melodies. This Navajo audience actually became participants in the tale as I danced out the characters. I could see the children swaying right and left throughout the performance.

Their teacher, the chief, and others who ran the tribal museum and gift shop invited, us in to the shop to pick out any jewelry we might want as a gift for the performance. Faculty from the tribal office said my music was not unlike much of their native music. I couldn't help but believe there could be a relationship between the Middle Eastern cultures and the American Indians.

I selected a bracelet and a necklace and Tom picked out a watch. At the tribal office, we were invited to feast on Indian bread and hot coffee. The bread was delicious and exotic.

We left Window Rock in the morning and traveled through more Indian country occasionally passing a herd of sheep tended by a Navajo. The peaceful life spread itself out before us and haunted me.

I knew there was another life to be had in the West. It would be some time before we returned to New York, but the thought occasionally gave me a jolt.

After Globe, Arizona, we traveled farther west, heading up through Utah for an engagement in Pocatello, Idaho, and a town called Moscow, at the University of Idaho.

As we passed through Brigham City, Utah, I noticed a large structure that looked like a theater.

"Let's stop here and see if they would like a free performance," I said. Tom agreed, and as we drove up to the gate, which was open, we read a sign which said, "Brigham City Indian School."

The principal responded warmly to my brochures and said. "We would be delighted, but there is only one problem. Our theatre seats only 800 and our school children average about 2,400."

"We'll give three performances," I said, overjoyed at the prospect.

The first half of my performance began with some classical pieces which were en pointe. The children made sounds as if they were frightened when I rose on toe. When I performed turns, they nearly screamed. They had never seen dancing like this, nor had they heard classical music.

During the break between shows, the children watched a movie with cowboys and Indians. We were amazed to hear the children boo the Indians and cheer the cowboys. As we snacked on some sandwiches and coffee, we could hear these reactions backstage.

The principal, a lovely Indian lady named Wilma, gave us some jewelry made by the older children. We left Brigham City, Utah with a warm feeling of friendship.

We were now on our way to California where quite a number of college dates waited for us. First we drove through Nevada. The desert terrain around Hoover Dam looked like the end of the world.

Vegas was a cultural desert punctuated by gaudy electric signs. It was exhausting just to walk through these casinos. I was impressed how much the Keno alcove resembled Mother's boardroom. After Las Vegas, we headed back into the desert, a retreat from the noise and bustle of jackpots.

The desert was an oven. It had a dryness that penetrates your very being. After being baked by the drive down these desert roads, it was a relief to dip into one of those motel pools at the end of the day.

Easter week was coming up, and as there are no college dates during that time, Tom had the idea to drive through Death Valley on our way to the coast. It was drizzling.

When we finally entered California, there was one small town which had a few one story buildings, but mostly trailers with picnic benches. Then there was a long winding drive through beautiful desert, with a faint tinge of golden sunset trying to come through the drizzle. We approached another small town, and to enter it, there was a sharp curve. An old gas station loomed into view, with pillars and a deep porte cochere.

"We need to get gas," Tom said. It was so dark, I could hardly see. Two donkeys were in a pen along side the filling station. A scruffy looking man filled our gas tank while Tom made small talk with him. I turned to look around, and what I saw was a long colonnade on the other side of a small park of trees and sage brush. There were a few people coming out of what appeared to be a hotel. The whole structure stretched around the entire park, like an enormous "L." This whole place was a one story adobe town, under one roof. Through the evening drizzle, it appeared like a mirage from out of the past. I immediately felt a great pull to the place.

"I want to come back here someday and stay for a long time," I said.

The little town made such an impression on me, but it was nearly forgotten by the time we got to the coast. We continued the tour, filling dates in San Diego and the Los Angeles area. Then we went on to Oregon and the state of Washington.

We managed quite a bit of sightseeing during waits between performances. In Tijuana, with only five dollars, I returned with embroidered lace blouses, a black lace dress, and beautiful pottery. However, using this Mexican pottery for anything more than decorative purposes I found was a mistake. The glaze came off in chips.

Returning to New York after the tour was a letdown. It always was. But somehow, following each season it seemed more so. During the summer of 1965, I began work on a new number. I had done the *Turkish Fairytale* to death, and needed something fresh for next season.

I decided on a full length work in which I would portray five characters from Vaudeville days auditioning for an agent who dreams he will bring back Vaudeville.

Tom had a collection of records from the 1920s and 1930s which were given to him by a neighbor. I selected five of them for the routines, and used dance school recordings for background, as if the rehearsal hall were surrounded by other practice studios, full of people rehearsing for their big dream.

I recorded everything straight from a microphone, to give it that tinny sound of old records on a gramophone. I found out by doing this, the street noises from Ninth Avenue came in on it, which made the tape even more realistic.

This was the very first large number I had attempted to create since I had married. Usually, Tom was at his print shop making signs, and by the time evening came, my shorter works had been already created and rehearsed by then. However, the vaudeville piece took all my time. Sometimes, when I was working on the tape for the background music, Tom would walk in after work and appear to be frustrated over the fact I was still working, and showed no signs of stopping. He would sometimes throw something against the wall and walk out.

I don't really think that these unpleasant interruptions were harmful to the finished work, but they certainly dampened my spirit. I soon found out it was better to work when Tom wasn't around. As I considered this, an idea popped into my mind. I will name it *Comeback Vaudeville, or Don't Call Us, We'll Call You.*

Now that *Comeback Vaudeville* was sketched out in my mind, I began working on the choreography. Mother came religiously every day to watch. She seemed enthusiastic over the project, and now, come hell or high water, it was time to invite Tom to a rehearsal. He hadn't seemed to show much interest in this new number. However, if *Comeback Vaudeville* was to be in the repertoire next season, he would have to see it. So I took the plunge and invited him.

The whole half hour work was performed in basic black leotard and tights to keep the costume changes as simple as possible. I went through all the characters until I got to Ted Benny, last of the Straw Hat Five. The only costume change I had thought necessary for him was the jacket, straw hat, and a clip mustache.

"Ted will have to be fired," Tom called out.

"I can't fire Ted Benny," I cried from behind the back drop. "He's my favorite character."

"The black tights look lousy," Tom called out again. "If you can't do something about covering your legs in a pair of trousers, it won't look right. You look like a girl doing a tap dance. It's all wrong."

"Tom," I called out to him, "You didn't even stay to see the end. If I do something about the trousers tomorrow, will you please sit and watch it again, please?"

I got a pair of men's trousers altered to fit me. No matter how long it would take, I would never fire Ted Benny.

That night when Tom came home, I practically ordered him to sit in the chair and see the whole number through with Ted Benny now in trousers. Tom admitted this was my best and most meaningful work yet. I felt triumphant. I saved Ted Benny!

Though I was putting together a new dance, I didn't give up painting. My first one-woman show was dismal when the opening was canceled due to the Kennedy assassination. I decided to try again when Park South Gallery in Carnegie Hall offered to give me a one-woman show. The exhibit was to be on November 10. I worked hard all that summer into fall on my art show. It was a small gallery, so I had to limit myself to four large paintings, and a dozen or so smaller ones.

While we were putting the final touches on the exhibit, the lights suddenly began to flicker and then go out. In a moment, the lights and signs outside went out. Suddenly New York was in total darkness. As the hour approached for my grand opening, there was no sign of any light returning. New York was bathed in solitary moonlight in what turned out to be the famous New York Blackout of 1965.

Disappointments came in dance as well. While I was rehearsing, I felt a terrible pang in the calf of my left leg. I pressed on, and it felt worse. I tried rubbing it, stood on it and began again, only to fall to the floor crying. I crawled to the telephone and called a Dr. Fleischer who treated dance injuries. He had me hail a taxi and visit his office. While I waited in his office, I listened to a desperate conversation he was having with a young dancer who was being told to take a break from dancing.

"Dancing is my life, my livelihood. I have to be able to dance in order to demonstrate to my students. I teach, and I cannot teach them sitting in a chair beating a stick," the patient said almost crying.

"If you don't lay off now, you will never dance," Dr. Fleischer said in a low but determined voice.

"I'm getting disgusted with dancers," he said when I came in. "All of you think this body is a machine you can repair by a quick visit to Mr. Fixit. A doctor is not Mr. Fixit. We deal with the human body which is a living mechanism subject to wear and tear, breakdown and buildup, if you give it a chance. None of you want to give it a chance."

"I know what you did. You pulled the plantarus muscle. That can be very painful, and you will have to stay off of it."

"But I'll get out of practice," I said earnestly. "I must work out every day."

He examined my leg. "Not only have you pulled the plantarus muscle, I see you have the beginning of Baker's cyst behind the knees. Do you do a lot of squatting? Deep knee bends?" he asked.

"Yes," I answered, "my *Turkish Fairytale* has many deep squats and knee bends."

"Come to me for diathermy treatments twice a week, that will help to partially dry the cyst; not completely, but a little. You'll have to give up doing your *Turkish Fairytale* if you want to continue dancing."

"I can't," I said again.

"Apply ice on your calf muscle, and then warmth with liniment, and then cover with a plastic wrap. If you do as I say, your calf muscle will heal in two to three weeks."

"What about the cyst," I asked. "Will it go away eventually?"

"You will always have the cyst," the doctor answered. "By the way, how old are you now Marta. I think I have a faint idea."

I was really 40, but that sounded so terrible to me, so I told him I was 39.

"Don't you think it's time to slow down?" he asked.

"I worked hard and waited too long to dance the way I really wanted to dance," I continued. "I will continue to dance one way or the other. My life is not yet over and because my life is dancing, I intend on living the rest of it doing just that."

I left Dr. Fleischer's office, and never returned. I continued to perform my *Turkish Fairytale* for a number of years after that. However, as time went on, even though I was able to keep the cysts under control, other ideas came into my head which eventually replaced it.

During the fall of 1966 we were preparing to go on another tour. It was to start right after the New Year, with a mix of concerts for universities, small colleges, and quite a few organized audience associations. The mileage jumps were large, and there were quite a few long waits between concert dates.

Our friend Dorothy Lake expressed the desire to give us a party before leaving New York for the tour.

"I have a friend, Rommey who is psychic, she's a musician, and has many cats. Lets all go to her place and have our fortunes told, have some tea, and just get together before you go away," she said.

Tom and I made plans to go with Dorothy to see her friend Rommey. She was beautiful and pale with pitch black hair that hung closely to her neck and curled upward at the ends. She wore a long black dress, and certainly looked the part of one who is psychic. We settled on her sofa while she held our rings and watches, and went into a semi trance.

The psychic took my ring, and didn't say very much. However, when she held my watch, she began.

"You will be leaving New York in a very short time," she said. "You will be moving to a very rural place, far away from here. I see a large letter 'A'," she said. "You will be doing the most satisfying work of your life in this place. I see a cow there and a pig."

Then Rommey stopped and just rested, still holding my watch.

Tom was negotiating for a tour in Australia and Argentina, both starting with the letter "A." However, both were for only three weeks. I could not possibly do the most satisfying work of my life in a matter of three weeks.

When I was in *A Tree Grows in Brooklyn*, I went with Oleg and some other dancers to the gypsy tea room. The tea leaf reader read our fortune from tea leaves and cards. She told me that I would spend ten years of my life in the chorus, and then break out into solo performances, starting with a dance with particular Oriental undertones. I would tour through many cities, perform in colleges, and later meet my future husband whose name would be "Tom Wi...," and she could go no further. She had said that there was a confusion here; two "Tom Wi...," as if she saw double.

To this day, I remember her prediction. So much of it was true. And yet, no one else's was true. She told Oleg he would be a marine.

Tom and I had often talked about the practicality of owning some kind of motor home for touring so that living expenses on the road could be cut to a minimum. Tom happened to mention this in front of Mana once and Mana offered to buy us a trailer.

I broke down and agreed to let him, and Tom and I went trailer hunting.

We found one we liked in New Jersey; a Covered Wagon, which seemed a most appropriate name for a vehicle that would take us out West.

Once it was bought, we had to decide where we should park it. Tom's parents did not take it lightly that we suggest parking it in the front yard of their Madison, New Jersey home. His mother felt strongly that trailers parked in front yards ruined the elegant appeal of upscale real estate. Mana came to the rescue when he and his wife offered to let us park the trailer at their New Jersey farm. As far as Mother knew, Tom had bought the trailer, and nothing more was ever said about the transaction.

We set out on a cold and snowy morning, picked up the trailer, and headed north for engagements in Maine and New Hampshire. The freezing cold caused havoc in the plumbing of our trailer, making us buy sea salt to throw down the drain.

At about four in the morning, there would be an enormous loud "ka-chug," which meant the sea salt did its work. We would then move silently and discreetly away from the scene.

After a performance at a Catholic college, the nuns were curious about our trailer, so we invited them in. We sat up until three the next morning conversing over wine.

After the few performances in the Northeast, we headed westward to Ohio, and then to Texas where we had a return visit to Del Rio. On our long layovers, Tom would visit a local college or university, and try and sell my program for the following season. I would do what exercises I could in the small trailer space, wash up, and ready myself for Tom's return.

We even brought along some of my paintings to show in the front lobby of the auditoriums where I danced.

The trailer was our permanent home on wheels throughout the tour. Howard, our hippo sat between us in the van. He amused many of the people we met on the tour.

Tom would often return from one of his promotional visits to a college, dejected. It was getting harder and harder to sell a soloist. The colleges and universities were booking big rock bands and large groups.

Still we felt better out West. It was the clear, cold air and brilliant, blue sky. As long as we were on tour, giving performances, we were fulfilling our mission.

ACT FOUR:
My Ship Comes In
In the Desert

SCENE ONE

Discovering The Opera House

om managed to book about three concerts for the following season but they were so far apart in time and miles that it seemed almost an impossible challenge to acquire pick-up dates in between.

With a few dates in Arizona, and then to San Diego, we finally approached Easter week and decided to camp in our trailer in Death Valley. We headed this time into Death Valley from Los Angeles along highway 395. It was hot, although it was only March. I remember thinking how cold it was in New York in March. I liked the heat in Death Valley. We went farther along and when we reached the area below sea level, we camped behind the visitor's center to Death Valley National Monument. Tom and I had our supper, and then joined the crowd in the museum auditorium to listen to a man named Dwight Warren talk about Death Valley.

The next morning, we woke up to a terrible wind storm. The dust in the valley swooped up and around making swirls and dust devils which spiraled single file down and across the highway.

"How graceful," I thought. They were like dancers.

As Tom prepared the trailer for departure, he noticed we had a flat tire, and inquired as to where it could be repaired. A park ranger suggested a garage at Death Valley Junction, so we slowly limped our way to the town. The sun was shining and the air was still hazed with dust from the storm. We limped on over to what resembled a Mexican village of adobe houses and then larger structures. We pulled over to the large garage which had a filling station out front. Tom proceeded to repair the tire on the trailer while I had a few moments to explore.

As I gazed down the long colonnade of what was known as the Amargosa Hotel, I remembered having seen it before. It was at the end of a tour in 1964. It was dusk then, with the damp mist of drizzle in the air. The adobe buildings were hardly visible. Now, as I stood in the noonday sun gazing at this long, beautiful colonnade, I recalled saying I wished to return. An invisible wall seemed to surround this place, impenetrable, creating a retreat from today.

I wandered down the colonnade to where it turned a corner. Smaller buildings with gates leading to possible courtyards continued and suddenly my eyes fell on the largest structure in the row. It looked like a theater. I couldn't believe it! Hypnotically I was drawn down to this structure. By now I had forgotten the tire. I walked over to the building, afraid to take my eyes off of it lest it should disappear.

I wandered around the back, accelerating my step until I found myself in a courtyard shaded by large tamarisk trees. There was a back door, possibly a stage door.

There was a hole in the back door, through which I tried to peer inside. A few sunbeams pierced the dark interior. Finally my eyes were able to make out a small stage with faded calico curtains hanging from a track. Debris was strewn all over the warped floor boards and several rows of wooden benches faced the stage. Some old roller skates lay up front, and directly at the foot of the sunbeam was a doll's head with its blue glass eyes staring back at me. Pockets of dust and sand provided a backdrop for kangaroo rats and desert spiders.

It was obvious the theater had been abandoned for some time. It seemed to be the only unused building in Death Valley Junction. As I peered through the tiny hole, I had the distinct feeling that I was looking at the other half of my life. The building seemed to be saying, "Take me. Do something with me. I offer you life."

Like the theater, I too was beginning to feel unused. A dancer cannot stay in form and be artistically fulfilled touring four months of the year with only twenty-one concerts. Road expenses and the cost of space to practice during the long waits in between were a high price to pay for the joy of performing.

I continued gazing through the small hole in the door knowing at that very moment I had to have that theater. I would find a new life in it and in doing so, perhaps I would be giving it life. Here I would have time and space to commission myself to do work no one else would ever ask me to do.

I ran down to the filling station where Tom had just finished repairing the tire. Words came out faster than I could articulate them. Eventually, Tom got the message. Soon we were both headed back to the theater, around to the courtyard where I pointed to the hole through which he would be able to see. Without a word to one another, we both knew that we were looking at our future.

Tom had always wanted to leave New York, so I believe my enthusiasm offered him the chance to leave sooner than he'd thought. For me, this tiny theater cast its spell. Now New York was no longer the center of the art world. At that moment, for me, the world could have New York. I wanted this theater.

The next day we went to Las Vegas for a mail pick-up. On the way, we talked of nothing else but the tiny theater in Death Valley Junction. From a letter from my mother we learned New York's great Metropolitan Opera House was slated for the wrecker's ball. Something about this devastating news strengthened our determination to return to Death Valley Junction and see if we couldn't arrange to rent the theater.

There was something positive about leaving New York now, not later when everything beautiful had been torn down. I wanted to remember New York with love.

We returned to Death Valley Junction the next day and located the town manager in his apartment behind the Amargosa Hotel.

"It's a mess," he remarked as he unlocked the double doors in the front of the theater. The swinging doors fanned out. A cloud of dust like a scrim lifted, revealing the spacious interior which yawned before us from its twenty year sleep.

After the dust had settled, I could see the tiny stage at the opposite end of the room. The once beautiful oak floor was warped from leaks and covered with debris. The wooden benches faced the stage and waited for the next performance. It hadn't occurred to me that the next performance might be mine.

I walked toward the stage. It too was warped from the rain. An upright piano stood directly under a hole in the rafters. The hole was so big you could see daylight. Rain water and sunlight had spilled onto the old keyboard, causing the ivories to fall and expose the wood underneath. The keyboard had the appearance of a smiling mouth with missing teeth, a grimace against the elements.

"It was tragic," I thought, "That somebody didn't know any better than to move the piano."

The keyboard with the missing teeth smiled back at me as if to say, "That's life, kid. Nobody around here cares until someone hauls me off to the dump."

"As for me," I thought to myself, "I don't have to wait for some one to haul me off, or offer me a better life. I will move myself to a better life here in Death Valley Junction before it is too late."

I felt as if I had just been given a shot of new life. I realized I had been slowly dying. The doors which had opened to me just a few years ago when I started touring in 1955 were closing. I will now have my own stage.

We made a simple agreement on a scrap of paper and gave the manager a dollar bill and a handshake. The manager, whose name was Ariel Taylor, was curious as to what kind of shows we planned. When I informed him they would be ballet and pantomime, his wife Mildred expressed hope I would give the town's children ballet lessons.

SCENE TWO

The Move to Amargosa

New York was cold when we returned in June. The anticipation of having to tell Mother about our plans to move to Death Valley Junction weighed heavily on me. She was devastated that I would consider moving to such a far away place without considering her welfare.

"Tom and I will move you out to Las Vegas, where you can be near us and see this wonderful place," I told her.

"I don't want to go to Las Vegas" she cried. "I don't do mechanical gambling."

Mana was glad for us, but sad that we were going to be so far away. Dorothy Lake was extremely sad about our move, and reminded us of what the psychic had said. Bert and Laura Gold were very unhappy, because they could see that this move meant fewer paintings for them to sell. Tom's parents were noncommittal.

Our plan was to pile into a big U-Haul trailer with all of our belongings and head west, staying the night at Tom's parent's on the way.

I bought a one-way train ticket for Mother. She was due to arrive in Las Vegas September 9. She wondered why she had to live in Las Vegas instead of with us. I informed her there was no boardroom there.

We returned to Death Valley Junction August of 1967. Beth Martinsen was behind the counter in the Lila C Café, and expressed a concern that we were never going to show up. I was so happy to be home, at last. I wished I had come long before.

We unloaded everything into the back door of the theater. Tom moved our trailer behind the building. We planned to live there while working on the restoration of the place.

That night as we slept, we could hear the munching of wild horses chewing mesquite beans by our window. At first, the whinny of a large horse would scare us out of our wits, but we got used to it.

It must have rained later that night, as there was the sound of dripping rain from a nearby spout. Our trailer was shaking too, quite violently. We looked out the window to see what it was. A large pig was rooting at the foot of our trailer, to welcome us, perhaps, to our new home.

We went inside the door of the theater to see what damage the rain had done. It was dripping everywhere, and the sounds of the constant rain drops echoed in the emptiness. We had so much work to do and a sum of $500 to do it with.

Later on in the day, I put on my tights, leotard, and ballet shoes, and hung on to one of our costume trunks and proceeded to practice in the yard. The local children came and watched as did some of the Mothers. It made me feel more like an oddity than ever.

We learned that we were only seven and a half miles from the Nevada state line. Down a dirt road was a bordello named Ash Meadows Lodge.

I was intrigued. There was another bordello toward Lathrop Wells called the Shamrock Brothel. There was also the Chicken Ranch. The place was dotted with these brothels. Otherwise, the area consisted mostly of ranches, farms which raised alfalfa and later on, ostriches.

Somehow, Tom had made the acquaintance of the madam at Ash Meadows Lodge, which also had a fine restaurant, where he secured a job there as bartender.

I began to teach the local children twice a week. They paid in blue chip stamps. With those, we acquired chairs for our theater, as the wooden benches were splintery and shaky.

Tom worked on securing the roof on the theater. I rehearsed each day, and sewed a red corduroy curtain for the stage. We could not afford velvet with the little money we had left. The back wall had been painted white by the Borax people years ago, as a movie screen. We decided to keep this wall as it was because buying gray corduroy for this expanse of wall was out of the question.

Outside, Tom painted the walls white. Even after they were painted a nice base white, the rains would come and leave their muddy streaks.

Tom built the stage out farther from the proscenium so that it measured about fifteen feet deep and twenty feet wide; small for a dancer, but better than if it was at only ten feet. This stage was going to be mine for as long as I could perform, which made it the biggest stage I ever had.

Tom put up the curtain and made theater lights out of used coffee cans. They worked well, and as the months went by, everyone in town became anxious about whether we would ever open.

Everyone in town was friendly, but regarded us with curiosity. These were rural folk, and we were from the big city.

There were three large families in Death Valley Junction: The Martinsens, with three children, grandchildren, and a visiting grandmother; the Smiths, with three children; and Ariel and Mildred Taylor who had several. Their son was married to Smitty's daughter who, still in her teens, had three children. Smitty was alone, and he ran the gas station.

Late that fall, I gave my first three shows. Everyone came to see my Death Valley Junction debut, including Smitty in his bib overalls. Even the old man who lived under the salt cedar tree across from the theater came. The children all came to these impromptu performances in their pajamas, and the very young ones, who were told to go to bed, snuck over and hung on the screen door at the side of the theater.

After the town folk had seen everything, I still had to go over all my dances, otherwise I would become rusty.

I would then rehearse to an empty theater, which didn't really bother me, because now I was beginning to create new dances and pantomimes which seemed more suited to the size and shape of my small stage.

After I had shown everyone in town my show, as they called it, they seemed to have a little more respect for me, although they treated me as more of an oddity than ever.

As fall turned into winter, I could see a change coming over Tom. He started wearing a cowboy hat, leather vest, and boots. He began talking rough. I wondered if he was trying to become like the locals, in order to fit in.

He wrote to Mana and mentioned that we were living in a Mormon town. Mana suggested Tom and I become Mormon so our new neighbors would take to us more readily. I disagreed. A little friction now and then was natural, and to be expected in a tight community.

Right behind the theater stood a house, one of seven, which had been built by the Borax Company to house the people who worked in the old

Amargosa Hotel and General Store. This particular house was known as house number two. A woman lived there whose name was Judy Tubb. Her grandfather had owned Death Valley Junction in 1907. It was a pretty rough place then, a tent town, complete with saloon and bordello. When the Pacific Coast Borax Company bought Death Valley Junction, they cleaned it up and made it into a respectable town of some 300 people.

Because of an editorial in *Harper's Magazine* written by Zane Grey, which revealed the deplorable conditions of this small mining town, the Borax Company was forced to improve conditions. An architect named Alexander Hamilton McCullah was brought in and designed a working company town of Mexican Colonial style. I'm convinced this town is the most beautiful company town that I had ever seen.

Judy's father was Bob Tubb. Judy was quite a character, had been married several times; each husband an ex-convict. She had a little girl named Nadine, who used to imitate some of my characterizations expertly. Judy worked at the Lila C Café making breakfast for a few miners and ranchers who came each morning.

"We're off and running," she would call out to the counter. I used to think if she could act like that in front of an audience, she would make a great character actress.

Tom and Mazie Bridges ran the Amargosa Hotel. Tommy would sit on the front porch at six in the morning with a percolator of coffee, inviting passersby to partake. My Tom enjoyed visiting Tommy Bridges, and I enjoyed visiting Mazie. Mazie ran the hotel and cleaned the rooms. After her housecleaning chores were over, she would sit in the lobby and answer the phone or take reservations. One afternoon as I sat with her, the phone rang.

"Amargosa Hotel," she answered. "No, we ain't got none of them," she said and hung up. After a short pause, she asked in a somewhat embarrassed tone, "Marta, what's accommodations mean?"

There were several occasions when Tom and I would have our supper al fresco in the yard behind the theater. No sooner would we sit down in happy anticipation of a lovely meal outdoors, a cat fight under the table would ensue. Then the local dogs in town would come snarling over bones from our chicken or steak scraps. The town folk did not feed their animals well, so we ended up filling that void.

I began feeling a great compassion for these strays. From that time to this day I have been surrounded by cats and dogs left in Death Valley Junction by people who have heard about me, "the paintin' an danc'n lady who takes in strays." Each spring I find a cardboard box full of kittens, or a pregnant cat left on my doorstep. At one time I ended up with forty-six cats. I never wanted so many cats, but what do you do, let them starve?

The hot summer of Death Valley Junction soon turned into an exquisite Indian summer with golden sunsets and balmy starlit nights. Cold weather did not set in until the first of November. The air became dry and crisp. The outlines of mountains in the distance looked like painted cardboard stage sets against the brilliant blue sky.

Even with all this beauty, I did not feel compelled to paint it. Instead I continued to send paintings back to Park South Gallery of occasional New York scenes, and allegorical subjects. These latter subjects seemed to surface in my imagination more prominently now that I lived in the desert. *The Waiting Room*, which resembled Grand Central Station, was filled with invisible souls waiting to board a train into their next life. *The Believers* was a large family painted to look like marble, all praying, with eyes closed. A small child up front was staring right out of the painting with tears streaming down her face. She was beginning to doubt.

We set out from Death Valley Junction to pick up Mother at the Union Plaza Station at the end of Fremont Street. We took our trailer in and parked at the Shady Acres Trailer Park on Main Street. I overheard the proprietor talking on the phone about some deal he was making in South America, and how nobody was going to find out what he was doing. Of course, the whole park was lined with shade trees, but still, the thought of something "shady" going on intrigued me.

Tom hooked the trailer up to electricity and water, and we prepared to have an early supper and then nap for a few hours before the train arrived at four in the morning. However, at three fifteen a.m., a great roar and whistle shrieked as a train pulled in at the Union Plaza Station.

"That's gotta be Mother," I exclaimed nervously. I began pulling on my clothes, but Tom insisted it was too early.

"I don't care if it is too early," I said frantically. "Even if it is too early, it's only forty-five minutes early. I've got to be sure. I don't want Mother to arrive in this strange town and not have us waiting for her."

Tom reluctantly dressed and we went down to the station. Fremont Street was like the Great White Way of Las Vegas. Casinos lined both sides of the street, with all the brightness of a sunny day, only at night. I was sure Mother would be dazzled by all this brightness, activity, and electric signs advertising jackpots of gold. The mere thought of Mother possibly enjoying this spectacular sight with all the milling crowds made me excited about the reunion.

When Tom and I found Mother sitting on one of those old wooden benches in the waiting room, she was absorbed in *Wall Street Journals* she had either found on the train, or in waste baskets. I was disappointed. I expected her to be at the front window of the station, gazing out on Fremont, the "Great White Way" to her new life!

She insisted on taking all the *Wall Street Journals* with her. We left the station and headed across the street for one of those great all night breakfasts for one dollar and ninety-nine cents at a casino called The Dugout. After we ate, Mother wanted to sightsee, although she didn't seem impressed with all the bright lights. Dawn approached, and Tom and I were tired. Mother seemed to pick up new energy and wanted to do more; see more. When it was nine o'clock, Tom and I decided to show Mother her new home, hoping we would install her there for a few hours while we could go back to our trailer and get a few winks.

Mother's new dwelling was a small one room wooden house which sat right next to one like it. It had a bathroom and kitchen facilities. Her landlady was a woman older than my mother, named Edith. As soon as Mother saw the big double bed in the corner of her rented house, she nearly screamed.

"I don't want that big bed in there. I don't need a bed like that. People will have the wrong idea about me if I have that bed. Can you exchange it for a cot?"

I was embarrassed to tears.

"I have a nice single bed, or a day bed," Edith said. "Would that do?"

"I don't want a bed at all, I want my Italian sofa. I'm used to sleeping on a mattress on the floor. I don't want a bed, period. And that's that."

At this point I wanted to sink in the floor. Mother wanted to go out and not come back until the big bed was removed. We gave in, and went out for another breakfast, which Mother ate heartily. When we returned, the big bed was gone, and in its place Edith had put a couch that opened up into a bed.

I never knew whether Mother learned to like her new dwelling or not. She had no stairs, and she could walk to a grocery market two blocks away. And, she had three different boardrooms in her neighborhood. I did all I could for her, but still it was not enough.

Tom and I finally made it back to our trailer where we flopped down and took a much needed nap. We had another day with Mother, and then we would leave her to go back to Death Valley Junction. It was heaven to return to our new home, to my theater, the desert, the wild horses and, most of all, my work.

We had made a promise to come into Las Vegas each week to visit Mother. This promise had to be made in order to leave Mother in her new surroundings alone. We also promised to bring her out to Death Valley Junction to see the theater.

I continued to teach the local children, and Tom continued working out at Ash Meadows Lodge. We set a date for formally opening our Opera House, which was to be February 10, 1968. It was now already January. The months seemed to fly by with slow progress.

I was surprised to see how cold it could get in the desert. It got so cold that we decided we should buy a stove for the theater. We bought a wood stove from an antique store in Las Vegas. It had once been used to warm a railroad station waiting room in Montana. How it got to Las Vegas, I never knew.

The day before opening night, I was inside the theater working, and Tom was outside on a ladder placed against the side of the building along the highway. He was busy painting letters which read, "Amargosa Opera House," using stencils Bert Gold had given him.

As Tom was concentrating on the job, a tour bus passed by and over the loud speaker a man's voice called out, "And there on the left is the famous old Amargosa Opera House." I even heard it inside.

The townsfolk already knew about the opening, but hardly any one else did. Tom distributed a few fliers down in Furnace Creek at the Visitor's Center, but outside of that, the only outsiders who knew were either guests staying in the hotel, or a few campers from across the highway.

On the afternoon of our opening night, Tom was standing out front of the Opera House, trying to solicit patrons for the evening.

A car drove up alongside the curb, and a man of medium height got out and surveyed the scene. "Opera House out here in the middle of the desert?" he asked. He had reddish hair and rugged features, penetrating blue eyes with extremely bushy brows that constantly moved up and down as he talked.

"Yes," answered Tom. "Come to the show tonight. It's opening night and we could use a few more in the audience."

"Oh, I wish I could," answered the man. "I have to go to work at four in the morning, and I still have a way to go. I'm from Trona. But I'll be back to be sure."

"What's your name?" asked Tom.

"My name's Tom Willett." the man answered.

Because the two Toms names were so alike, they got into further discourse, and discovered that they both were interested in flying. After learning that Tom Willett owned an airplane, my Tom suddenly had great admiration for him, and invited him to come to a performance any time as our guest.

Opening night came, with an audience of twelve souls huddled up against the cold. The potbellied stove did what it could, but failed to warm up the stage where I danced my full repertoire as if I had a full house. This first performance was the first of many for which I sometimes danced for an empty house.

The curious came; a few tourists, some locals. But when the weather was bad, there was no one. I continued to perform. To stay ready to perform, I must dance whether there is an audience or not. I now had my stage, and so a schedule of Friday, Saturday, and Monday evenings was made which faithfully carried me through season after season.

The important thing for me now was to do my thing. Whether anything would come of it was not important.

The winter remained cold and dry. I had expected warmth all year round, but then, one always expects more than one gets, and with the wonderful theater I had to work in every day, the weather was unimportant.

We lived in our trailer parked behind the Opera House for the next four years. After performances, it was nice to slip out the side stage door and flit into our warm abode.

We adopted two stray cats who appeared in town, an orange striped tom cat I named Rhubarb, after the cat that starred in the movie of the same name, and a black and white female with long hair whose markings resembled a tuxedo. Naturally her name became Tuxedo.

When the spring season came around, we decided that for the summer, performances would be limited to Saturday evenings. This gave me more time to create new stage works, and do some easel painting. I created *The Garden Party*, a three character comedy to Strauss, and started a new work entitled *The Good Daughter*, a kind of autobiographical dance-mime about a middle aged woman and her mother who run a boarding house along the railroad. It very much resembled Maude Firestone's life in Harrisburg. This work was an excellent vehicle for me to vent out some of my frustrations with my own situation with Mother.

We were still considered odd by the townsfolk. After all, if hardly anyone came to performances, they would think, "Why should we bother?" When no one was around, they often closed the Lila C Café, or put a closed sign up at the hotel. I felt, if you're going to do something, do it. So we did, well into the future.

I was happy that at least Tom continued to announce my show enthusiastically whether any one came or not. He was away from New York, and was becoming acclimated to the West, and enjoyed making friends of passersby and out at the bordello where he was making money for us to live on.

He wrote long letters to Mana, who returned the correspondence with even longer letters. Mana was critical of our move, and fretted over our apparent low living standards. He was appalled to learn Tom was working out at a bordello to help make ends meet. In actuality, Tom enjoyed working at the bordello. He saw the other side of life.

To my dismay, Mana decided to make the trip to Death Valley Junction to see for himself what we were doing in what he thought was a godforsaken place. His wife came along, and Mana's old cat, Dinah, was brought in her special carrying case with the necessary medications which supposedly kept her alive. Dinah was very old, and really had no business being taken on this lengthy trip. I was sorry that Mana decided to come out so soon, before enough had been accomplished. We had only been here for some six months. There was still so much to do.

Tom went in to Las Vegas to meet them and bring them out. When they arrived, I was amazed at how out of place they looked in the desert setting. Mana, wearing a dark "citified" suit, holding a valise in one arm and a large cat carrier in the other, looked like a preacher or doctor on his way to visit a patient. His wife stood beside him, wearing a dark suit as well, with a white ruffled blouse. Her glasses reflected me in both panes, and although she was smiling, I could not tell whether she was happy at being here, or not.

Following our greetings, we marched over to a room in an adjacent apartment where Dinah the cat could be kept. Then we took them to the hotel where we had reserved a room for them. Several times a day, Mana would go to visit Dinah, who had about seven bowls of different cat chows, canned food, and medicines. Dinah was not happy, and I felt sorry for her.

Spring was on the way, and although the temperatures here were far warmer than they would have been in New York at this time, Mana complained there was no green grass, no green trees, and no flowers.

"Why would you pick a place like this?" he asked.

"Because I have my own space here, my own time," I answered.

Mana regarded the whole thing as the most foolish decision I ever made. I told him that I had not time yet to accomplish anything and hoped he would come out again in a year or two.

During Mana's stay, he quietly paid a visit to the Ash Meadows bordello. He walked the whole way. His wife never knew, but here was my father, adamantly against red light districts and yet so fascinated he was pulled like a magnet to this house of ill repute.

One of the most tense moments of the visit was my performance. It was cold still, and it was one of those evenings when no one came. I warmed up behind the curtain and heard Tom let two people in the front door. I hoped it was someone other than Mana and his wife, but it wasn't. I peeked through the side of the curtain and saw them walk down to the front row. They sat down stiffly and waited for something to happen.

Tom, in his tuxedo, promptly at eight fifteen p.m. came down the aisle, faced the empty house and announced the opening lines of the show. I felt numb, but like a robot, I started the tape recorder and Tchaikovsky filled the air. Tom then dimmed the lights, I took my place center stage and the red curtain opened. The lights then went up and I performed *Romance*, a classical dance I always began each program with. It felt like an audition. Tom made his announcements in between my dances, and his voice sounded hollow in the empty hall.

We did the entire program going through each selection to the end which included *Slavonic Dance*, and the twelve minute version of *The Mirror, the Carpet and the Lemon*. There was no applause.

The day for their departure back east came not too soon. Tom took them back to Las Vegas and to the airport which would whisk them to their New Jersey farm in a few hours. Mana promised to write, and Tom said he would write as well. I was alone at the Junction to contemplate the visit.

Spring had finally come, and hot days with it. Easter week is a big thing in Death Valley, so there were quite a few people around to catch our performances in the Opera House.

We were starting to be talked about.

Lee McGowan, Ash Meadows Lodge madam, asked Tom if it would help our audience to grow if I performed at her Easter party. He said he thought it would, so it was arranged. I decided to perform *Gossip*.

It was a large sprawling place with many trees. There was a pond in front with ducks and a large swimming pool behind the lodge. The building itself was a ranch style wooden structure with a roomy porch, behind which was the dance floor, a pool table and then the restaurant. Way over to the left was the famous cathouse itself, a long wooden building with several rooms, and a big black cat on the roof.

The place was jammed with people. Farmers, ranchers, hundreds of children, the local sheriff and highway patrol, and quite a few folks from Las Vegas were giving a big barbeque, along with an Easter egg hunt.

The ladies of the night were over to one side of the front lawn, dressed in colorful chiffon culottes. They had decorated the Easter eggs and although they joined in the festivities, they stayed together in a group. You knew who they were the minute you saw them.

I had expected to meet a madam who would look more like Mae West than Lee McGowan did. She was an imposing woman with dark hair, white skin, and painted eyebrows that started below her real brow line, and then went way up almost to her temples giving her a permanent surprised look. Her speaking voice was beautiful, and almost dignified, which was unexpected. She was very motherly when it came to her girls, but firm.

Everyone at the lodge gathered around the dance floor to see my skit. I received a huge round of applause.

From that event, our audiences grew, not to huge proportions, but enough that we could start to depend on some revenue which was stuffed in a huge paint can which was painted gold. This revenue was in the form of donations, and still is, to this day.

Lee McGowan decided to bring her girls to a performance at the Opera House once a month, for culture.

Summer finally came. It was suddenly hot; 112 degrees. It was dry, which made it bearable. Our trailer was burning hot, as the sun shone on the roof all day long. The theater became hot and stuffy. I continued to work in spite of this.

One afternoon I was rehearsing *Comeback Vaudeville*. I was timing my costume changes, for they had to be very fast in order to return as the next character without too long a wait after the one before it. I heard a loud noise up in the projection booth which was used during Borax days.

"Hey, Norry," I heard a young man's voice say from up in the booth. "Come on up here, there's a woman changing clothes over and over again down on the stage. Hurry Up."

There was a great commotion going up the ladder out front which led up to the booth on the outside. I stopped my rehearsal and ran into the trailer to tell Tom.

Without a word, Tom rose to the occasion, anger showing in his face, and went out to find the culprits. I believe the confrontation was quite violent. The two men left in a hurry and Tom put a large padlock on the trapdoor leading to the projection booth. Nothing like that has ever happened since.

When the temperature rose to 115, we pared down our performance schedule to Saturday evenings only. A smattering of people came; no more than ten. I continued to paint and send my work back to Park South Gallery in New York, but because I was not actually there to see what was going on, my work was being sold at discount, the reason being that business was bad.

I finally gave up sending work, and asked for the paintings that were there to be sent to me here at Death Valley Junction. A large painting of Gypsies waiting to tell fortunes was sent back, slightly damaged due to insufficient packaging. The other, three children dancing around an organ grinder also did not fare too well. This painting was older. It was dated 1948. I was glad to have them back, like old friends.

SCENE THREE

Flooding and the Murals Begin

One day I was giving a ballet class to the local children. The side door to the Opera House was open. It had been raining around us, up in the hills and the Greenwater Mountains. One of my small boy students looked out that door during a moment of rest and said, "Look, we're having a flood." We all stopped what we were doing and ran to see. Sure enough, we could see waves of muddy water topped with foamy lumps of alkali heading straight for town.

"We'd better stop class and pick everything up off the ground before it gets in here," I said.

Everyone scurried in four directions as soon as they got out the front door. I ran into the trailer to look for Tom. The waters soon came in the back yard to the stage door of the Opera House. The muddy water oozed through the yard and into the small apartment next door. Soon, the brown stuff ran into the side door of the Opera House, finally filling the gigantic room with sixteen inches of mud. I couldn't find Tom anywhere, so I tried getting around the side of Opera House only to find myself standing in mud about ten inches deep.

It took me twenty minutes to find my way down the colonnade which by now was standing fifteen inches deep in mud. The farther down I got, the deeper the mud, for that part of Death Valley Junction was lower than the north end. By the time I got to the hotel entrance, the lobby was flooded with muddy water. Everyone was hurrying to lift things off the ground and save whatever could be saved.

To wade through this mess was frustrating. The top of me wanted to go faster, while the bottom of me stuck fast in the brown glue. If I tried in any way to move faster, I might end up on my face square in the mud.

When this flood had finally finished its job, it stood still in town and all the buildings for several days. The smell of wet clay was sickening.

All the small houses, which had their first and only floor ground level, were standing sixteen inches in mud. The apartment next to the theater was also deep in mud, as was the theater. We had some valuable things stored in the apartment. Everything was ruined; books on bottom shelves, albums of photographs of paintings I had done in the past, shoes, the legs of furniture, and clothes that hung on lower hooks.

The trailer was livable, because it stood high up off the ground. However, the entire Opera House was flooded. The stage was untouched as it stood high above the main floor. But its masonite covering was warped from the moisture. It was uneven and rumply. Everywhere we went, we were barefoot. It was impossible to wear shoes. They would fill with mud and become so heavy you couldn't even lift a foot to take the next step.

One afternoon, the muddy waters decided to leave town. We stood at our apartment doorway and watched the waters leave the front room carrying photographs, books, pieces of furniture, and mementos with the speed of a river. We were helpless to save any of it. Our past was erased by the waters from the Greenwater Mountains.

A few days later, we tried mucking the mud from the theater in time for Saturday evening's performance. A man and his wife came through Death Valley Junction at the moment we shoveled out a big wad of mud, and saw our dilemma. They were wearing evening clothes, and were on their way to a party at Furnace Creek Inn. They offered to bring squeegees the next day to help. They were Mr. and Mrs. K.C. Den Dooven of Las Vegas, the publishers of the books on Death Valley and other national parks.

While we were using the squeegee that next day, I looked up at the blank white walls of my Opera House and envisioned an audience of the Renaissance sitting in gilded boxes and balconies, conversing with each other, some gazing down at the stage, some laughing and drinking wine, and others just with rapt attention.

"I think I will paint an audience on these walls," I said to Tom. He didn't quite believe me, but the next day I repeated what I said, and insisted we buy scaffolding so that I could get on with the project. For twenty-five dollars we rented a scaffold. Later we bought a scaffold for $125.

I began painting with almost a drunken frenzy. I made a sketch, or cartoon of the rear wall, scaled it on the wall making one inch of my sketch into a foot for the mural. I painted everything in brown and sepia before putting in the color. I played baroque and Renaissance music as I worked, and became obsessed with preserving the past through my art.

Each afternoon, I would climb the scaffold to the top rung which to me was heaven. I was happier and more fulfilled up there than anywhere else I could imagine.

A king and queen appeared in the center of the highest balcony, and on each side of them were seated ladies and gentlemen of a royal court, with a few clerics in the background. Below, on the left, I painted a Spanish bullfighting family absorbed in wine, eating mangos, and laughing among themselves. On the lower right balcony were more ladies and gentlemen of the court. I began with the Spanish Renaissance because, architecturally, the whole town, including the Opera House, was styled after Spanish Colonial design.

In each corner, below the balconies, I painted Rhubarb the cat seated on a red velvet cushion, and Tuxedo also seated on a red velvet cushion with her kittens. She and Rhubarb had a litter.

Tom would come in now and then to see how things were going. He seemed overwhelmed by my obsession. He worked every night at the bordello from about eight at night until four in the morning, which meant I had those hours to myself to work. I would spend hours up there with only one light focused on what I was painting. Rhubarb and Tuxedo draped on the scaffold with me.

After a long session, I would climb down, go over to the lake that was across from the theater and put my tired feet under a pipe that had water running out of it. The moon would be overhead, and as I sat there basking in the serenity of the scene, I would watch the wild horses at the other end of the lake enjoying the cool water.

By three thirty a.m., I would wrap it up and take a cold shower and fall exhausted into my trailer bed. I would be dreaming of my mural, when Tom would suddenly come in the door. He always seemed to be in a mood for lovemaking, or sex as he called it now. I was not. The world I had immersed myself in was not conducive to feeling sexual. Tom, on the other hand, had just been in an atmosphere geared to sex, and more and more he intimated a need to satisfy this urge.

As the beautiful summer turned into fall, and this schedule continued into the next season, irritation grew between us because our working hours were driving us further and further apart.

I was beginning to feel inadequate as a wife. My art was starting to irritate Tom, and yet, I could not abandon my mural before it was finished just to make Tom happy.

It was about this time that a couple of "flower children" moved next door to us, in what was the old hospital for Borax. Tom and Diane Ryan had been working at Furnace Creek Inn. She as a salad girl in the restaurant, and he was a barber. Wanting to go in business for themselves, they decided on Death Valley Junction.

Diane opened a boutique, selling sand candles and long dresses. Tom opened a barber shop.

Smitty married Lucille, the cook who worked out at the bordello. And they got a long haired Persian cat named Snowball. Rhubarb became enamored with Snowball and it wasn't long before Snowball delivered a litter of Kittens underneath the lid of their couch. Smitty had it in for Rhubarb after that.

Many friends came to visit Tom and Diane Ryan. They were all flower children, and two of them, called Little Paul and Big Paul, had been associated with Charles Manson. Often there were pot parties and droves of hippies would visit and do their thing into the night. The sweet smell of grass wafted through the air, and the mixture of various scents and rock music unnerved me so that climbing up the scaffold into my heaven was an escape.

My Tom frequently visited the flower children, and if I should walk in on them unexpectedly, all conversation stopped. I was beginning to feel unwelcome except in the Opera House, the world I had created for myself.

As time went on, the mural grew. Audiences became a little larger, and the curious came down from Amargosa Valley, and from below in Tecopa, to watch the mural become more populated. One well-meaning group from Tecopa came to see what damage the flood had done to the Opera House. Then there were those who were curious about what kind of performances went on inside. The floor of the auditorium had become terribly warped from the standing flood waters, and people had to be warned not to trip over the wooden waves of floor boards.

In November, I premiered a new stage production. I was inspired to create a full length work to the music of Offenbach's *Orpheus in the Underworld*.

The scenario was simple. A marquis decides it is time to give his annual party in the public garden. He has invited a wide variety of characters to attend. They are the master of ceremonies, a flirt, a dandy, a young girl who must say farewell to her lover who must go off to war, the young girl's lover, a revolutionary and an aristocrat in an argument, the marquis who announces the entertainment for the evening, and three cancan dancers in succession.

The piece was called *An Entertainment*. I had worked on this opus all summer. Between this stage work and painting the mural, Tom and I spent more time apart than ever. I was frustrated. After waiting some forty years for my ship to come in, I began having feelings of guilt because the world I was creating demanded all of me. I felt alive for the first time, and the sky was the limit. Tom on the other hand, was letting me know that he was being left out, my role as a wife had failed, and his attentions wandered elsewhere.

An Entertainment was a big success. I performed it as the second half of each program for the next thirteen years, alternating at times with *Comeback Vaudeville*, and the *Turkish Fairytale*.

The Opera House was gaining a following, and we now had some very good patrons from Las Vegas, Indian Springs, Los Angeles, and Death Valley National Monument. The mural was growing larger, and now it was time to turn the corner and start on the east and the west walls.

The madam would come over to inspect and shake her head in disbelief. Tom was discouraged when I started on the two side walls. The more involved I became with what I was creating, the unhappier he became. I loved what I was creating and the larger it grew, the more I became obsessed with it.

One late afternoon as I was painting a figure clothed in Renaissance armor standing in a niche, Tom Willett came in the front door of the Opera House. He stood there watching me paint for a while, and then said, "Holy mackerel, you're not going to cover the entire walls, are you?"

"Of course," I answered. "Wouldn't it look awful with some of the walls white?"

"I suppose it would," he answered, "But what a job, what an undertaking, to tackle something so big." He stood there for a while, watching me paint. After Tom Willett watched for a while longer, he left, saying that he would be back for another visit to see how the mural was coming.

One very cold evening when we were giving a performance that no one came to, I was dancing *Four Romantic Dances* to Chopin, when I noticed the front door opened and four figures walked in. "Oh good," I thought as I continued to dance, "An audience. We'll finish the entire performance." At the end of the performance we discovered that Dwight Warren, Chief Naturalist in Death Valley, his wife, and two people from the *National Geographic Magazine* had been our audience that evening.

That evening was a very exciting one. The gentleman from the *National Geographic Magazine* was Rowe Findly, who was slated to do a story on Death Valley for the January, 1970 issue. This particular performance took place early in the winter of 1969. It takes that long after a story is planned for publication for it to finally be made public. I was so happy, and Tom seemed to be happy too. A photographer was sent out in two weeks and took pictures.

Tom and Mana continued to correspond. Mother came out on the bus occasionally to visit. Her eyesight had become so poor, she couldn't see the mural I was working on. At my performance, she would sit in the front row with opera glasses to watch my every move.

I had finally written Mana to inform him that I had begun the large mural in the opera house. I even sent him a Polaroid photograph of the back wall. He wrote back and chastised me for spending my time painting the walls of a building I didn't even own.

"You can't sell that," he wrote, "How many more things can you embark upon that are senseless," he continued.

Tom bought a small printing press to print fliers and circulars to advertise our Opera House. I thought this was a great idea, and it saved money in printing bills at a commercial print shop. Tom preferred to buy the stock for his press in Los Angeles instead of Las Vegas. He would go to Los Angeles every other week.

We would go to Las Vegas for groceries and banking. These trips also provided the opportunity to visit Mother. We would pick her up at her little house, and Tom would go do some shopping, while Mother and I did Fremont Street which included a Woolworth, a J.C. Penney, and dozens of casinos.

When I tried to please Mother, Tom was bored and was now showing resentment. When I was practicing or painting, Tom showed annoyance.

I was tired of trying to be a good wife. I had been a good daughter for so long now; what I really wanted to be was a good dancer, a fine painter, a good me.

After a while, Diane went along with us on trips to Las Vegas. They would let me off at Mother's little house. I did not think anything about it as I was left in Mother's driveway, and they drove off. Then Diane started to accompany Tom to Los Angeles.

About this time, Mana talked to a man from *Life* magazine about the Opera House. The man, a John Frook, decided to come check it out for himself. I was teaching a ballet class for the local children when Mr. Frook showed up.

When I finished the class and the children had dispersed, he introduced himself, and told me he was from *Life* magazine, and would be staying for the performance. Regardless of Mana's intervention, I started to become excited and felt that this performance must be extra special. Maybe this will convince Mana that I am worthwhile after all.

The performance went very well. I remember doing my *Curtain Raiser*, *The Garden Party* and the *Turkish Fairytale*. Afterward, John Frook seemed very impressed, and said he would be out very soon with a photographer and writer for a story. In the meantime, a week later, there was a letter from Mana saying that he had heard Henry Moscow of *Life* magazine say, "This Marta Becket is of astounding talent, and we will do a story." I couldn't believe it. Finally Mana heard from someone he knows and admires, that his daughter has talent.

The next week, John Frook and the photographer came out to do their picture story. One large photo was planned on top of Death Valley Junction's tailings pile, where the entire view of the town can be seen behind us. At four in the afternoon, everyone in town was told to meet for a portrait. Tom was to be dressed in his tuxedo, me in my pink classical costume, Smitty in his greasy overalls, Beth and Don Martinsen in their workaday clothes, and the children seated down in front.

No one turned up for the shoot. Only Tom and I did. We were disappointed because we thought it a great idea. When we later asked Smitty why he didn't show up, he grumbled, "I ain't gonna be in no picture for *Life* magazine, got too much ta do in the garage." Don and Beth Martin pretended to forget. I think it was because the story was not about them.

I remember Beth saying, "Why didn't they write a story about the café?"

"An opera house isn't necessary out in the desert," the locals would grumble. "A cafe is necessary. *We* should have the story, not them."

The local people couldn't understand why the public was beginning to get so interested in our Opera House.

"You don't do nothin' that's necessary," they would say. "You dance, you paint, what else do ya do that ain't necessary?"

I wouldn't begin to tell them about my composing. That was a thing of the past anyway. I had no piano, and would probably never have one again, so I never mentioned that side of me.

We waited and waited for the *Life* magazine story to appear. Mana would write and ask if we had heard anything. At this time, the story of Charles

Manson was big, and John Frook called and told us one day that our story would be put on hold because of the Charles Manson coverage. I was let down, but other stories started to come out in the *Las Vegas Review-Journal* and the Associated Press. Then there was the *National Geographic* to look forward to in January of 1970.

Losing Mana and Finding Marie

ana was not well, and I was hoping that the *Life* magazine story would appear soon so that he could see it. Tom and I planned to send Mana a subscription for a year of *National Geographic* so that upon opening the very first issue, he would see the story called "Death Valley: Land and Legend." He would see my picture painting the mural he scolded me for spending so much time on. This was to be a surprise for him.

It was a week before Christmas, 1969, and we were in the middle of a performance one Saturday night. At intermission, Smitty came in with a telegram. Tom wasted no time after he read the news to inform me Mana had died. I couldn't finish the performance. Tom sent the small audience home, and for the rest of the evening, I sat by the big potbellied stove and sobbed.

Matie wrote a week later to say a funeral service for Mana would be held at the Community Church in Manhattan. She gave us the date, which was early January. Mana would have been eighty years old. Tom jumped at the idea of us going to New York to attend this service. Flying to New York and back seemed like a financial nightmare to me, and we wouldn't be in Death Valley Junction the night of the first performance after the *National*

Geographic had come out. We already had eighty-seven reservations; more than we ever had. I was heartbroken.

We made arrangements with a lady who lived in Indian Springs to be at the Opera House the night of the performance when we would be in New York. I couldn't help but wonder why my father had to pass away just before he had a chance to read and see my story in the *National Geographic*.

We took the midnight flight to Chicago and changed planes to New York. The midnight flight was terrifying. Once on the plane, we were all advised to strap ourselves in and we were given instructions about the oxygen masks that would fall from overhead in case of emergency. Then there was the thrust into the air which I thought would surely catapult us into the next world.

There was a blond woman who sat on the other side of me in the row. She was very nervous. She had boarded the plane in Las Vegas and looked like a showgirl. She began to cry. She opened her fur coat to reveal she had nothing on except a string of pearls.

"I hope this plane will crash because I've lost everything, money and my boyfriend," she said.

An airline stewardess came and quietly removed the woman to where, I didn't know.

The memorial service was teeming with people, admirers of my father's who read his columns faithfully for years. There were a few I knew, but not many. No one there knew I was Henry Beckett's daughter.

They were trying out some music on the record player that my father wanted played at his service. Suddenly, Fritz Kriesler's *Caprice Viennois* soared through the air and I started to silently cry inside. Then *Schoen Rosmarin* with its delicate opening waltz strains invaded *Caprice Viennois*, and I could hardly stand it. I was trembling all over at the memories and the passing of those wasted years of misunderstanding between me, my father, and my mother. I wanted so to tell my father I loved him for what he did for me, if nothing else but to introduce me to the arts for which I have made my life.

I wanted to tell Mother I loved her for the lifetime of artistic freedom I had. I wanted to love them both, and yet, they were so far apart. The woman standing next to me was my father's wife, but she showed no emotion at the sounds of the music my father loved.

For the first forty years of my life, I tried so hard to make my father and my mother proud of me. Now it was over. My father was gone, and my mother could hardly see me and my work any more. It was up to me now. I was on my own.

I suddenly looked up and around me. There was Louie and Ellen Crooks.

They came forward to reintroduce themselves to me. I was stunned. Too much was happening. I wanted so to talk with Louie, but this was not the place or the time.

After the memorial service, Matie seemed depressed because none of the family from Hamilton came to Mana's service. Tom and I were the only family who came, and the Beckett family is large. Certainly someone could have come and shown their respects. I guess it was a good thing that we went to New York. Mana would have had no one, just his admirers from the paper, and from his list of fans.

When we returned to the sunny desert, I knew that this was where I belonged! I never wanted to leave again. Nearly one hundred people turned up to the Opera House for the performance I missed. They were sympathetic, bought cards and a few souvenirs, and said they would be back. Seeing the murals helped. Unfinished as they still were, they made people interested in seeing the completed project.

As audiences grew, Tom became resentful. When people from the audience would address him as Mr. Beckett, it was the final blow to Tom's ego.

After the *National Geographic* came out, our audiences grew. We had given up on the *Life* magazine story, when NBC decided to include the Amargosa Opera House in their magazine show, *First Tuesday*. Even Smitty consented to an interview in front of his gas station. It was a beautiful show, produced and directed by Bill Hill.

Finally, this was followed by *Life* magazine which came out with a colorful spread of two pages. There we were, on top of the tailings pile in our show finery. There also was a shot of me performing from backstage, showing a sparse audience of twelve of our neighbors. They sat there, with stoic expressions on their faces, as if listening to a sermon. I wished it had been one of our regular audiences, but writers seem to get excited about my dancing to my painted audience, or a small rural group. They do this to this day.

I remember after one show, a lady out front said in a loud voice, "I'm so disappointed! The paper said I would be the only one in the audience, and here there were over a hundred!"

As time went on, more stories about the Opera House came out either in local papers, *Sunset* magazine, *Desert Magazine* and *Wild West* magazine.

Life continued the same in town. Tom and Diane spent more and more time together while I was completely lost in my mural. I was at home on the second rung of my scaffolding. As the faces continued to pour out of my imagination, the concern for what was going on around me, or behind my back, seemed less important. The walls insulated my world like a time capsule.

The performances went on, the audiences grew and the mural was almost completed. Diane and Tom Ryan would attend some of the performances, and the flower children who visited them came, also. I did not feel comfortable around them, but Tom continually tried to enter their circle.

When June 1972 arrived, Tom and I had been married for ten years. Margaret Grodt, an Opera House guild member, invited us to a tenth wedding celebration for our anniversary at the Tropicana in Las Vegas. Margaret's husband arranged a table with flowers for us. We dressed up for the occasion. I wore an organdy dress and Tom was in his tuxedo. Tom went through the motions of this celebration like an actor who says his lines, but is thinking all the time of something else. I was trying to enjoy an evening that should have been a happy one, but underneath it all, there was a resigned sadness that hung over the occasion like an ominous vapor.

The evening went well, like a smooth performance of a play that has lost its heart. We drove home in silence.

Once we arrived home, Tom broke that silence to tell me he was leaving me for Diane.

"Times have changed. One woman cannot possibly satisfy a man any more," he continued. "You have your art, you don't need me. Diane needs me and we are in love."

Tom stood up, looking down at me as I sat on the bed weeping with my head in my hands. I lay down on the bed, weeping with my head still in my hands, and exhausted as I was, dropped into oblivion. It was a momentary escape from the nightmare I was now living. When I awoke, the sun was just casting its morning glow through the window. Tom was still standing at the foot of the bed, looking down at me.

Suddenly, I became angry. I sat up, and Tom said in a sort of monotone, "I just want some one ordinary. I can't cope with this any more."

I got up out of the bed, still in my organdy dress from the night before, and ran outside into the dawning day. Standing there on the edge of the lake, I wondered if it would be better to just jump in and end it all. As I looked up and saw my Opera House across the highway, it seemed to have large cracks in it. It seemed as if they were getting larger and that possibly the building would crack and crumble the way my heart seemed to be breaking. No, I didn't have the courage to jump in, and the possibility of my not getting the job done made me turn away and decide to live with whatever consequences there would be in the future.

I returned to the apartment, and then went into the Opera House and sat there, alone. The mural was almost finished. As I looked up and around at all the faces I had created, the golden balconies, and the ceiling which was waiting for its central dome and bands of dancing cherubs, my best friend said something to me. "You will stay and finish the mural. You will stay and dance and perform into a long future. It is you who have created this world. You must not abandon it now."

I went about my daily chores forcing myself to go through what had to be done so that I would not lose what I had worked so hard to attain. I did my daily workout. After a brief lunch, I mounted the scaffold and made some finishing touches on the mural, and then worked on some costumes which I needed for a new ballet I was working on called *The Summerhouse*. I deliberately stayed away from Tom.

I knew that being happy added to my inspiration. Sadness, on the other hand, subtracted from inspiration. Because I felt that everything was now falling down around me like a house of cards, being mechanical about my chores was the only way I was going to accomplish anything. I was adamant about not wasting time, and I was not about to let tragedy waste any of it.

Tom was over at Diane's boutique. I didn't care. I was determined to move ahead. All I had now was my art. I must not let this incident make me be a failure to my work, my best friend.

Late that evening Tom returned, and told me he had called it off with Diane.

"Why," I asked.

"I told Diane that you would fall apart if we went through with the divorce. I can't let that happen. The Opera House would fall apart, too."

"Why should that matter?" I asked.

The Opera House is more important than any of us," Tom said.

"How did Diane take it?" I asked.

"She's heartbroken," Tom answered.

Diane's husband was out of town during this whole conflict. Rumor had it, he was having a nose job done to treat a bad case of asthma. Right after my Tom told Diane it was all over between the two of them, she entertained a string of young men who would visit her day after day; hippies, wayfarers, road runners. You name it; they all came, one after the other. Then finally she chose one fellow who looked halfway decent, named Jack. He worked for a mine down the road, and became the most frequent visitor of all. Tom would sit on a bench in front of the Opera House and watch the parade of men visiting his former lover.

"Was Diane worth hurting me?" I asked.

"No," Tom answered. He would sit there all day and just watch.

I, on the other hand, continued to work. My feelings for Tom were changed. I still loved him, and wished it could be like the old days. However, I felt that his love for me was no longer there, because I had failed as a wife.

He told me he wanted someone normal, ordinary. If I am not normal, does that mean I am incapable of being loved, or incapable of loving someone? Am I just some sort of creative machine? Does this mean that I do not have feelings? If I was void of feelings, emotions. and compassion, I could not be an artist.

In a few days, Diane's husband, Tom, returned from out of town and could tell immediately that something had gone wrong. That afternoon, Lee McGowan, the madam came over to tell me my husband and Diane were having an affair.

"I already know," I said, "Tom told me himself on the night of our tenth wedding anniversary."

"Oh," responded Lee in a sigh. "Well," she continued, "I'll just go over and tell Tom Ryan in case he doesn't know yet."

I watched as she told Tom Ryan. It was a stab in the heart which caused him to sob hysterically.

I ran over to him and we both sobbed together. No one else was around, so we could just let the tears flow as they may.

"We have a performance to do tonight," I said, "and we must not let this stop the show from going on. You must open the boutique, just as if everything is all right."

"I can't," he answered, still sobbing. "You will," I said. "Don't give in to your hurt. You must go on living."

My Tom immediately straightened things out by telling Tom Ryan that their affair was no longer on, and that Diane was now carrying on with a man named Jack.

Diane soon went off with Jack. Later on, a nice Jewish girl named Heidi came along, and lived with Tom Ryan. She loved him, and things turned out for the better. However, the flower children continued to visit Tom and Heidi by the droves. My Tom did not go over there any more, and to take Diane's place, he got interested in buying an airplane, which he did. Tom also became interested in riding around with our local deputy named Don Ward, I never understood why.

I was beginning to become afraid of Tom. He would throw dishes against the wall if he was displeased with what I served him for supper. He even threw my cat Tuxedo over the roof of the shed behind the Opera House. Tuxedo survived the ordeal, but that did not excuse what Tom had done.

Tom told me that if I wanted to hold on to him so he wouldn't stray, we should have more sex, sometimes two to three times a day. Hoping for the old Tom I knew and loved, I complied. However, it wasn't the same. It was mechanical, and scheduled. I knew he had been with Diane for some time, and was beginning to wonder about others he had been with. I was no longer special to him. I was convenient.

My creative work became stilted, and I was not feeling happy with myself. I felt cornered in a helpless situation. I needed Tom. I couldn't run the theater alone. I didn't drive. To run simple errands, or repair stage lights, or help with the mechanics of running the theater, I needed Tom. Mine was not a situation I could run from. We had married some ten years ago and had vowed to be true to each other.

When Mother visited, Tom would pick her up at the bus station at Lathrop Wells, Nevada. He showed impatience and resentment at having to do these things for me. If I could drive, I would have been happy to go get Mother myself. As things were, I had no way of learning to drive. Tom would not teach me, and no one else in Death Valley Junction had the time.

Tom would say, "Waddya need me for if you learn how to drive?" He also intimated that I did not have the mechanical mentality to learn how to drive a car. Every ordinary person can drive a car, but I was different, all I could do was dance and paint.

At least in New York I could go out and get on the subway or bus myself, or walk to the Metropolitan Museum. I could get away from Mother or from Tom when we lived there. Here in Death Valley Junction, I was trapped. Tom always knew I was here.

I mentioned to Tom one day that it would be nice if the Opera House had a piano. "Perhaps we could get a donation of one if we made an announcement about it," I said. Tom did make announcements following the next few performances, and a week later we received a letter from a Mr. Ellsworth Johnson from Spokane, Washington, offering us a nine foot concert grand Mehlin piano. It was built in 1914. Mr. Johnson said he would ship the piano at his expense by Allied Van Lines.

About three weeks later, the piano arrived. Everyone in Death Valley Junction came to witness the great event. It seemed strange to see my Tom and Tom Ryan together helping to assemble the various parts of the piano.

"Now play something," a voice said from the rear. I looked around. I guess I was the only one who could play, but it had been so long, I didn't remember a thing. I timidly walked to the piano bench, sat down before its sparkling white and black keyboard, and wondered for a moment what to play. I decided to compose something on the spot which made it easier than trying to remember something from fifteen or twenty years ago. The sounds that came out of the piano were beautiful, mellow, and yet brilliant. I improvised something in a Chopinesque style, and as I pressed the keys and delighted in the singing quality of what came out. It was as if an old friend had come back into my life and I knew then that I would be spending many hours in the theater alone with this piano.

When I got up from the piano, everyone applauded except Tom. He seemed to look troubled. However, I tried not to let it worry me. I wrote a letter of thanks to Mr. Johnson, and told him that when I had composed enough selections, I would send him a tape.

I began playing and composing in earnest. I also practiced scales, arpeggios, and exercises to regain the playing facility I once had. It took me about one month to be able to play the way I had some twenty years ago. I dug out my old music manuscripts, but looked in vain for the tapes I had made of the music I composed while at Radio City Music Hall.

"Where are the tapes of my music from New York," I asked Tom. He acted as if he didn't know what I was talking about. "The tapes from the Music Hall, the tape of me on the *Paul Whitman Show*, the *Lorraine Day Show*, where are they?" I cried. I was desperate, as if my child had been kidnapped.

"I have no idea where they are" he answered coldly with a smirk. He left the room and somehow I saw it was fruitless to ask him any more about the lost tapes.

One afternoon, I got a call from a woman in San Francisco.

"I don't know whether you will remember me," she said. "My name is Marie Kaufmann."

"You mean Mrs. Zelak Kaufman?" I asked.

"Yes, that's right," the woman answered. "Zelak and I saw you on television twice, a year or so ago. He was so happy that you found someone, I refer to your husband, and that you are fulfilled in your work and art. Very few have found this."

"How is Zelak," I asked.

"Zelak passed away last year," Marie answered. "He had lung cancer."

Although Zelak was from my long ago past, I had never forgotten him. It was a sudden pain to realize that he was no more. Marie said he had been playing with the San Francisco Symphony.

"I am so very sorry," I finally said. "He was always inspiring to me. When I knew that he was playing in the orchestra that show, I always danced better. I was hoping your call would mean that you were both planning a trip to the Opera House, but now, I guess you won't."

"I want to come to see you alone," Marie said. "I need to visit the desert and I want and need to see you again."

I told Tom about Marie's planned visit, but he hardly looked up from his printing press. He knew about Zelak, but considered the whole thing a girlish crush.

My life with Tom was becoming more of a business relationship, filled with tension. The fact Zelak had remembered me gave me a silent comfort, a hint of a romantic encounter that remained in the heart, if not in reality.

It was a Wednesday morning when Marie's bus stopped promptly at ten in front of the Opera House. The people filed out and came into my theater for a talk about my murals and a brief history of the Opera House itself. As they all filed in, I desperately searched for Marie. There she was, at the end of the group, carrying a valise in each hand. She looked pretty much the same, so I recognized her immediately. We stood gazing at each other for a few moments. However, the presence of the tour group alerted me to the fact that it was now time for me to give my talk. I turned and faced the small crowd and told my story.

The tour group sat in the folding chairs facing the stage, but Marie stood over by the piano staring at me, still holding her valises. My talk was like a recording, while my mind was on Marie. When the tour was done, I turned and faced Marie.

"Zelak talked about you all the time," she said, staring at me with tears in her eyes. I was somewhat overwhelmed and felt sadness for Marie at having to hear Zelak talk about another woman so much.

"Do put your bags down," I said. "Perhaps we can be alone and talk a few moments. Then I can take you over to the hotel." Marie put her bags down by the piano and came over and sat on one of the folding chairs beside me.

"I brought a tape you might like to hear, a string quartet playing Schubert's *Death and the Maiden*. Zelak plays first violin. It was his favorite. Perhaps we can listen to it while I am here. I will want to take it back with me when I leave."

"Oh, I want to hear it very much, perhaps tomorrow evening," I said. "The performance isn't until Friday, so we could have the theater to ourselves tomorrow night."

Marie talked a little about her two sons, who were now grown and living in San Diego. She mentioned Raoul, who she said disappointed Zelak when he liked rock music. "Neither of the two boys is musical," Marie continued.

I took Marie into the apartment where Tom and I lived, next to the Opera House now. He was there, reading a book. When I introduced them to each other, he was cordial enough, but went back to his book.

We planned on having dinner together the nights Marie would be here. I would do the cooking, but my cooking was nothing spectacular. Marie seemed to understand how much I had to do.

The next night we went into the theater to listen to Zelak's tape; just Marie and I. The sounds of the strings drew out of the air memories of a longing I had to know Zelak better; to know more of him than the handsome musician holding his violin, poised to play *Kiss Me Again*.

Death and the Maiden continued, melancholy, making me aware of time lost, never to be recovered. I followed the violin, picturing Zelak there up on my stage, playing. I was sobbing now, and so was Marie. We sobbed together, silently for a man who was gone, but also for both of us, very much present.

When the music stopped, we both sat for a long time in silence.

Marie stayed to see all of my performances. She said the show was much better than she ever expected. Perhaps Zelak was there with us; who knows? That following Tuesday morning, Marie left Death Valley Junction and I never heard from her again.

Marta plays the new piano, 1974.

Scene Five

Finding Freedom

We celebrated the completion of my murals in August of 1972. It had taken four years, but the work was well worth it. They were my dedication to the past. A shimmering statue painted in the mural holds a scroll printed in Latin that says it all, "The walls of this theater and I dedicate these murals to the past without which our times would have no beauty."

In a way, the celebration held for the mural completion was bittersweet. For me, it marked an end to a creative endeavor that had both caused and eased the pain of Tom's infidelity.

When the party to celebrate the murals was over, everyone said their goodbyes and went off into the night. I felt dejected until suddenly I looked up and realized, the joy I had experienced those happy four years could be extended; perhaps for two or three years more.

Immediately, I got to work on a sketch for the ceiling. My scaffold was extended upward and for the next two summers, I spent every day reaching up to create my own sky, my own heavens filled with blue expanses, dancing cherubs, billowing clouds, and the four winds; one in each corner.

Within a central dome, I painted sixteen golden ladies playing antique musical instruments. The ceiling was completed with seven doves flying overhead expressing my hope for peace.

Things with Tom weren't good, but I realized the fortune teller in New

York had been right. Even without his approval, I was doing the most satisfying work of my life here in Amargosa. Perhaps this place had been my fate all along.

I know people think I am eccentric. I have been called a recluse. Is it eccentric to love your work so much that you would go anywhere in the world to do it?

In 1974, I completed the ceiling. My dancing and painting (now on canvas) continued. And Tom had taken up a new pursuit, filmmaking. Over the course of several summers, he set out to film my entire repertoire from *The Mirror, The Carpet, and The Lemon* to *Gossip* and more. We would spend hours in the sweltering theater, which I have never air conditioned, for fear of damaging the murals. Though sweat poured down my face and stung my eyes, I continued to dance. The film footage was later damaged by rains, floods, and improper storage, but after much restoration effort, it remains today. Much of the footage was compiled into a set of *Performance Tonight!* video tapes.

My many supporters helped me realize a need to preserve the Opera House, and my paintings with it. With legal advice from friends and the help of the Trust for Public Land based in San Francisco, Tom and I formed Amargosa Opera House, Inc. We bought the Opera House and later, using the corporation, took out a loan and bought the entire town of Death Valley Junction. I hoped that buying the town would create friendly and sympathetic surroundings for the arts.

The surroundings with my murals were friendly, but my home life became worse with Tom. He was away much of the time in Los Angeles, supposedly getting his film developed. But I never knew what he was up to.

There are so many times when I've been left alone in this town with the wind blowing. I'd go to the postmistress and ask her, "Why does Tom do this to me?"

She'd smile a knowing smile and say, "Nice day ain't it?"

Eventually, he moved a woman named Jody into one of the houses in town; house number 10. She was his mistress and he loved to parade her around town in front of me, showing her off to everyone. He would introduce her as his mistress to patrons waiting in front the Opera House. I was humiliated and hurt, but still powerless to make things better.

I went to a Pahrump marriage counselor in 1978. I was in great pain—psychological pain. I didn't know why my husband was doing what he was to me. The counselor said he brought another woman to make a threesome to diminish my power because of his jealousy over my abilities.

"He's tried to hurt you by bringing another woman that you can not compete with," he said.

That was Jody, or as I called her, the fat woman. Tom found out I went to see the counselor and became upset. He learned a photographer friend in town had advised me to go seek help. He confronted the photographer screaming, "How dare you meddle in my life by taking Marta to a counselor."

"I was helping Marta." He defended. "She's in a quandary. She's in pain and needs psychological help."

"You're still meddling; leave her alone," Tom continued.

Tom meanwhile, was out to make me lose my mind. He would leave audio tapes on the table right in the open. When I listened to one, it was a session with the psychic with Jody and Tom talking about me in the most disparaging way. No mistake, he left them there for me to find.

During the time of my struggles with Tom, I remember the front doors were open and a limousine stopped. A very well-dressed man got out and came into the Opera House. He said his son would like to have look. He brought his son in a wheelchair. The boy's head fell back. I don't know what kind of illness it was.

The father looked around and began to shake his head, "How can your husband stand you surrounded by this?"

"What to do you mean? I haven't done anything ugly," I said. I didn't know what he was talking about.

They came to the Saturday show. When it was over, the father asked Tom how he could stand living with me. "I wonder myself," Tom said.

Does being an artist mean I'm carrying a disease that makes me unlovable. I don't know why Tom wanted to marry me in the first place. I have always had this talent, this drive. Maybe he expected to change it.

In spite of my injury and hurt, I thought I still loved Tom and I didn't want to lose him. I went to see a psychic who shared with me her secrets to preserving love. I filled our house with candles as I slept as she had suggested. I was determined to do whatever I could to make Tom stay with me and make him love me again the way he did when we met following the circus elephants.

Perhaps I should become more like Jody. Maybe if I was less like me, he would love me again.

One night as I slept in the room with the burning candles, a figure covered in white with a surgical instrument came toward me and was about to operate. As the instrument was about to touch me, I screamed and woke-up.

The candles flickered; the smoke from the burning wax was asphyxiating. The cats jumped off my bed and I suddenly realized how thankful I was to be me. I no longer wished Tom to love me, and threw away the candles.

In 1983, Tom decided he needed more help around the town. Tom Willett had been laid off from his job, so my Tom invited him to come stay in Death Valley Junction, as a maintenance man. Tom Willett, who we lovingly called "Wilget," willingly agreed.

Wilget had a ball living in Death Valley Junction. He had a little four-wheeler he used for chores and entertainment. He would cruise up and down the road barking like a seal, laughing, and spinning in circles.

When Wilget would sweep up the colonnade, he did a little dance with the broom that always made me laugh. Suddenly I wondered, "Could he entertain audiences the way he entertained me?"

At this time, I was working on a new stage production for myself. It was called *The Inheritance*. I remember Wilget coming over to help film the production. Tom came and tried to introduce it, but fluffed it three times because the show touched on infidelity.

Shortly after this, Tom told me he hated me. He hated my talent. He wanted to take the piano out to burn it. But it was my talents that were giving him bread and butter. I knew I couldn't take much more.

About that time, a young artist named Dan Britton came to town. We became quick friends.

Dan decided to teach me how to drive. It was a challenge to learn, but a need for independence and his patient lessons got me through. To thank him, I painted him a huge piece called *Self Portrait*. The painting featured a dancing marionette surrounded by her husband, her parents, and others, all pulling at her strings. In the distance was a car, ready to drive her away from slavery and into freedom. It was painted on an impulse. The finished painting sat in my studio with the paint still drying, but Dan never got to see it.

Tom had never showed any interest in my paintings before. Even back in New York when I had put on the show in our loft, he walked out on it. One day he burst into my studio, pulled the sheet from my canvas and said "What's the meaning of this!"

I could see the rage in his eyes. I could see it would become more unbearable than it was, so I slashed the painting with a butcher knife and burned it! But I never gave up the freedom that painting represented.

Using my newfound freedom, I drove to Las Vegas, took the bus to L.A. and filed for a divorce.

Finally, the day came for Tom to leave. Our board members were there.

We had a full house and I was scared stiff that on his last performance he would introduce me and say something humiliating to destroy me but it was the best performance he gave. It was almost like his old self, like he had turned from one character to another. Three days later, he was to be gone and I was to open with Wilget as my master of ceremonies.

As I was preparing for my opening night with Wilget, Al Bell called to say house number ten was on fire. Tom had poured gasoline over an old can behind house ten and filled it with papers he wanted to destroy. The whole thing went up in flames and there was not a bit of evidence left. He drove out of town with Jody. It was like a nightmare finally ending.

Once Tom was gone, I returned to my stage for comfort.

Wilget took to the stage like a duck to water. He was a natural and the audiences loved him. Soon I loved him, too. He loved to act the clown, and I loved to create for him. We were soulmates.

Mother never met Wilget. By this time, she was in a nursing home, The Beverly Manor in Las Vegas. The last few years of her life, she became someone else. Even when she came out to the Opera House, when she was more lucid, she didn't comprehend the murals. She was healthy, but her mind was somewhere else.

When Mother died, she was buried in Death Valley Junction, in a small family graveyard. The only person who came to Mother's ceremony from out of town was a preacher from Tecopa. I was joined by Al Bell, the postmistress, Dan, and Wilget. I was sad, but Mother lived a long life. She was ninety-six.

Dan and Mother suffered a similar fate, but Dan died young, at only twenty-three. He is also buried down there with Mother. I don't know why it was that Dan had a connection with my mother, he died on her birthday.

My performances continued in spite of the sorrow around me. And now, I no longer put on a one-woman show. I had a performing partner in Wilget. He willingly put on a hoopskirt and picked up a fan in *Gossip*. His best turn was as Miss Victoria Hoops in *Looking for Mr. Right*. He made an adorable Cherub in *Cupid's Mistake*. While I wore a tutu, Wilget said he wore a "four-four."

From the beginning of our partnership, we put on nine shows beginning with *The Second Mortgage* and continuing through *Cupid's Mistake*, *Comeback Vaudeville*, *A Farewell Letter*, *Command Performance*, *Looking for Mr. Right*, *On With the Show*, *The Goodtime Cabaret*, and finally our last show, *Masquerade*.

Wilget never seemed threatened by my painting, composing, or choreography. We never tried to spend every moment of every day together. We did take all our meals together, and each night we would go to his little home at Death Valley Junction and watch Lou Dobbs and a program called *Classic Art Showcase* on the Arts Channel. When the program was over, I would go back to my house.

Wilget had hobbies of his own to occupy his time, while I was creating. Besides working to keep the Opera House and town in order, he indulged in his favorite hobby — garden scale railroad models. The tracks of his trains wended their way through rooms and walls in one of the houses here.

In addition to the railroad, Wilget was a big fan of music. He created a music machine. A sort of mechanized pipe organ that played several instruments at his command. Audiences loved it when we would open the music room to them after our performances. Wilget would put on a little show of his own. He loved the attention and people loved him. He didn't steal the show, I gave it to him.

The Opera House, Wilget and I continued to draw attention with articles, television spots, and radio show attention. In the 1990s, a film company came out and created a documentary about my life and the Opera House and Death Valley Junction. *Amargosa*, written and directed by Todd Robinson, was released in 2000. The film features my dancing, Wilget's antics, and comments from fans and people around town. Author Ray Bradbury, plays a large part in the film as he tells of his joy in first discovering Death Valley Junction and my dance-mimes. *Amargosa* became an Oscar-nominee in the documentary category.

My friend Charlotte Barclay wrote stories for the ballet in New York City. She had once been a dancer as well. She agreed to help me out. I would work on pages and then send them to her for editing. She would send back corrections which Wilget would type up for me on an old typewriter, in all capital letters. Wilget didn't like to worry about which letters to capitalize and I had no typing expertise myself. We figured that anyone who was truly interested in my story would just put up with the hand-typed job we had done. When Charlotte died, I lost a friend and an editor.

While performing *The Good Time Cabaret*, I was beginning to have a great deal of pain in my left knee. I visited a doctor who told me I would need knee replacement surgery. But I suspected if I had my knee replaced, I wouldn't be able to walk again, let alone dance. The surgeon told me with therapy, that might not be true, but I decided to press on and work with the knee the way it is. "On with the show!"

In 2001, from September to November, the Las Vegas Art Museum exhibited a retrospective of my art spanning six decades. The paintings were on loan from a variety of private collections. For me, it was like a happy reunion since I had not seen many of these paintings for years.

My most recent production, *Masquerade*, took at least three years to create. While working on it, I would create the dances and then bring Wilget in and show him his parts. During every show, he learned his dances faithfully, but when the curtain opened, he had made them his own. He would always add little sparks of his own. As the show progressed, he would elaborate on his own and add little steps here and there. They always seemed to fit, so I didn't mind.

As the years went by, he continued to dance, but he seemed to slow down. I noticed a diminished sense of energy.

Every morning, I would phone Wilget at his place to wake him up. He would snooze, while I got the answering machine. To rouse him, I would imitate a menagerie of animals, all common to Death Valley Junction. My sounds consisted of burros, cats, dogs, geese, chickens, peacocks, and more. Finally, he would stumble toward the telephone, pick up and say, "Alright, alright, I'm up." I think he looked forward to my calls. I know I did.

On April 14, 2005, I made the call, went through my entire routine, but Wilget never picked up. On the other end of the phone I got nothing, just the blackness of silence.

"Wilget! Wilget!" I screamed into the phone. I ran over to his house and he was down on his bed trying to move his legs to get up. He was mumbling something I couldn't understand, something about animals to feed and work to do. He got up, stumbled into the front room and fell down into a winged chair.

I called Dennis Bostwick, our town manager. Dennis looked at Wilget and said, "He's had a stroke."

We called 911, but it took forever for the helicopter to come. I don't think it would have made any difference if it had come sooner. We drove to town after Wilget and arrived at Valley Hospital in Las Vegas.

All along, I was thinking, "Will he recover? Is this serious, or is this the end?" He had been in the hospital before with a pinched nerve and kidney stones, but this was different. He continued to mumble about the work he needed to do back in Death Valley Junction. He expressed a need to go to the hardware store. I convinced myself his ambition meant he would be okay.

After spending the day and much of the night at the hospital with Wilget, we all went home to get some rest. We had planned on returning Friday morning. But Friday morning, we got the call from Valley Hospital. Wilget had died. Gaila, Tom's daughter and Dennis came to my house to tell me. All I could do was cry. God, it was awful. No matter how many years have passed by, you still never expect death. You're never prepared for it.

Wilget's funeral services were held in Pahrump at the Neptune Society of Nye County on Monday, April 25, at eleven in the morning. So many people came and cared. Cards, letters, and phone calls came rolling in the moment people found out.

I didn't want to see Wilget when they had him on view. I just didn't want to see him that way. He was buried in his black velvet suit and the sparkle derby hat he was well known for. He was taken so suddenly. But we would watch television and see Terri Schiavo's case rolling on and Wilget thought it terrible to keep her hooked up on tubes for fifteen years.

"This is cruel. She would not have liked that at all," Wilget would say. We both agreed the best way to go was to go at once. That's the way Wilget went. But I still can't believe it. He was here so recently, right here!

Now that Wilget is gone, my show, again, is a one-woman show. The Saturday after he died, I couldn't go on. A ballet school had made reservations to see me dance. I had been looking forward to their visit all season; a rough season since the rains and floods had washed our main access road out for several months. Yet, I still couldn't risk breaking down in front of them.

The students understood when they heard what happened. They went to the gift shop and watched my performances on video tape. Thank heavens for film.

Wilget was memorialized in the *Pahrump Valley Times*, *Los Angeles Times*, *San Francisco Chronicle*, and more. After missing one performance, I vowed to get back up on the stage and go on. I knew Wilget would have wanted that.

My return to the lonely stage was difficult. My show was written for two. I explained to my audience that where there were pauses and music playing with an empty stage, that's where Wilget would be performing.

My first night back on the stage, many well-wishers brought me flowers. Going back out on stage was a challenge, but the moment the music began, the magic of the theater took over and I was better, until my final bow amid an eager ovation.

I have seen ghosts here in the Opera House and about Death Valley Junction. I wonder if Wilget is still here. I just wish I knew where he was and if he is alright. I guess we'll never know about the life after this one until we get there.

I listen for Wilget in the wind, even though I never liked the wind. He hated the wind, too. You never get used to the dust no matter how long you live here. But you learn to live with it. Now I'll have to learn to live without Wilget.

After a summer off to rewrite my show, this time for only one to play, I will again face my stage alone, performing all the parts myself.

Without Wilget, without Tom, without Mother, or Mana, I must keep going, alone. I often wonder what I'll do when I can no longer dance. I'm determined to keep going as long as I can. I'll dance on one leg if the other one stops working.

Making plans for the future keeps me going. My next show will be a circus carnival featuring characters you would find on publicity posters. I've been planning it for some time. I expect it to be ready in 2008. It takes longer than you would think to put on a new show. I have to choose music, choreograph dances, paint backdrops, and make all the costumes.

Wilget will be painted into the circus backdrop. Audiences will see him on the left as the lion tamer and as a strong man. Perhaps, I'll make a clown figure that I will dance with at the end. I will write on it, "Wilget the clown." He *will* be in the show.

Now I will have to play his part, but his image will remain in the background.

Though I've long thought I could hold back time through dance and creativity, I know that one day life will catch up with me. I won't last forever, I know. One day, I too will haunt this place, dancing like a dust devil in the wind.

When I ache, when I'm tired or just lonely living in the town on my own, I know I have to keep on going. I walk into my theater and see my stage which still calls out to me and pleads with me, "Use me. Create for me." It's there ready to offer itself for more creatively. It is up to me to use it again. My theater says to me, "Take me. Do something with me. I'm ready for the challenge. Give me something to live for; something to look forward to."

I am grateful to have found a place where I can fulfill my dreams and share them with the passing scene for as long as I can.